THE LIGHT OF HIS COMING

THE LIGHT OF HIS COMING

KESWICK MINISTRY

Edited by David Porter

Keswick Convention Council, England

British Library Cataloguing in Publication Data

Light of His Coming:Keswick Ministry
I. Porter, David
236.9

ISBN 1-85078-204-0

OM Publishing is an imprint of STL Ltd
PO Box 300, Carlisle, Cumbria, CA3 0QS, UK

Typeset by Photoprint, Torquay, Devon
and Printed in the UK for
OM Publishing, PO Box 300, Carlisle, Cumbria, CA3 0QS
by Cox and Wyman Ltd, Reading

CONTENTS

'The Light of His Coming'

CHAIRMAN'S INTRODUCTION

The thrilling truth of our Lord's oft-repeated promise concerning His coming again has never been far from our minds at Keswick, particularly in the final Communion Services at the end of each week when we 'proclaim the Lord's death, until he comes again' (1 Cor. 11:26).

But 1995 saw the theme of the two Convention weeks centred specifically on 'The Light of His Coming', and it was a rare treat to have our minds stirred, our hearts warmed and our wills steeled by this rich doctrine. We can only thank God for such an outstanding Convention fortnight, and in these pages you can have a taste of the banquet which was spread for us by the Lord. In the end pages you have details of the audio and video tapes of the addresses—of which the printed versions here are necessarily précis records. Happier still if you were one of the thousands fortunate enough to be there! We thank David Porter and all responsible for enabling us to have and enjoy this printed record. This little book literally travels the world. May all who receive it find blessing from it.

If there is a regret in my mind it would be the realisation that the thrilling teaching about the Second Coming seems to be a Cinderella doctrine amongst evangelical Christians today. I confess I feared that we might get bogged down in worthless speculation—a tragic trait of the handling of the doctrine by some in past decades. We were mercifully preserved! Instead, what we saw was godly eagerness to hear the truth expounded. I believe there will be many who will pray 'Thy kingdom come' with far greater understanding and far greater conviction in the days ahead as a result of Keswick 1995.

When you read these pages may I ask you to thank God for His continued blessing on the Convention, and to pray for that blessing to continue still, as we move on from 1995's 120th milestone? Big is not necessarily beautiful, but the truth is that the Convention would find continued increased attendance somewhat hard to handle. This is never more true than in the growth of numbers of under-20s attending (whose activities and teaching programme is not mentioned in this book). The children's and young people's activities strain accommodation to the limit. (In the second week one in three of those attending was under 20 years old.) There are some far-reaching decisions to be made by the Council in this connection. But the problems are those of God-blessed growth and life—and those are the happiest problems to have!

Keith A. A. Weston
Chairman of the Keswick Convention Council

EDITOR'S INTRODUCTION

It has been a privilege once again to work on the material which you will find in this book, and I would not want to delay you on your way to another annual feast of Keswick ministry. But it is important to run through the usual editorial matters, for this is an edited transcript of a spoken occasion, in which most of the speakers have graciously waived the right to check the edited version of their material. This speeds up the production process enormously. A representative of the Keswick Council reads the proofs to ensure that no accidental errors or misrepresentations have crept in.

The material is necessarily abridged: if you want to savour the authentic atmosphere of the occasion or to find out the full details of Rev. Alec Motyer's disastrous experiences with azaleas, I recommend the tape and video libraries mentioned on p.13. All Bible quotations have been retained, though some have been edited or even included only as references. Each has been checked against the appropriate version. Speakers' paraphrases can usually be recognised by 'cf' in the reference, or by the fact that Scripture quotations do not follow the Keswick house-style of capitalising pronouns referring to the Persons of God. You will certainly benefit most from this book if you have your Bible by you as you read.

I have tracked down as many literary quotations and allusions as I had time to (if you want to hunt for the rest I can assure you it is an edifying and interesting experience), and I have tried to retain as much as possible of individual speakers' personalities and the atmosphere of the occasion.

I would like to thank my wife Tricia, who transcribed all

the tapes this year, our daughter Eleanor who brightened up the summer with her 'A' level results, our younger daughter Lauren who tolerated yet another Keswick-dominated August, and Wade and Chryse Bradshaw who were kind enough to lend me a word processor at a crucial stage in the editorial process.

David Porter

THE BIBLE READINGS

‘Living for the Day’
Paul’s First Letter to the Church of Thessalonians

by Rev. Alec Motyer

1: The Church in the Father and the Son
1 Thessalonians 1:1–10

Years ago my wife and I bought two azalea plants. We were attracted by the colour and scent of the blooms. We were assured that they were perfect plants in good health, hardy, good growers—everything you would want in an azalea. We brought them home and planted them. Almost at once they began to look sickly. Overnight the blooms faded and eventually dropped off, and the leaves began to shrivel and soon they dropped off too. Finally the branches themselves withered and died.

The problem was, that we had given them the wrong soil and habitat. They had died for lack of a proper ecosystem.

Paul’s Greeting (1:1)

To the church of the Thessalonians
Paul tells us in Acts 16 that he decided to leave Philippi in response to the local magistrate’s request. He headed south-west, a journey passed over in Scripture but actually a hundred miles long, until he arrived in Thessalonica (Acts 17:1–9).

When they left Thessalonica a very short time later—possibly hardly more than four or five weeks—there was something that is called in 1 Thessalonians 1:1 'the church of the Thessalonians' [lit. 'a church of Thessalonians']. J. N. Darby's translation calls it an 'assembly', rightly; a church is an assembly that has been officially and properly convened and called out for the purpose. Who called it out this assembly? We'll return to that question.

It was an assembly not of 'the' Thessalonians—for there were Thessalonians who weren't called out and didn't belong—but an assembly 'of Thessalonians'. We will see how they came to be part of that properly constituted and called-out assembly, 'the church of Thessalonians'. Paul only uses such language in the Thessalonian epistles. Elsewhere he speaks of 'the church at Corinth' or 'the saints at Philippi', but only here does he use this expression: 'a church made up of Thessalonians'.

A people-emphasis runs right through this letter: how we become all that we ought to be, in character, conduct and community; how we can be a church of Thessalonians in our day. There's a marvellous stress on individuals being gathered into the community of the people of God. We are going to learn together those remedies, recipes and ways which God has provided for that purpose.

In God the Father and the Lord Jesus Christ

This is where the azaleas, which you've all been wondering about, come in! The church of Thessalonians 'in God the Father' has been transplanted out of the wilderness of the world in which they grew up, and have been brought into a new situation. And unlike our azaleas which we planted in the wrong soil, they have been planted in an ecosystem that is perfectly suited to the new nature they have been given. They are 'in God the Father and the Lord Jesus Christ'; they have been planted into a new habitat which will feed them with all the vitality, energies, elements and trace-elements which are necessary for their perfect growth. Every believer is a transplant, in just the same way, transplanted into a habitat specially designed to cultivate growth, development and fruitfulness, 'in God the Father and the Lord Jesus Christ'.

When Paul says that we are 'in God the Father and the

Lord Jesus Christ', he doesn't mean that we have been brought into *being* by God, but that we have been brought into *union* with Him, like transplants planted down into the soil that matches us and is conducive to our growth. It is the same biblical image as that of the vine and the branches: the branches are in a system perfectly designed to maintain their health, growth and fruitfulness. So with the body and the members: the members are in a system perfectly designed for their health and holiness, their development and usefulness. We have been planted into God the Father and the Lord Jesus Christ.

Paul in this very early (perhaps his earliest) letter links our Lord Jesus Christ with God the Father in a unity of deity. The NIV is correct in translating the verse so that one preposition—'in'—governs all that follows: 'in God the Father and our Lord Jesus Christ'. In such cases in New Testament Greek you can hyphenate all that follows. These Thessalonians are bound together by this one preposition, *in* God the Father and the Lord Jesus Christ—one unity of deity.

All the life of that one God surrounds us as soon as we become Christians, and is there for us to put our roots into and draw our nourishment from, so that we grow straight, true, clean and fruitful. God the Father and our Lord Jesus Christ feed us with the perfect elements and trace elements for life and growth.

Grace and peace to you

'Grace' is not something God *gives*. There is a hymn which wrongly talks of 'a higher gift than grace', but there is no such thing as grace apart from God. It's not something external to Himself, that He hands out like medicine. Grace is God being gracious. It is the free undeserved unmerited movement of God sharing Himself with His people as Father and as our Lord Jesus Christ.

From God our Father and the Lord Jesus Christ (NIV margin)

'From God our Father'—it is a movement of the Father, the God who is rich in mercy for His great love wherewith He loved us, who saved us by grace (cf Eph. 2:4)—a movement of the Father now coming to us to offer the perfect setting into which His transplant can be established for life and growth. All the eternal God's fatherly love, saving mercy and eternal power surround us.

And the Lord Jesus Christ (NIV margin)

Always pause when Paul uses that fullness of title. He is *Lord*, in the fullness of His deity, because the word 'Lord' reaches back to the God who is revealed in the Old Testament, who can be called by name, Yahweh. The word 'Lord' in the New Testament declares that Jesus is Yahweh, God Himself. And He comes to us not only as Lord, but as *Jesus*—that is to say, in the fullness of His humanity; Jesus, the one who perfectly understands us and can perfectly minister to our needs. And He comes to us as Christ, the one who was anointed to be the totally perfect Saviour of sinners.

Are you beginning to feel like a protected species? That great God reached out into the wilderness of the world, and took us up so gently out of that habitat in which we were living, and brought us into Himself—God the Father and the Lord Jesus Christ—nourishing us with grace which is God Himself being gracious.

Peace

Of course peace begins with peace with God; but peace also means 'peace and fulfilment in our own being'. It would do no harm if we remembered, every time we saw the word in our Bibles, to put alongside it the word 'fulfilment'; that is its meaning, especially in the Old Testament. When He ministers peace to us, He is ministering to us all those things which will bring us to fulfilment and full maturity: peace with God, the peace of a truly fulfilled humanity; peace in society, peace in fellowship with our brother Christians; and then reaching out beyond them in lives that grow into full bloom in relation to God, to self and to the church.

1 Thessalonians 1:1 will serve as a title for the whole letter. It's about being God's transplants, about living in this new habitat, this new plant pot in which God has planted us.

It tells us how we got there, how we live there, what we are going to be, and the harvest that's coming.

The Model Church : The Four Sides of a Square (1: 2–10)

Let us continue the gardening metaphor, as we look further at these Thessalonian Christians.

The fruit is right (1:2–3)
Their faith is producing work, their love is producing labour and their hope is producing endurance. They have been transplanted into God the Father and our Lord Jesus Christ, and they are finding this new habitat so rich and nourishing that Paul can give thanks that already they are bearing good fruit.

The root is right (1:4–6)
The fruit is right because the root is right. Verse 4 is a key verse. 'Brothers loved by God.' Dear sisters, I'm afraid that the word 'brothers' is in the text, but it is used in its wider sense of children together in God's family. So we are all included, as His dear, beloved children. 'We know,' says the NIV, ' . . . that he has chosen you.' The AV renders it: 'Knowing . . . your election of God.' You have been chosen and picked by God.

The transplants spread (1:7–8)
Because the root is right God's transplants make good ground cover. They spread and they cover the earth. So he tells us (1:7), 'You became a model [AV: "ensamples"] to all the believers in Macedonia and Achaia. The Lord's message rang out from you.' The plant is growing, spreading and beginning to fill the earth.

The plant is a hardy perennial (1:9–10)
Finally, this plant is secure against all eventualities. Nothing can ever kill it; not even 'the coming wrath' (1:10b), because it is a plant surrounded by the saving efficacy of the Lord Jesus Christ. It is hardy, it is perennial: it will go on and on for ever and ever. This model church is secure for all time

and eternity because it is secure in the saving work and care of Jesus.

The Square Examined in Detail

So there is a quadrilateral of genuine Christian life and experience, a reality of which the four sides are going to be our study for the rest of this morning. Notice, Paul is talking about basics. He's not saying, 'These things are true if you're lucky', or 'These things are true if you enter into this or that experience'. He's saying, 'These things are true because they are basics.'

So when in verses 2 and 3 he talks about the fruit of work, labour and endurance, he says, 'We continually remember'. He doesn't say, 'I hope you will soon begin to produce fruit'. He looks back at that church, the immediate fruit of his evangelism, and sees it there and then as a fruit-bearing constituency. It's part of the basics. In verse 5 he goes back to their conversion. They 'became' (not 'will become') imitators. In verse 9 he looks back to the report of 'the reception you gave me'. Throughout our passage there is a constant looking back to how things have been from the very beginning. So I say to you, this is the quadrilateral of genuine Christian experience: not a proposal for a future blessing, but a statement of existing reality.

So let us come to the first side of the square.

The evidential side (1:3)

You will find verse 3 put more bluntly in the older translation: 'Remembering [as we look back to those early beginning days] your work of faith, and labour of love, and patience of hope in our Lord Jesus Christ' (AV).

John the Baptist illustrates this. He said to those who came to him, 'Bring forth fruit worthy of repentance' (cf. Matt. 3:8). We all know what that means. It means that if you are truly repentant, it will show. John was enunciating a principle: spiritual experience is not a matter of claim but of evidence. The work of faith is there to be seen, the toil of love is there to be seen, so that the outsider looking at us and how we conduct our lives would say, 'He must be a believer.

She must be a loving person. They must be entertaining a great hope. Look how they live!' The evidential side of the square of Christian experience shows the reality of the faith, love and hope which are the cardinal points of our Christian experience. Faith upward to God, love outward first of all to our fellow believers and then to all, hope onwards to our Lord Jesus Christ.

Three dimensions, three directional pointers—they're not steps on a ladder to be ticked off—'Right—I've done my faith bit for today . . . Now, let me get on with my love bit . . . And, if the day lasts long enough, I'll get through to my hope bit.' No. In every situation there are three directional pointers: upward to God in faith, outward to others in love, onwards to Christ in hope.

It is dramatically striking, in the light of much that is said and done and claimed today, that Paul makes no apology for the fact that in those early days with the Thessalonian Christians their faith demanded work and toil and endurance. He doesn't say, 'Dear friends, I'm sorry it worked out like that—I wish it could have been easier for you.' He speaks as if it is quite natural that being a Christian should demand work, toil and endurance. How very different from the instant coffee that is placarded as Christian experience today!

'Work' and 'toil' may, I think, be legitimately thought of as synonymous. But perhaps we can define 'work' as 'energy put out; labour', and 'toil' as 'tiredness felt as a result of energy put out'. The Christian is a working Christian, who is fatigued by the exercise of being a Christian, who is enduring by looking onwards to our Lord Jesus Christ—in every situation faith, love and hope.

How often, when life turns strange or difficult, do we say, 'What is God *thinking* about?' I'll tell you. He is thinking about the fact that He calls us to live by faith, to live in love and to exercise hope. He's calling us to be what we are. The troubles and toils of life which demand the exercise of faith and the putting forth of energy unto fatigue and tiredness, which demand endurance—these are not unnatural experiences. They are the conditions of life and growth in which we live.

In every situation, faith (that is, what I did in that blessed moment of my conversion: putting my faith in Jesus, exercising faith for justification) is to be the pattern of all my life. I must say to myself: 'If faith solved that most difficult and truly insoluble of all problems of how to be right with God for all eternity, is there any problem faith will not solve?' So whatever the day brings forth, let your first reaction be, 'Lord, I trust you. If it is your will for this illness to go on and on and become terminal, I trust you with that. Lord, if it is your will that this trial in my family will not be solved overnight but will live on the top of my head like a bag of sand—very well, Lord. So be it. I trust you with it. Faith solved my eternal problem; faith will solve every problem en route.'

I will toil away at loving my fellow believers. And it's going to be toil, because I'm called to love them like I love myself. And how do you love yourself? Do you wake up in the morning and look at that poor bleary face in the mirror and say, 'Oh! How I love you'? No, you look at it with extreme loathing. But you take it to the bathroom and wash it, don't you. That's what love is! Not the stirring of the heart, but of the will, to look after every obvious declared need. That's how we love ourselves. We reach out in love to our brothers and sisters in the church. 'There is a need, and I'm going to meet it.'

Finally, the endurance of hope. We used to sing a great hymn in days gone by:

> Hold the fort for I am coming
> Jesus signals still
> Wave the answer back to heaven
> By Thy grace we will.

That's the endurance of hope. How awful it would be if, under pressure and the call to endure, we failed to endure —and that very moment, He came back! No, we fix our eyes on the returning Lord, and we endure.

The spiritual side (1:4–5)

I'm going to call this the spiritual side even though it contains visible, audible realities. Verse 5 speaks to us of the word that came 'not simply with words'; but it did come with the audible reality of the word. And there's the visible life of the preacher: 'You know how we lived among you.' Those two factors had an important part to play in your conversion. Indeed the middle of verse 5 is linked to the end of the verse in a way that the NIV unfortunately omits; it should say that the word 'came bringing conviction to you', and continue, '*just as* you know how we lived'—as if to say, 'The depth of your conviction is in proportion to the reality of the life we live.' So there were audible and visible realities at work.

But there were also great spiritual and invisible realities at work in their conversion.

The verses do deal with the visible and the audible, the word and the life of the preacher; but mainly they deal with the love and choice of God, the invisible power of the Holy Spirit which He attaches to His word, and the conviction that is wrought in the heart and mind of the hearer.

First of all, *Election as God's choice (1:4)*. We start with the mystery of election and of the love of God. I use the word 'mystery' in its biblical sense, of a revelation that has been made but which is beyond our understanding. The Bible has revealed to us the love of God and the choice of God. We are often troubled by the question, 'If I have been chosen by God, what room does that leave for my conversion which I remember so clearly? What room does that leave for me to say to Jesus, "I choose you as my Saviour"?'

So first of all we must recall how we were placed before Christ. The key phrase is in Ephesians 2:1—'Dead in your transgressions and sins'. That's the situation that God sets out to solve in salvation: one in which we could not possibly be contributing partners, nor exercise repentance and faith, because we are dead—helpless, hopeless, without a spark of spiritual life, and with no inherent capacity for it. We are dead in trespasses and sins, just as people hooked on a drug have lost a whole area of liberty, even though they may *feel* the liberty is still there and may say, 'Oh! I could kick that habit any time I want . . .' The onlooker knows that death has taken hold. The liberty no longer exists. That is what sin has done to us; we are so hooked on sin, we have no liberty to return to God.

Into that situation, He came in love and choice. That's why Paul goes on in Ephesians 2 to introduce one of those great 'buts' that occasionally come in his letters: 'But because of his great love for us, God, who is rich in mercy, made us alive in Christ' (Eph. 2:4–5). The boot has to be on God's foot, the initiative has to rest in His court. There is no way we can come to life in Christ until He first gives us life. He does so because of the great, inexplicable factor: He loved us. He says, 'I want you to be my son, I want you to be my daughter.'

That's why the Bible speaks of it as adoption. If you have a child in the ordinary course of events, you are delightfully lumbered with the children born to you. But if you adopt, you say, 'Yes—that one. I want that one.' Because of His great love, God said, 'Yes—that one.' Because it springs out of His love, it means that there is a great sufficient and eternal reason for it. But He doesn't tell us. 'He loves you because he loves you' (cf. Deut. 7:7–8). That's all that we know.

Secondly, *Election applied to human beings (1:5)*. How does it actually work out on the ground level, where we are lying dead in our trespasses and sins?

1. The gospel was preached. Verse 5, 'Our gospel came to you not simply with words.' That just means there were other factors besides words. The gospel certainly did come to them by words, as we read in Acts 17, where Paul reasoned from the Scriptures to make their meaning plain, and proclaimed unto them Jesus as the Messiah. There is the work of the preacher: an address to the mind, a fundamental resting upon Scripture, and a focusing upon Jesus Christ.

2. Power was at work. The gospel came 'not simply with words, but also with power'. Paul the preacher saw that something else was going on. Power was going on. 'Faith comes from hearing the message, and the message is heard through the word of Christ' (Rom. 10:17). The word of God was beginning to do its life-giving, quickening work. It was beginning to rouse the person who was dead in trespasses and sins, to create in us the capacity to hear.

3. The Holy Spirit came. What power was this? It wasn't demonic. It wasn't the power of eloquence, personality or persuasion. It wasn't inward in the hearer, the power of hysteria. It was that greatest of objective realities: that quiet, unobtrusive, un-self-advertising divine Person, the Holy Spirit. He came, bringing to us what by nature we could never have—a vision of Jesus, a gift of repentance and an ability to believe.

Did they not say to Peter after he had been to the house of Cornelius, 'God has granted even the Gentiles repentance unto life' (Acts 11:18)? It's His gift. In Ephesians 2:8, does it not say, 'It is by grace you have been saved, through faith—and this not from yourselves, it is the gift of God'? The Holy Spirit comes bearing heaven-sent gifts of repentance and faith. Now you can become a Christian! The word of God in its power has brought you to life, and the Holy Spirit has shown you Jesus and given you the gifts of repentance and faith. Now you are home and dry.

4. Conviction was created. Acts 17:4—'And some of them believed, and consorted with Paul and Silas'(AV). Or as Thessalonians puts it, the word came 'with deep conviction', convincing us of its truth and saving power.

So then God's election works outward, from the inner reality of His love to the outward preaching of the gospel: the exercise of the power of the word of God, the energy of the Holy Spirit, producing conviction and giving the ability to repent and believe.

The response side (1:6–8)

They truly, and actually, responded. Jesus says, 'You did not choose Me, but I chose you.' (John 15:16) And I reply to Him, 'Well honestly, Lord I did choose You. I remember it well, 23 February 1940, 7.15 p.m.—I know I did.'

'Yes,' He would reply to me, 'Of course you did, but you couldn't have done so if I hadn't chosen you first. Your choice was inherent in Mine.'

And so we come from that glorious truth of election to the reality of the response which they made. Verse 7 expresses their response by saying that they became a Model Church.

It will help us if we study their response by asking the question: what makes a model church?

1. They focused upon the word of God. That was how they became Christians (1:6). They focused on the word of God as the way they became Christians, and they discovered that this related them straight away to the apostles and to the Lord Jesus. They were living in the great system of imitation; they were now apostolic and dominical Christians. In receiving the word of God, they aligned themselves with the apostles, the men of the word, and with the Lord Jesus Christ, that great Man of the word of God. They had the likeness of the apostles and the likeness of Jesus stamped upon them—because they welcomed the word of God. Read 2 Timothy: Paul would say that this was his whole purpose as an apostle—to bequeath the word of God to the church of God. (2 Timothy 1:13,14; 3:10,14; c.f. 2:15; 3:15–17; 4:2). And as for the Lord Jesus, come with Him into the Garden of Gethsemane. When Peter drew his sword and wanted to make a fight of it, Jesus said, 'Do you not think that even now I can ask my Father and he will send me twelve legions of angels? But how then should the Scriptures be fulfilled?' He submitted to the absolute direction of the Scriptures.

Not only so,

2. They persevered with the word of God. They received it in severe suffering with the joy given by the Holy Spirit.

I want to tell you that the Scripture Union portion for the morning Paul wrote this letter to the Thessalonians was the parable of the Sower! That's where he got it from, because the Lord Jesus Christ said in that parable that those who have today heard the word of God, lay hold of it and bring forth fruit with endurance. The fact that endurance was imposed upon the Thessalonians by outward opposition, persecution and that kind of suffering is not the point. In the mercy of God, many—probably most—of us will live long lives without any such experience. But none of us will receive the word of God without our reception of it being tested for reality, to see whether we will follow our reception of the word by our perseverance in the word.

But the Thessalonians' perseverance was not a mere grim determination: it was full of joy because the Holy Spirit was there, annexing Himself to the word so as to bring them the spiritual joy of knowing the truth. In Genesis God's Spirit is depicted as 'hovering', waiting over the waters. Waiting for what? Waiting for God to speak His word so that He might annex himself to that word and make it work. And when God said 'Let there be light' there was light—because the Spirit was there to effectuate the word. So it is every time we open our Bibles: the Spirit is hovering at the ready, waiting to annex Himself to the word; and when He finds in us a determination to persevere in the word, He at once imparts His own joy.

3. They trumpeted the word. Verse 8, 'the Lord's word rang out'. Verse 8 should begin with the word 'because': they are a model church (verse 7) because of this trumpeting! They 'welcomed the message'/'received the word' (verse 6) and they share it (verse 8)—the great hallmark of a model church, its focus upon the word of God. To them the 'word' was what we call the Old Testamment, plus the apostolic teaching derived from it and given fulfilment and substance in the Lord Jesus Christ. It was this word that constituted the church. Without the word of God calling it out, converting its members, giving centre to its life and substance to its message there would be no church at all. The church is the people of God focused down upon the word of God. To us, this word is the whole Scripture which we possess in its entirety. And Paul would challenge us, his present-day Thessalonians, by asking: Are you really Bible people? Are you really persevering in the word of God? Are you trumpeting the word abroad? Are you a model church?

But we must notice that in verse 8, Paul says 'your faith in God has become known everywhere'. In other words, the 'trumpeting of the word' includes how we respond to the word—with all the reality of simple faith, accepting God's truth, believing His promises and trusting His Son. This is part of our message: the saving message is accompanied by an invitation to saving faith. The dying thief at Calvary is the normative believer; he is not an exceptional arrangement made for exceptional circumstances. Why? Because he is shut up to faith pure and simple. He is nailed to a cross, and faith is his only option. There's no good saying to him, 'You've got to perform good works before you become a Christian . . . You've got to be baptised before you can become a Christian . . . You've got to come to the Lord's table before you become a Christian.' The only option open to him is to look to Jesus and live.

> Just as I am, Thou wilt receive
> Wilt welcome, pardon, cleanse, relieve,
> Because Thy promise I believe.

The eternal side (1:9–10)

Verse 9: 'They . . . report'—about their conversion, 'you turned to God'; their separation, 'from idols'; their commitment, 'to serve the living and true God'; their continuance and perseverance, 'and to wait'—to wait on and on and on, says the Greek. And they tell of their expectation, 'to wait for his Son from heaven', and of their concentration, 'whom he raised from the dead—Jesus, who rescues us from the coming wrath.' Isn't that a lovely verse? Very human realities are here: decisive conversion and commitment, a determination to go on with God.

But the main thrust of verses 9–10 is that an eternal issue has been raised and been settled:

> The wrath of a sin-hating God
> with me can have nothing to do.[1]

That's why I call these verses the Eternal Side. And it is all down to our Lord Jesus Christ.

Firstly, because of *the proved efficacy of His work of salvation*. Jesus, 'his Son . . . whom he raised from the dead'. The resurrection of the Lord Jesus Christ is the Father's 'Amen' to the Son's cry, 'It is finished'. 'Amen,' said the Father, and

---

1. This is a paraphrase of two lines from Augustus Toplady's hymn, 'A debtor to mercy alone'.

raised Him from the dead. The resurrection is the confirmation from heaven of the work of Calvary, the proved efficacy of the work of salvation.

Secondly, because of *the lasting consequence of His work of salvation.* He is 'Jesus, who rescues us from the coming wrath'. Notice that present tense. It does not mean that the work of salvation is still going on. It was done once and for all upon the cross, and it needs no re-enactment by Him or anybody else. It is the one eternally efficacious work of salvation, the cross of our Lord Jesus Christ, confirmed by His resurrection. He is the one who still is our rescuer. He is not forever rescuing, He simply rescues for ever. So when Paul looks forward to that dread reality of the Day of Judgement and of standing before God, the Christian has no fear. He has been rescued from the coming wrath.

And how have we entered into that eternal benefit?

O my beloved, listen to me! It all happened the day you were converted. 'You turned to God,' he says, and he uses the lovely dramatic past tense; you did it, you can probably date it. Maybe you can't—but you know you did it, you turned to God. What happened on that day? You entered into a finished work of salvation, and an eternal security in which 'the wrath of a sin-hating God, with you can have nothing to do'.

It's all down to that one single, blessed, central, all-sufficient person: our Lord Jesus Christ.

2: The Church Worthy of God
1 Thessalonians 2:1–16

The most important word for our understanding of 1 Thessalonians 2 comes at the beginning of verse 1, but you will need one of the older versions of the Bible to find it. It is the word 'for' or 'because'. The AV reads, 'For yourselves, brethren, know.' Chapter 2:1 is an explanation of something in chapter 1 (of course in Paul's original letter the text was continuous).

What is being explained? Verse 1 gives a clue: 'entrance' (AV) or 'visit' (NIV). The same word occurs in 1:9, where the 07AV says 'They themselves show of us what manner of entering in we had unto you.' The NIV translates it as 'reception' but that is wrong; it means 'an entrance'. It is the passive counterpart to 'exodus', which means 'a road out'. Thus, 'you remember how we entered in among you.'

Chapter 1:9 tells us what an extraordinarily fruitful, positive thing that approach was. Immediately people began to be converted—'You know what manner of entering we had unto you, and how you turned to God.' It was one of those occasions which was productive of real, actual, lasting conversions.

Why was that? Well, that is to be the link between our two chapters. Paul is setting out to explain how we can arrive at an effective evangelism which bears fruit in positive, unmistakable, lasting conversions. That is the point of the word 'for' in 2:1. 'I'm going to explain to you the background of something that you know well; that my first visit to you was the occasion on which you individually became converted true Christians.'

Beloved, are you tired of belonging to a shrinking cause? Are you tired of preaching the gospel and seeing no results? Are you tired of a church that is failing to grow? Then prick up your ears, because in the design of God, through the ministry of Paul, the answer is here in Holy Scripture. What is the secret of church founding? What is the secret of church growing? What is the secret of true, real, practical, lasting conversions? It's here.

Let's look on into the chapter and discover what Paul has to say to us. Verses 2–4: 'We had previously suffered and been insulted in Philippi, as you know, but we were bold in our God [NIV: "with the help of our God"] we dared to tell you his gospel [lit. "the gospel of God"] in spite of strong opposition [lit. "in much conflict"]. Our appeal does not spring from error or uncleanness, impure motives, nor are we trying to trick you. On the contrary, we speak as men approved by God to be entrusted with the gospel.' There is an all-important truth factor, which Paul calls here 'the gospel of God'. You'll find those words in the AV and the dear and great RV; you must put them back into your NIV. It's not just 'His gospel'; that buries the drama of what Paul is saying. It is the 'gospel of God'.

Paul brought that great and mighty truth factor to the Thessalonians in the context of a dedicated and holy life, and in the context of a heart of which God approved. He said, 'We suffered beforehand . . . we were treated outrageously . . . but we dared to bring you the gospel of God.' There was dedication—and there was holiness: 'Our appeal to you' he said, 'did not spring from error or uncleanness.' He goes on to say that when he was entrusted with the gospel of God, it was by a God who had tested and proved his heart [2:4b].

Look forward to verse 8. 'We loved you so much that we were delighted to share with you not only the gospel of God'—there it is again—'but our lives [own selves] as well, because you had become so dear to us.' Besides the truth factor, the mighty gospel of God, there is the personal factor:

a loving, caring, yearning ministry. That is the context in which truth is presented—a loving heart and a self-sacrificing life and a yearning spirit.

Now verses 10 and 12. The NIV's 'urging' (2:12) is a very bad translation; the word means 'bearing testimony'. Bearing testimony in the Bible is bearing witness to the truth as it is. So here is Paul yet again amongst his dear Thessalonians, as one who is appealing to them and who is ministering a word of comfort to them—but also as one who is always leading them back to the word of truth.

But what sort of man is he? 'How holy, righteous and blameless we were . . .' This truth rings right through the chapter. Paul is saying 'Do you know why our entrance to you was fruitful? Remember how we came among you. What was the character of our entrance amongst you? We came among you with dedicated committed lives, with hearts under divine approval. We came among you as those who are willing to share our very souls with you. We came among you holy, righteous and blameless.' Personal commitment to the gospel, yes; personal commitment to holiness, personal commitment to the gospel, yes; personal commitment in love to those to whom we minister the gospel, oh yes! Personal holiness and blamelessness!

So it's no surprise when in verse 13 we see that 'when you received the word of God, which you heard from us, you accepted it not as the word of men, but as it actually is, the word of God,' because they saw the lives, dedication and loving hearts of the people who were speaking this word to them. Paul said to his dear Timothy, 'As for you, take up your permanent address in the things which you learned and of which you have become confident, knowing from whom you learned them.' (cf 2 Tim. 3:14). The quality of life commends the reality of the message.

We can look at the Thessalonian situation like this. In 1:7 Paul calls them a model church. In 1:8 he tells us part of that model, because, he says, the word 'rang out from you' into every place. A model church is one that shares the word of God. But Paul longs for them to remember something else as well, as he recalls his effective evangelism among them. 'Yes, it was the word of God—and you', he says, 'are fair marvels at that! The word of God is thundering out from you. Well done, you are a model church. But your evangelism will not be fruit-bearing evangelism, unless you wrap up this word of God in holiness of life.'

Let us now look more closely at chapter 2. First,

Our Relationship to the Gospel of God in the Work of Evangelism (2:1–4)

I have chosen this heading because we are going to allow Paul to address us, as he would like to, as his dear Thessalonians; and we are going to reap from his example something for ourselves.

The heart of this section is the two strongly-related ideas which we have already noted. First, *the gospel of God* (2:2). Paul uses many parallel expressions. For example, he speaks of 'the gospel of His Son', by which he means that the Lord Jesus Christ is the sum and substance of the gospel. He is the great subject of the gospel, He is its great content. Similarly, when elsewhere he speaks of 'the gospel of the grace of God', he means that the gospel message is a ministry of imparting the grace of God. But here by 'the gospel of God' he means origin and ownership. Here is the dignity and awesomeness of the gospel. It originated from God Himself, and He is the owner and master of it.

The other key idea here is that *the gospel is something given in trust to people.* It is not just a verbal formula that anybody can take up and prattle at will. It is the gospel of God, given to those who are 'allowed of God' to be put in trust with the gospel (2:4, AV). The implication is that God chooses His trustees: 'I will entrust my gospel to you.' The word 'allow' gives the right idea, but it's not the best translation. Look at the NIV: 'We speak as men approved by God.' That immediately relates to the end of verse 4, where we find the idea of testing the heart. The word translated 'allowed' or 'approved' is the same that is translated 'tested'.

Let us put all those ideas together: 'We speak as those who have been tested and approved to be gospel trustees.' Effective gospel ministry belongs to God's trustees. Effective gospel communication requires more than knowing the facts.

It requires being qualified to pass on those facts; it's a trusteeship given by God.

We are going to go through the verses in turn now, to explore that idea of trusteeship.

In verse 1 the point Paul is pursuing concerns success and failure. In verse 2, having said that 'our entrance into your lives was not a failure', he goes on not to describe the fruit of that entrance, but to consider the factors which make for fruitfulness in the gospel.

In verse 2, the first mark of the trustee: *a conscious reliance on divine strength*. 'We were emboldened in our God', as I suggest to you it should be rendered, combines the ideas of free-flowing liberty of speech and the courage to speak. Actually, there is another English word that well holds both ideas together: 'forthright'. 'We exercised freedom to express the gospel, and exercised the courage to do so.' It was not human stoicism, nor was it a dismissal of suffering as though the flogging and the imprisonment in Philippi had been a light thing. It was an emboldenment in our God; conscious reliance on divine strength.

Secondly, still in verse 2, *a simple presentation of the divine good news*. 'And', said Paul, 'we came among you and we chatted to you.' The word Paul uses is the ordinary word for chit-chatting.

Thirdly, *a ministry of self-subordination*, a ministry prepared to accept risks and live within our hesitations. We chatted away the gospel of God to you, says Paul, 'in spite of strong opposition' (2:2, NIV). The word, however, refers not only to dangers 'out there', but also to dangers and threats within. Paul said, 'I came from that chastising experience at Philippi. I knew there'd be more opposition "out there", but I had something else to deal with: hesitations "within here". I didn't want that to happen again.' How human the apostle was!

Fourthly, *integrity of mind, emotion and will*. Our appeal 'does not spring from error or impure motives, nor are we trying to trick you' (2:3). The AV is much more literal: 'it was not of deceit, nor of uncleanness, or in guile'. The word 'deceit' refers to playing false with the truth, 'uncleanness' to playing false with holiness, and 'guile' to playing false with honesty and honourable methods. 'I came before you,' he said, 'with integrity of mind, because there was no error in what I conveyed to you: it was true. I came to you with integrity of conscience, because there was no uncleanness involved.' In Paul's day travelling lecturers were obsessed with sexual gratification; they loved to get women into their power. Paul says, 'You know it was not like that with us. We weren't out for uncleanness or wrong sexual gratification. We were holy in our conscience. Nor did we practice deceitful methods. We didn't indulge in any sort of evangelistic trickery to get you to make a response. We came to you as people of total integrity . . '

The fifth mark of the trustee is this: *a heart-desire to please God*. 'On the contrary, we speak as [those] approved to be entrusted with the gospel, [Lit: "Not as pleasing men, but God who tests our hearts"]' (2:4). 'God tested us,' says Paul. 'All that suffering in Philippi—He was testing our reality. Are you committed to your own comfort and safety, or are you committed to my gospel?'

Beloved, we say there's no explanation for suffering; but Scripture is full of explanations for suffering. It's just that it's not the kind of explanation we want. We want logic; Scripture presents us with the practicality. If Paul not been flogged in Philippi he would not have known whether he was going on in the gospel for his own purposes, or out of a pure desire solely to please God. He had to be tested.

How do we know whether that travail through which we have just passed or are passing, or the one that may start today or tomorrow, may not be God qualifying us for a trustee-ship of the gospel? If we accept His divine discipline and chastening, if we hold on to Him and love Him with a heart of pure desire for His glory, how do we know that it will not now issue out into such an effective Christian life as we've never experienced before?

Our Relationship to Those to Whom We Present the Gospel (2:5–12)

Now Paul turns to the other side of the coin. The evangelist must relate to the gospel in all the ways we have been considering, but he must also relate to the people to whom he is going to present the gospel. Relating to the truth must be matched by relating to people. If they don't like us, why should they listen to us?

The right to speak must be matched by the right to be heard. The former lies in our relationship to the gospel, the latter in our relationship to people. My ministering brothers, our right to be heard on Sunday depends on how we use Monday to Saturday.

Two illustrations

Paul divides his treatment of this great topic into two sections, verses 5–9 and verses 10–12. At the centre of each section, there is an illustration to help us.

The Nurse-Mother. The first illustration comes in verse 7: 'As apostles of Christ we could have been a burden to you, but we were gentle among you like a mother caring for her little children.' The AV has, 'even as a nurse cherishes her children'. So let me suggest: 'even as a nurse-mother cherishes her very own children'.

A mother will certainly cherish her children. Sometimes we are so enthusiastic as parents it's a marvel our children survive! But a nurse is trained. And in this illustration she is not now a nanny in somebody else's house but is looking after her very own children. You see the quality of tenderness and love and care. Paul says, if you are going to be evangelists, there's this vital matter of un-self-seeking devotion.

Before that illustration, in verses 5–6, Paul speaks of shunning self-advantage. Verse 5, 'You know we never used flattery'—the word means 'cajolery'. It means using words to gain advantage from the people you are talking to. 'Nor did we put on a mask to cover up greed'—the word is 'covetousness', an insatiable desire to possess more. It is often used in the New Testament for sexual greed and insatiable sexual appetite, but here it is used simply of the desire to possess more and more; a desire that is never satisfied. Thirdly, 'We were not looking for praise from men, not from you or anyone else. As apostles of Christ we could have been a burden to you.'—'We didn't allow you to put us on a pedestal. We have that right, for we are apostles of Christ, members of a unique chosen band; we are different, unique, special; but we did not allow you to put us on a pedestal.'

The particular pedestal he had in mind was the pedestal of receiving support for evangelism. It was a matter of principle for Paul that though he would gladly accept support from an established church, he would not accept support for evangelism from the people he was evangelising. The ministry had to free, like the gospel.

In verse 8, on the other side of the illustration, he says, 'We loved you so much [AV: "affectionately desirous"] that we were delighted to share with you not only the gospel of God but also our own souls [AV] because you were dear to us.' Verse 9 speaks of costly self-sacrifice: 'Surely you remember, brothers, our toil and hardship; we worked night and day in order not to be a burden . . . while we preached the gospel of God.' What a picture! If on one hand he avoided self-advantage, on the other he pursued their advantage, both by his willingness to lay down his soul for them and by his willingness to work day and night so that the gospel might be free to them.

The Father. Paul's second illustration comes in verses 11. He was a mother—and he was a father. And where the illustration of the mother draws attention to un-self-seeking devotion, that of the father draws attention to holy living and encouraging teaching.

The father first *presented to his sons a life that they could see.* 'You know how holy, righteous and blameless we were; you know what you saw in us' (cf 2:10). That's what a father should be. Do the words 'holy', 'righteous' and 'blameless' have particular significance? Probably not; they are probably simply heaping up the idea of holiness. What an emphasis!

Secondly the father *encouraged his sons and pointed them in the right direction.* Verse 12 holds together encouragement and exhortation: 'We pointed you in the right direction with positive encouragements. And when you tripped up as you tried to follow our encouragements and our directions, when you fell flat on your face, we were there to kiss your bruises and make them better. We were there to console and to comfort, just like a father. But all the time, undergirding our exhortation and our pointers and comforts, there was a testimony to the truth. We were there to share the truth with you. And what's more, we were there to hold God up before you, that you should walk "worthy of God who calls you into His kingdom and glory".'

There are three things about God's call. He calls; He calls into His kingdom; and He calls into His glory. The call of God in Paul has a very special meaning. Those of you who remember National Service will remember Call-Up Papers. They were not a gracious invitation by the Sovereign to enter his service, such that you could take time to consider whether or not to accept. They were not an invitation, but an appointment. The call of God is His appointment. By His call He brings us into that blessed, transplanted situation where every need is met, in the elements and sub-elements of the soil we live in, in God the Father and the Lord Jesus Christ. So, as a father exhorts his son, Paul reminds them of the sufficiency of God, of the obedience that is due to the great King, and of the glory: he reminds them of the promises that will entice and attract them forward like a great divine carrot—keep going, the prize is yours! The sufficiency of God, the obedience that is due to Him and the promises that lie at the end of the road; the Father, holy encouragement, and teaching.

'I don't think evangelism's my calling,' we say. Before we leave these verses, consider: Paul doesn't mention a large-scale evangelistic campaign. He's not leading Mission England, Mission Greece or even Mission Thessalonica. Did you hear him saying anything about pulpits and platforms? About advertising campaigns or appearing on television? We must be careful not to get the wrong picture in our minds when we use the word 'evangelism'—and yet he was an evangelist: verse 9, 'We preached the gospel of God to you.' Isn't that evangelism? But how did he do it?

One, it was *love evangelism*. Evangelism carried on by

cultivating personal, tender, caring relationships, like a mother with her children; evangelism based not upon a gift that some may have and others not, but upon a virtue common to all Christians. To love like the love of Jesus.

It was *workplace evangelism*. 'We preached the gospel unto you as we worked day and night.' The bench at which he made his tents was his evangelistic hall and platform. He chattered the gospel as he dealt with his customers. It was workplace evangelism, evangelism in the office, the home and workplace, the ordinary place and the launderette.

And it was *report evangelism*. 'We preached unto you the gospel of God.' It is the town crier's word. Go to a town crier and ask him, 'Why are you shouting at the top of your voice? And why are you saying what you are saying?' He will point to the town hall: 'Because they told me to shout, and they told me what to shout.'

'We came to you,' says Paul, 'as a town-crier with the gospel of God, because he told us to do it and he told us what to say.'

Isn't this *domesticated* evangelism? Can we now side-step the challenge?

Our Relationship to the word of God (2:13–16)

Paul's last topic matches that with which he opened. In verse 13 you see how he is broadening the matter out. We are people who are not narrowly related to one brand or branch of truth, awesome and marvellous though it may be; we have a whole Bible to relate to. We are people relating to the word of God. Paul says, 'Oh how I give thanks! We brought the word to you, but you saw at once that it was more than our word, it was the word of God.'

The nature of the word

So let us think about the nature of the word of God.

This word, says verse 13, is 'at work in you who believ [lit. "effective in you who believe"]'. The word of God cannot but achieve its purpose. It is effective. Why? Simply because it is the word of God, and it remains the word of God in the fullest sense, even though it came through human agents; it remains the word of God, undiminished by the fact that it is also the word of man. 'It is 'the word'—let me change the NIV here—'which you heard of us . . . of God.' Paul quickly corrects himself, you see. It was a human word, with human agents and a human voice, inflexion and accent—'which you heard of us'. But it is also, and more importantly, the word of God and it has remained undisturbed, uncorrupted, undiminished as the word of divine truth. It came through human agents but it is the word of God. And that's true, beloved, of that whole Book.

The response to the word

What does Paul tell us about their response to the word of God?

He says, 'When you received the word . . . you *accepted* it.' To 'receive' is the technical word for recognising something as authoritative. But, adds Paul, you went beyond that. You welcomed it as something lovely. So there are two immediate elements in our response to the word of God—recognition of authority, leading us to receive it, and opening of mind and heart, by which we welcome it.

And the word is effective 'in you who believe'. Our third response to the word of God is to believe it, to believe its teaching and its promises, and in the obedience of faith to act upon its commands.

Fourthly (2:14), 'You suffered.' We've already had this thought in 1:6. As before, it's not the form in which the testing comes that matters, but its inevitability. Their reception of the word was tested by an onset of persecution. The word of God is always challenged. Part of our true reception of the word of God is not only to receive it as authoritative, to welcome it as lovely, to believe it and to obey it, but to persevere in its truth in the face of any odds—even the odds of our own desire to stay in bed in the morning. True reception of the word of God is persevering reception.

This, then, is the effectiveness of the word of God in those who believe. But in 2:15–16 there is the dreadful effectiveness of the word of God in those who reject it.

Paul says here about the Jews that they 'killed the Lord

Jesus and the prophets and also drove us out' (2:15). They had the word of God in the loveliest personal form of Jesus; they had the word of God in the inspired form of scriptural prophecy; they had the word of God in its up-to-date form of New Testament apostleship—and they rejected it out of hand. Furthermore, they rejected the word of God in its evangelistic benefit for the whole world. 'They wouldn't have us speak to the Gentiles that they might be saved' (cf 2:16).

We must handle this passage with great care. Paul is not, despite some commentators' suggestions, indulging in a sudden outburst of anti-Semitism. Nor is he contradicting any of what he says in Romans 9–11, where he longs with all his heart for the conversion of his countrymen and promises that for them as for everybody else turning to Christ is the way of salvation, and forecasts for them before the coming of Christ a notable turning of Israel according to the flesh. But he *is* saying that where there is rejection of the word of God—as there undoubtedly was on the part of the Jews he has in mind—where there is refusal of Jesus, rejection of the prophets, driving out of the apostles, barring of the evangelistic message; where there is that great four-fold rejection of the word of God, there cannot be anything else but the utmost judgement of God. That is the dire reality of rejecting the word of God.

He is not anti-Jewish. There is no polemic, simply a basic statement of a dreadful but an inescapable fact: that when people reject the word of God, they come under judgement in its final and full form. And these words are written here in Scripture, beloved, in case you or I might sit easy or loose to our own attitude to the word of God or to our God-given task to qualify as evangelists. For what Paul says was true of some people whom he had in mind is true of persons whom you and I know. And judgement will come upon them to the uttermost, unless they hear of Christ. Perhaps nobody can get close enough to love them, and care for them, and chat the gospel to them, but you or me.

Turn that last passage on its head. Listen to this. Receiving the Bible we receive the verbal portrait of Jesus. Receiving the Bible we receive the inspired word of God through His chosen agents, prophets and apostles, the very word of God. Receiving the Bible we receive the message of salvation. Dwelling on the verbal portrait of Jesus, by embracing His word we embrace Him. Dwelling on the inspired word of God, embracing the inspired word, we bow in reverence before its author. When we embrace the message of salvation, and in that way embrace Holy Scripture, we are bringing into our lives all the nourishments of the gospel in grace and peace, which will enrich us and enable us to be God's transplants in a wilderness world.

3: The Church and the Holy Will of God 1 Thessalonians 2:17–4:8

Our passage this morning is the story of Paul's love affair with the Thessalonian church: how deeply he loved them, how deeply he felt being separated from them, how deeply he wanted to get back among them again.

The Love Story in Five Steps

Let us briefly step through this love story.

Step one: Paul's separation (2:17–20)
'But, brothers, when we were torn away from you for a short time . . .' (2:17). He uses a very strong word, 'like orphaned children taken from you'. We saw yesterday that he expressed his relationship to the Thessalonians as a nurse-mother and then as a caring, directive, loving father. We have already noticed, as we will again on Friday morning, how frequently he addresses them as brothers—in fact he uses the address 'brothers' more frequently in the Thessalonian letters than in those to any other church. He's a mother to them, he's a father to them, he's a brother amongst brothers, and now he's a child bereaved of its parents. How greatly Paul loved these Thessalonian Christians!

It was no formal or pretend relationship: being snatched

away, bereaved, for a short time—'in presence, not in heart' (AV). His heart is engaged in this relationship. He longs for them with what the NIV correctly renders as 'intense longing'. Indeed he says (2:19) that the prospect of the coming of the Lord Jesus Christ itself would be a less a matter of hope, joy and glory if Paul thought they weren't going to be there ready.

How deeply, how affectionately, how from the heart Paul loves his Thessalonians! And of course at the moment we are his Thessalonians, so he loves us like that. He has that earnest desire and longing that we should be stable in Christ, growing in Christ, and ready and acceptable to the Lord when He comes again.

Step two: Timothy's mission (3:1–5)

Things became too much for Paul and he was ready to make some considerable sacrifice. 'We thought it good to be left at Athens alone.'

If you are one of those hardy people who can go abroad to strange places without batting an eyelid, then perhaps you won't feel Paul's sense of worry and fear at being alone in a strange city. King George V would have: he once said to a friend, 'Abroad is awful: take my word for it—I've been there.' Paul had that sense of dread and isolation, of being under threat in this great cosmopolitan and foreign city. But he accepted that burden and he accepted being parted from his beloved Timothy. Verse 2: another member of the family lost.

I think the AV is possibly slightly more correct here than the NIV, but it isn't important; what is underlined in verse 2 is that the person sent was a special person, but that Paul was willing to accept that separation and bereavement. He sent him 'to strengthen and encourage you'. He himself needed the comfort of good news about them, as we shall see in a moment; but his whole thought in sending Timothy was to establish and comfort them. The word 'strengthen' might be translated 'buttress you'—'In case your fabric was in danger of collapsing, I sent him to be a flying buttress to hold you in place.' His whole thought was for their welfare.

Step three: Timothy's return (3:6–10)

Timothy came back, and oh! what a tonic it was for the apostle. 'Brought us good news' is exactly the same word used for preaching the gospel. It was like hearing the gospel all over again. 'It brought me a gospelling joy when I heard good news that all was well with you, good news of your faith and of your love and that you have a good remembrance of us, and desire greatly to see us.' It was lovely news that Timothy brought back from Thessalonica. 'Now we really live, since you are standing firm in the Lord'—it's like an injection of life to him, to hear good news from Thessalonica.

A picture is building up of such a loving relationship, such a concerned apostle, such a tender heart towards the Thessalonians whom he had led to faith in our Lord Jesus Christ. 'Indeed,' he says in verse 9, 'I don't know how to thank God enough . . . What thanks can we render?'

Step four: Paul turns to prayer (3:11–13)

There is a lesson to be learned in all this which we should note if only in passing.

Paul had felt that their spiritual welfare was largely dependant upon him being there to minister to them. 'I feel desperate that I can't get to you,' he has been saying. 'Is all well with you, has the tempter tempted you, is your faith collapsing?' He thought that they so deeply needed his tender, loving care. But Timothy came back and said, 'They've been getting along very nicely, thank you, without you.'

Paul returns to a place where he has been all the time: the place of prayer. Verse 10: 'Night and day we pray most earnestly that we may see you again and supply what is lacking in your faith.' But now he returns to it in a new spirit, leaving it entirely to God whether he ever gets back to Philippi or not, for now he sees that really it doesn't matter. He goes on praying for it, of course, but he leaves it to the Lord.

'Now God Himself and our Father and our Lord Jesus Christ direct our way unto you' (3:11, AV)—but whether I get to you or not, what does it matter? God is looking after His people. So 'the Lord make you to increase and abound in love one toward another, and toward all men, even as we do toward you: To the end he may stablish your hearts unblameable in holiness . . .' (3:12, AV). The welfare of the church rests in the hands of a sovereign and loving God, Himself concerned for His people.

How strongly and dramatically that thought came in! Can you sense the difference between Paul's prayers as reported in verse 10 and as written down in verses 11 and 12? 'If the Lord brings me back, great! But if He doesn't, He's there and He will make you perfect in holiness, and He will make your faith and your love go on increasing and out-reaching. You're all right. You're in the hand of God, and I'm happy to leave you there.'

Step five: Paul's conclusion (4:1–8)

You would think, because the NIV uses the word 'finally' in 4:1, that this was a separate, concluding section. But that is not actually its sense. After all, Paul still has a long way to go in this letter, so why would he say 'finally' in the middle, when he knows he is nowhere near the end? That should make us be suspicious of that rendering.

The AV, on the other hand, says 'furthermore', suggesting a link back to the preceding subject and an intention to pursue it further. In addition, neither NIV nor AV translate a word, 'therefore', at the beginning of 4:1. There is a real link created between the end of chapter 3 and the beginning of chapter 4: 'therefore, to proceed'. He's going on with some subject on which he has already touched, and is taking it on to the next step. What is that subject?

Let me tell you. At the end of chapter 3 Paul prayed 'To the end that he may stablish [buttress] your hearts, unblameable in holiness.' Now he says, 'Furthermore, having raised that point of holiness with you, I have more to say about it.' This is his topic as he goes on into 4:1–8. It is announced at the beginning of verse 3: 'This is the will of God, your holiness.' I've more to say to you about it, says Paul. Holiness is not just something that God will do for you, it is a will of God which you must obey: your holiness.

In 3:13 'holiness' is the end product, completed holiness, but the slightly different word 'holiness' in 4:3 is the practical and progressive holiness that the Christian is to experience in the course of living in this world: 'This is the will of God, that you should go on being and becoming his holy people.'

So Paul brings the love story to a very particular point. It is like his teaching on marriage in Ephesians, where he says that the task of a husband in loving his wife is to present her perfect in holiness, without spot or blemish, like a true bride of Christ (cf. Eph. 5:27–28). That is what he wants for the Thessalonian church when Christ comes again.

Paul's Key Themes

Now let us go back through our passage, because in each of the five steps there are key ideas on which we must dwell a little more closely.

The reality and power of Satan (2:17–20)

The subject of these verses is Paul's earnest longing to get back and why he couldn't do so (2:18). So we must pause in this tiny section of the letter and note the reality and the power of Satan in relation to believers on earth.

When it says 'Satan stopped us [AV: "hindered us"],' it is like our expression 'stopped us in our tracks'. 'Here am I,' says Paul. 'My bag is packed, I've noted the time of the train I want to catch, the taxi has been ordered—but do you think I could get out of the house? Satan stopped me in my tracks.'

We need to get Satan into perspective. I must say to you that in my opinion we hear far too much about Satan and demons in Christian conversation today. It is too much, because it is out of proportion to what we find in the New Testament. Satan is mentioned by name only nine times in Paul's letters. Compare that with the hundreds of times that Paul refers to 'Jesus', 'the Lord Jesus', 'Jesus Christ', 'Christ Jesus', 'the Lord Jesus Christ'. Let's get a sense of proportion!

The second thing I would say to you to keep this question of Satan and his power in a biblical perspective and proportion, is that Satan in the Bible does not operate as a free agent but only within the sovereign purposes of God. Even in so striking a passage as Revelation 20 where Satan is let loose, you will discover that he is let loose only to do what God predetermined that he should do. The opening chapters of Job contain all that the Bible wishes us to know on this point. In Job 1:6–12 Satan is depicted as coming to be debriefed by God. 'Where have you come from?' says the Lord. 'From walking up and down on the earth and going to and fro in it.' What happens next? Was it Satan who said to God, 'I'm going to have a go at your servant Job'? No. It was the Lord who said to Satan, 'Have you noticed my servant Job?' Now Satan has been given a little liberty to operate. 'Let me have a go at him. If you do I'll soon expose him as a fraud.' 'All right,' says the Lord, 'have a go at him. But you mustn't touch him in himself, you mustn't damage his health.' You see the limitation. Job loses his children, his home and his goods. 'The Lord gave and the Lord has taken away, blessed be the name of the Lord.'

Satan comes back to the Lord. 'Have you seen my servant Job? Just as perfect as ever, isn't he?'

'Of course; but you've set a hedge about him. Let me have a real go at him. Skin for skin, yea all that a man has, he will give for his life.'

'Right,' says the Lord, 'you can lay your finger upon him—but you mustn't take his life.'

In all this Job maintained his integrity and didn't sin. But the point we need to notice is that Satan is hemmed in. In the whole of the book, we are not told what purpose the Lord had in mind in directing Satan's attention to Job. All we know is that somehow great eternal issues are at stake, and can only be solved in this way; and Job is the arena of this conflict. Satan can only operate within the permission and direction and limitation of God.

The Bible tells us that God runs history in a similar way. Isaiah describes it as being rather like a horse and rider (Isa. 63:13–14). The horse has the energy to jump a fence, but will not get over it unless the rider directs him to it. So there is a force and an energy, and there is a force and a direction. That's the way the Lord runs history. He sends the Assyrian careering to Jerusalem—that's the horse—and on its back is the great divine rider, directing all that sinful power and energy to perform holy purposes.

Satan always has the Lord on his back.

So let us get this into proportion. There is supernatural power ranged against us. There is ceaseless malevolence, the god of this world, the blinding of eyes lest people see the glory of our Lord Jesus Christ and the light of the gospel. And here in Thessalonians 2:18 there is that power putting a road block across Paul. How did he do it? We're not told. But in the hand of God, wasn't it marvellous that Paul couldn't get back? As a result they had a much better and richer experience; as independent believers, living for themselves with God, entering into His blessing and learning that, apostle or no apostle, ministry or no ministry, God was looking after His church.

It's a terribly frustrating thing to be Satan! We can begin to attempt to guess why the Lord directed him to put up the road block: so that Paul could learn, so that the Thessalonians could learn, so that we could learn that our spiritual welfare rests in the hands of God.

The Christian in the arena (3:1–5)

Paul has not finished with Satan. Now he expresses his real fear, on account of which he sent Timothy: 'For this reason, when I could stand it no longer, I sent to find out about your faith. I was afraid that in some way the tempter might have tempted you and our efforts might have been useless' (3:5).

Christians are in a certain arena where they face the power of the tempter, working along a certain line that is revealed here. Paul says he was afraid lest 'anyone should be moved by these afflictions' (3:3, AV). The word 'afflictions' is the ordinary trials and troubles of life. It may be the persecutions referred to in the NIV, it may be simply the ordinary troubles, difficulties and botherations of life which come upon every Christian; under those trials, there's the danger that we would be moved.

The word translated 'moved' started life as a word for a dog wagging its tail. It came to mean 'cajolery', towards a particular end, as when a dog wags its tail to cajole you into taking it for a walk or giving it its supper. The word acquired connotations of influencing, agitating, unsettling, stirring up. 'I was so afraid,' says Paul, 'lest with the onset of the trials and tribulations of life you might be perturbed, and this would be an opportunity for Satan to leap into your lives and to mar your progress in faith.'

Isn't that where we often are? Don't the trials and tribulations of life begin by putting doubt into our hearts and lives? That dread question 'Why?' is so often the question of doubt. (Incidentally, if you want a biblical question to ask when trouble comes, don't ask 'Why?', because you won't be told the answer. Ask 'Who? Who did it?' Out of the Bible comes the answer, 'None other than the Lord Himself, you're safe in His hands, trust Him.')

With trouble come doubt and a shaking of faith, and the pressure of Satan to lever us away from a firm and believing attachment to the Lord Jesus Christ. Paul says, 'But didn't I fortify you by knowledge?' Look in verse 3: ' . . . so that no-one would be unsettled by these trials. You know quite well that we were destined for them. In fact, when we were with you, we kept telling you that we would be persecuted. And it turned out that way, as you well know.'

Oh, will we learn it, dear friends? James says, 'Consider it pure joy, my brothers, whenever you face trials of many kinds' (Jas. 1:2). But we pay no heed; we don't count it joy. Peter says, 'Think it not strange concerning the fiery trial that is to try you.' And we don't believe him either, we think it's very strange indeed. And we go on with our 'Why? Why?' and our doubting of the goodness of God.

But Paul says, 'We must go through many hardships to enter the kingdom of God' (Acts 14:22). The word 'must' means not only that it is necessary, but that it is right and proper. Here is a Christian inevitability. Don't be knocked off course. Don't let Satan enter in and tempt you when trials come. Grasp today, and hold from today, the fact that this is not strange, but a Christian inevitability; and for the Christian, a right and proper thing.

And it is a sphere of discipleship. Verse 3: 'we are appointed [NIV: "destined"]'. When Paul wrote to the Philippians from his prison he said, 'You know my imprisonment, contrary to what you might have expected, is becoming a real testimony to the gospel, because they know that I am in prison for Christ—I am on duty for the gospel' (Phil. 1:17). It is the same word here. Suffering is where we are on duty for God; it is the appointed sphere of our discipleship. So the real question should not be 'Why?' or even 'Who?', but 'What?'—'What shall I now do so as to exercise in this situation my Christian discipleship, my devotion to our Lord Jesus Christ?'

In the only situation that has touched myself and my wife in our forty-seven years of marriage and could come anywhere near being called a real trial and tribulation, a loved and respected friend wrote to us: 'You will never pass this way again. Make sure there is something in it for Him.'

It is the sphere of our devotion, discipleship and duty to our Lord Jesus Christ. But it's all in the sovereign hand of God. *Why* are we appointed to it? *Why* is it a Christian inevitability? Because that's His way. Sometimes, in mercy, it's all green pastures and still waters, praise the Lord. Sometimes it's the dark valley, the valley of the shadow of death. Do you remember what Psalm 23 says comes between the two? *Why* is our portion the green pasture? *Why* is our portion the dark valley? What does the Scripture say? 'He leads me in paths of righteousness, for His name's sake.'

What is a path of righteousness? It is a path that makes sense to God. You see, we think the only path that is proper is the one that make sense to us, and when suffering or trials come we say, 'It doesn't make sense.' Yes, it does. It makes sense to Him. That's all that matters.

The Christian victory (3:6–10)

There is a difference between heavenly victory and earthly victory. Heavenly victory is the greatest exorcism that's ever been seen; it is the final complete ousting of Satan eternally into the lake of fire, never again to raise his head or tempt the people of God nor even be noticed in our eternal existence. But on earth the believer does not experience that kind of exorcism; satanic temptation is our inescapable earthly lot. So when Paul goes on to speak of the triumph in

Thessalonica, he doesn't say anything about exorcising Satan. He doesn't say, 'I'm so glad you all got together and had that mighty service of praise and worship, and claimed the victory of Christ and banished Satan from your midst . . .'; nothing of the sort.

Neither are heavenly circumstances like earthly circumstances. In heaven we will live in the paradise of God, and everything will be totally and unimaginably perfect. There will never again be anything in our circumstances to challenge our faith or make us hesitate in our faith; no more trials or tribulations—glory, glory all the way in the paradise of God! But it's not like that on earth. And God has given us no way, and very little permission, to go about trying to change our circumstances. They are to be accepted first and foremost from the hand of God, until He is pleased to raise up some way of changing them.

Living on earth is so different from what it will be like living in heaven. So Paul doesn't say, 'What a mighty victory you have scored in driving Satan out, Thessalonica, and in so dramatically changing your circumstances in answer to prayer.' That's not the essence of earthly victory. And yet they scored a triumph, for Paul says, 'It was just as good news to me as the gospel', 'It was like a fresh injection of life', and, in verse 9, 'I don't know how to thank God enough.' Whatever they did, it was magnificent.

So what was their victory? I can tell you in two words. Their victory was Christian *stability*: verse 8, 'we live if you stand fast in the Lord'. And their victory was Christian *virtue*: verse 6, 'Timothy brought us the good news of your faith and your love—and your standing fast.'

Where have you heard those before? In 1:3. 'I look back,' said Paul, 'and I remember how your faith was at work and your love was labouring and you are steadfast because of your hope in the coming of Jesus.' Faith, love and stickability. 'And it was like the good news of the gospel to me, it was like water falling on thirsty ground, I didn't know how to thank God enough.' Christian stability, Christian virtue. Beloved, that's the Christian victory.

R. W. Dale, a great preacher of the last century, wrote a marvellous book called *The Atonement*. He says in it that love is not love until it actually bestows benefit on the beloved. 'I might say to Mrs Dale, "My darling, I love you so much I'm going down to the railway station to throw myself under a train". And Mrs Dale would say to me, "I'd far rather you stayed at home and did the washing up." ' Christian victory is not in the drama but in faith and love and stickability in the ordinary realities of life.

The Christian walk (3:11–4:8)

We've seen Paul talk of the power of Satan, and in the two middle sections we've seen how Christians are called in the arena of conflict to maintain their stand and their virtues of faith and love. So our passage begins with the power of Satan, moves into the Christian arena of conflict, and ends with the power of God. 'God is on your side, beloved,' he says in verse 13.

Christians are a kind of spiritual sandwich-filling. There they are in the middle of things, in the arena, contending with Satan in the circumstances of life, striving and struggling to maintain faith and hope and steadfastness. On one side is Satan to devour them and on the other side is God to perfect them. You see the shape of our passage, and the message that shape contains. Now; who do you think's going to win? The Satan whose power is limited to the purposes of God—or the God whose purposes are growth in faith and holiness, until we are ready for the coming of Jesus?

Our section begins with a prayer and in chapter 4 proceeds to a plea. The prayer is in 3:11–13, and the plea in 4:1–8. The prayer is that God will perfect them in holiness—we have looked at that already—and Paul is so certain that He will. And the plea, brothers and sisters, is that they will get on with being holy. Being a Christian is not a dressing-gown-and-slippers exercise. The New Testament never uses that model, but it does use that of an armed soldier. And even though it is true that in the last day we will give all the praise to him—'Glory be to the Father, the Son and the Holy Ghost', we will say, and all the holiness we will then enjoy is the work of His merciful and gracious hand—yet He brings us to holiness as we commit ourselves to realise the holy will of God in our own lives.

'Therefore,' Paul says (4:1), 'I beseech you and I exhort you'—you have to get involved in this God-given exercise of pursuing holiness—'that as we have told you how you ought to walk, even as you are walking . . .' Walking is one of the early signs of life. 'Is the baby walking yet?' we say. And it is something that requires initiative on the part of the person concerned. Paul says, 'I beseech you and exhort you' to start your walk of holiness (4:1, AV).

Five things about that walk.

It is to be *a directed walk* (4:1–3). It consists of obeying God. Paul says, 'You received of us how you ought to walk.' The verb 'received' means 'Here is a truth that came to you with authority.' He goes on, 'You know what commandments we gave you.' The word belongs in a military context: a command that brooks no argument. We are commanded in the way of obedience. It's an apostolic command, because this is the will of God; not just what the apostle wants, but, through him, what God wants. We should be up and walking in obedience to His commandments and in pursuit of holiness.

It is to be *an informed walk* (4:4–5), to be carried on by knowing God. 'That everyone of you should know how to possess his vessel in sanctification and honour' (AV); Paul is here talking particularly about sexual offences. Maybe Timothy had reported that some of the Thessalonians were wobbling in their morality and were inclined to sexual lapses. Maybe Paul was simply addressing the condition of the church in a menacing world which was as sexually alert and as sexually insane as the world is today. Maybe he was just saying 'Look, there is a cardinal way in which you can show your separation from the world and your dedication to God: keep clear of sexual offences.'

And he says in this regard, 'Everyone of you should know how to possess his vessel in sanctification and honour.' There are two equally valid ways of understanding 'vessel'. It may be one's own body, specially in relation to its sexual powers. Or it may be a metaphor for one's wife, not at all derogatory, and mean that 'each one of you should obtain his own wife and marry her in sanctification and honour'. There is a strong implication that, according to the apostolic command and the will of God in relation to holiness, sexual activity is confined in, and restricted to, monogamous marriage. When he says, 'This is a great thing you've got to avoid', he also says, 'Here is a remedy, that you should know how to enter into possession of your sexual faculties and enter into the possession of your own wife in sanctification and honour.' He continues, 'Not in the lust of concupiscence, even as the Gentiles which know not God.'

Now without losing the primary reference of sexual purity, we want to broaden the matter out into the general concept of Christian holiness. Verse 4 begins with the idea of 'knowing how', and verse 5 ends with the idea of 'knowing God'. If only the Gentiles knew God, they wouldn't behave like that. Knowing God is the clue to knowing how. So, my brother or sister, if we are plagued with sexual temptations and lapse into sexual sin, if we lapse from the way of holiness, the key is to be an informed believer.

It is to be *a reverential walk* in the fear of God (4:6). 'Let no man go beyond and defraud his brother in any matter: because the Lord is the avenger.' We need to recover our concept of the fear of God.

It is to be *a trustful walk*, believing God (4:7) 'For God hath not called us'—watch the translation here—'unto uncleanness'—that is to say, as an external objective—'but he has called us in holiness.'

Yesterday I compared the call of God to receiving one's Call-Up Papers. Call-Up Papers put a young man in a different situation from that in which he was in the moment before they arrived. 'Then I was a civilian, now I am a soldier. Of course I don't know how to be a soldier, I've got to learn that yet. I have yet got to become what I am.' And when it says here that God called us in holiness, it means that by His call He put us within the context of holiness, and we say, 'We are not yet holy.' No—but we've got to become what we are. Holiness is not an external objective but the reality to which we have been brought, and with which we are surrounded by the fact that God has conscripted us.

So we say to Him, 'Lord, I'm desperately unholy in all my inclinations, I desperately want to be holy. I believe that You have given me all that I need to be, therefore it is worth struggling and striving.'

Finally, it is to be *an enabled walk* in which we are to enjoy the presence of the Holy God resident in our hearts. Verse 8: 'He therefore that despiseth,'—if you feel like sitting loose to this call to holiness—'despiseth not man, but God.' It's God who holds out this objective before us and has surrounded us with this reality so that we may live it out. It's God's will for us.

And what else has He done? He has given us His Holy Spirit. The holy life is the life of enjoying the inward residence of the Holy God, respecting that Holy One and drawing upon that holy life which God has made to reside within us. He is the giving God, says the Greek; He is the giving God who keeps on ever giving us His Holy Spirit. And why is He called the Holy Spirit? Because His task is to administer holiness to us, as we walk with God.

4: The Church Listening for the Trumpet 1 Thessalonians 4:9–18

In one way, Paul's letter is like any letter between loving friends: the outpouring of impressions, opinions and facts. But always in Holy Scripture there's another factor at work: the inspiring Spirit of God. So while we trace out what Paul said to the Thessalonians and try to follow his train of thought, we are looking at the same time for the mind of the Holy Spirit in building up a body of truth that reaches from the Thessalonians of those days to us, the Thessalonians of today—a coherent presentation of scriptural truth.

So before we turn to verse 9 of chapter 4, it is good to look back and remind ourselves of how we got to this point and then to look forward to what follows, so that we may begin to see how this letter is a unity around certain great related truths. So start with me again, please, at what I think bids fair to be the entitling verse of this letter considered as a statement from the Holy Spirit to the church—1:7, 'You became a model.'

We saw that the church's status as a model depended upon its relationship to the word of God—1:6, the word to which they responded; 1:8, the word they immediately began to spread. Then in chapter 2 Paul elaborated that idea of the church reaching out with the word of God; he tells the Thessalonians that effective evangelism is the reaching out with the word that God speaks, but is also a reaching out with that word in the context of holy living. And yesterday we saw Paul developing that point from the end of chapter 2 on into chapter 4. He does so by telling them the story of his love for the church, but we saw that beyond and beneath that human story were great spiritual realities—warfare with Satan, the church in the arena; and above all, the call to be, by means of faith, love and steadfastness, the holy people according to the will of God.

So even when Paul seems to be telling a simple human story of how he loves the church, he is also, in the hand of the Holy Spirit, pursuing this great truth that if we are to share the word of God effectively with the world, we must become God's holy people.

The first dimension is the word, the second is holiness. But there is a third dimension. In 2:7–8, Paul speaks of himself as a mother. Love must come to exist between the evangelist and the evangelised. 'I came to you,' said Paul, 'with parental longing.' The sharing of the gospel of God in the context of a holy life is not a remote detached exercise, but one in which the heart must engage in love with those to whom the ministry is being offered.

It's that aspect which he begins to take up now in 4:9 as he introduces the topic of brotherly love. A very important little verse, 3:12, which we had to skate over yesterday, puts the idea into its proper wider context. Paul is praying that God will prosper the Thessalonians spiritually: 'May the Lord make your love increase and overflow'—listen—'for each other and everyone else.' Love must overflow for the world if we are to win the world. But we must learn love in the context of the church. It is only from the base of a loving church that we can reach out in love to the world. That's why in 4:9 Paul first launches into the topic of creating a church base of love, from which there then can be an outreach of loving evangelism and the drawing of a needy world into a heart of love already beating in the local church.

The question therefore in evangelism is always this: Is our church worth joining? Have we created here a basis of Christian love, with all that goes along with that, into which the world can be drawn as we go out in love and holiness to share with them the gospel of God? I want you to see how this topic of mutual love amongst believers now dominates Paul's thought.

In 4:13 he moves to another topic which he announces in the same way: 'about those who fall asleep'. He intends to deal with that question by teaching us about the return of our Lord Jesus Christ. But see in 4:18 the point to which he leads that great truth: 'encourage each other'. Even the great truth of the coming again of our Lord Jesus Christ is bent to this end, that we should belong to a mutually loving, mutually caring body, the church of our Lord Jesus Christ.

In 5:1 he announces a third topic: 'about times and seasons'. When is Jesus coming? He ventures into the area of the undatable return of our Lord Jesus Christ. But again in 5:11, the point to which he returns, having dwelt on the truth that we do not know the date: 'Therefore encourage one another and build one another up.' He is dominated by this thought of mutuality in church life: mutual love, mutual encouragement, mutual upbuilding. And indeed, as we shall see tomorrow, this continues right through to the end. Take one verse, 5:26—'Greet all the brothers with a holy kiss.' Love is to find expression when we meet each other, not just in verbal greeting, but also in Paul's day, with a 'holy kiss'—or, today, says John Stott, rather austerely I think, with 'a culturally appropriate gesture'.

The model church is the church of brotherly love, and has to be, if it's going to reach out in love to the world around. In fact Paul in 4:9 says, 'You have no need for me to say anything to you about this, for you yourselves have been taught by God—but that's not going to stop me!' Why? Why spend valuable space writing to them about something that they know very well already? It is Paul once again, under the guidance of the Holy Spirit, building up a body of truth. There is something that they—and we—must learn even if they, and we, know it already. So here it is: 'Now about brotherly love . . . you must love each other.' He must put it on paper because it is part of the model for the church as long as it is on earth.

Mutual Love: a Call to Personal Responsibility (4:9–12)

'In this matter of mutual love,' says Paul, 'you have been taught by God'. I take that in two ways. First of all, when they became Christians they began, without knowing it, to share the mind of God—or, putting it better, God began to share His mind with them. So Christian intuitions began to govern their relationships: 'You were taught by God.'

But for them, and certainly for us, there is more involved than a feeling that 'this is right'. Our feelings must be instructed by Holy Scripture. And for them, as for us, there was the direct teaching of the Lord Jesus Christ (e.g. John 13:34). It's not just a matter of intuition, but intuition confirmed, strengthened, directed and controlled by the teaching of the word of God.

This matter of love within the family of God constitutes an endless, unceasing obligation. God has taught you to love each other: 'You do love all the brothers throughout Macedonia. Yet we urge you brothers to do so more and more' (verse 10). It's not a requirement that can be set on one side, it's for now; it's not one that can be exhausted however it reaches out into Macedonia, it's something that must be always on the increase, more and more abounding, an immediate and endless obligation for the people of God.

But Paul, most interestingly, goes on to say that there are certain implications of trying to live this out. Verse 11: 'Make it your ambition.' This is not a separate thing; it flows on from what he has said immediately about brotherly love. At the end of verse 10, 'We urge you to do so more and more'—and now—'Make it your ambition.' He's pursuing the same topic. It's very important, if you use the NIV, that you keep alongside it one of the old, more literal translations. Otherwise you will lose these necessary connections, and think that Paul is beginning another topic.

It's a lovely word: to 'make it your ambition'. Its basic meaning is to 'love this honour'. But then it came to apply to 'ambition' (the AV 'study' is not so good here). Make it your business, says Paul, to —what? Well, to lead a quiet life, to mind your own business and to work with your own hands.

There are three things here that could spoil love within the church.

Frenzied activity: Contemplating this endless duty of love, Christians could become restless and frenzied. Our obligation is for now, for ever, without end. Aren't we going to be busy people! We might become over-busy attempting to live out this obligation.

Interference: Love within the family can be spoiled if it's seen as a licence to interfere in the lives of other people. Sometimes it is. I know of church fellowships which are governed by a group of elders who are nothing more or less than nosy-parkers; under the guise of pastoral care they are downright interferers in the personal lives of those committed to their charge. But brotherly love is not a licence to say, 'You know that I'm only poking my nose in here because I love you so much.' It can be marred if it degenerates into undue interference in the lives of other people.

Trading on good will: Love can be spoiled and corrupted if it is seen as a licence to trade upon the good-will of the church: 'Oh I don't have to work, they'll look after me.'

And that's why Paul says these things here. First, make it your ambition to be tranquil, a person easy in your mentality and your temperament. The translation here 'to lead a quiet life' is all right, but the Greek word means 'tranquillity of temperament' rather than 'tranquillity of circumstances'. Make it your ambition to be a tranquil person, to face life and to accept life and to enter into a relationship in an easy manner, amenable.

Second, mind your own business. First and foremost, give yourself to your own needs. There is no more needy person in the fellowship than you! And so all of us have enough on our hands to look after ourselves.

Third, work with your own hands. Earn your own living. These three things are very directly related to the preservation of a true brotherly, sisterly, family concern for each other. They are the safeguards of the reality of the virtue. And Paul goes on to say that if you live like that, two things will follow.

Firstly, the world will respect you. You will 'win the respect of outsiders'—and isn't that the main priority in evangelism? Aren't we hampered in our evangelism primarily because we know so few non-Christians? Now, Paul says, here's your way in: belong in a loving fellowship. But safeguard that love, by your own tranquillity of temperament, by your willingness to mind your own business and by becoming self-supporting so that you are not trading on the good-will of others. The world will respect a fellowship in which it sees those qualities.

The second thing that will happen is that 'you will not be dependent upon anybody'—that's a bad translation in the NIV—better, 'you will not have any need', which means need among the fellowship. The background to this is Acts 2–4. Paul is reaching back to that example of the early church where there was nobody in need. Why? Because nobody considered any of the things he possessed as his own, but distribution was made according as anyone had need. That's what he's talking about here.

If we are tranquil in temperament, if we mind our own business and earn our own living, we will have opportunities to be loving brothers and sisters to those in need. The world will sit up and take notice, and we will be in a position to cultivate and cherish and support a loving fellowship. Christian love is the recognition of need and the determination to self-sacrifice to meet that need.

Mutual Comfort: a Call to Hope (4:13–18)

This passage starts (verse 13) with the people of God facing the sorrows of life, and ends (verse 17) with them enjoying the glories of heaven in eternal joy and eternal security. Paul says we can face the sorrows of life and look forward to the glories of heaven because we are knowledgeable. Verse 9: 'I do now want you to be ignorant'—a phrase he uses several times in his letters. It is always lovingly linked with the words 'brethren', 'dear children of God', and is always said to quell a fear or correct a misapprehension.

As an apostle of Christ, he is bringing us into true knowledge. Not only have we got the apostolic word, but (4:15) 'the Lord's own word'. No wonder therefore we are to 'encourage each other with these words' (4:18). We are in the know, we have been taught by the apostle, we have been taught by the Lord Himself; we have a sure and certain word of comfort to share with each other.

Our characteristic before death (4:13)

It is typical of Paul, with his loving pastoral heart, to start off where people are, sorrowing over dead friends. By implication we can learn something about Paul's attitude to the second coming. We know from 1:10 that the return of our Lord Jesus Christ was part of his converting message. So right from that early moment he was lifting up their eyes to a coming Lord. But he must have been lifting up their eyes to a soon-coming Lord, must he not, if they immediately got anxious when they saw brothers and sisters dying? They must have been led by Paul to cultivate a real spirit of immediacy in their expectation. Otherwise why would they say, 'Oh, dear sister, she's going to miss the coming, she died too soon.'

Paul had that expectation himself. That's why he says in verse 15, 'according to the Lord's own word we tell you that we who are still alive, we . . .'—he doesn't say 'they' he says 'we'. What does he mean? Is he precisely dating the second coming? Certainly not. Remember 5:1—'About times and dates we do not need to write to you, for you know very well that the day of the Lord will come like a thief in the night.' Paul subscribes to the teaching of Jesus that nobody knows the day of the coming. You remember, Jesus said, 'No man knows, no angel knows, the Son doesn't know, only the Father' (cf Matt. 24:36) Not even the Lord Jesus as the Son of God knows the day of His coming. I can't fathom that mystery within the Holy Trinity, but it's what He said.

So Paul is not claiming to know the date of the second coming. It is not, as some commentators say, that he taught that the Lord was coming soon and events proved him wrong. No; *he taught them to live in moment-by-moment expectation of an undatable event.* And he was right to do so. That is how every Christian should view the coming again of our Lord Jesus Christ, and that is the spirit of expectation that we should cultivate by day and by night, every day and every night. We do not know when He is coming—but I'm longing for it, I'm living in the advanced good of it, and I'm expecting Him now.

Our state at death (4:13–14)

'I do not want you to be ignorant about those who are falling asleep, in order that you may not grieve like the rest of people who have no hope. For since we believe that Jesus died and rose again, so God will bring with him those who have fallen asleep through him, through Jesus' (cf 13–14).

Death has been transformed. 'Those who have fallen asleep' is a reference right back to Jesus and Jairus' daughter (Mark 5). They laughed Him to scorn knowing that she was dead, but Jesus said, 'No, she's only asleep.' Why? Because to us death is the impenetrable and irreversible reality, but to Him it is a sleep from which He will at once shake us awake.

Grief has been transformed. 'We do not want you to grieve like the rest.' How is our Christian grief unlike others'?

It is sharper, because in Christ our emotions are sharper than the unregenerate emotions of a person who does not know Jesus. Our grief in bereavement is sharper than the world's grief, because we feel it with sharper emotional capacities. Christians are often upset, indeed shocked, by the abundance of their tears. No! Paul said that the Lord spared Epaphroditus so that he would not have 'sorrow upon sorrow' (Phil. 2:27). That's the Christian experience in bereavement; free-flowing tears, loving emotions sharpened by the regenerating work of the Holy Spirit.

But our grief is different also because it is grief in the context of eternal hope. And therefore while we weep, we hope; while we are bereaved, we have the glorious expectation of a joyful reunion. Therefore our tears are gladdened.

And *hope* has been transformed. Here is the world in which Paul grew up. One contemporary writer said, 'Hopes are among the living, the dead are without hope.' Another writer said, 'We, once our brief light goes out, must sleep in endless night.' And even when some perceptive minds in that ancient world reached forward and began to speculate that there might possibly be something beyond this life—as Plato and Socrates did—it's speculation, not hope. For as you know, when the New Testament uses the word 'hope', if we are to catch the sense of it we must prefix it with the words 'sure and certain'. As a word it doesn't need that, but as a translation it does, because it contains that idea of sureness and certainty.

It's quite different to our use of 'hope' when we say 'We hope it will be fine for Kate's wedding.' That's wishful thinking. By 'hope' the New Testament means something sure and certain. And we have the sure and certain knowledge that after death there will be a transformation. Paul says, 'We believe that Jesus died and rose again . . . God will bring with Jesus those who have fallen asleep in him.'

There's a reference here to the death and resurrection of the Lord Jesus. Naturally, our thoughts first turn to His death as the finished work of salvation and His resurrection as a divine ratification. So when we look forward we are resting upon the finished work of Christ. Our minds also turn to the truth that when Jesus died and rose again, by the Lord's wonderful working we were then and there associated with that death and resurrection, so that we both died with Him and rose with Him. So already in that great package of full salvation which is ours, we possess in ourselves the realities of dying with Christ and rising with Christ.

And of course, thirdly, we look back to a Jesus model. Paul uses here the human name, 'Jesus'. In His full humanity, did He not go down into death, and did He not come out in resurrection? This is the pattern for the true humanity which God has created in Christ. It will be for them like it has been for Him; they will follow through the Jesus model. When we die we pass to be with Him. Isn't that what 4:14 says? Why will He bring 'those which sleep in Jesus' with Him? Because they've been with Him since they died. They've gone to be with Christ, which is by far the best.

But there is something else here. Verse 14 literally says: those who sleep not 'in', but 'through' Jesus. That's a lovely thought. Why isn't it in our Bible versions? It means that our death is stage-managed by Him; that the circumstances of our dying have been organised by His sovereign hand and that the timing of our death has been decided in heaven. It is all through Jesus. Through Him we go to be with Him. And going to be with Him, we have a guarantee that we who have died before He comes will none the less share in His coming, because God will bring with Him those who sleep through Jesus. If that should be His portion for us, we will not miss out on any of the glory of the second coming. We might even have a better view of it! We will come with Him, having been with Him.

Our confidence about the undated future (4:15)
Again, Paul is so sensitive. He begins by touching upon the problem that's upsetting them. He's already dealt with it: 'Your dear dead are all right. They'll come back with Jesus, they won't miss out.' But he comes back to it again, pastorally, sensitively, reassuringly. 'We will certainly not have any advantage over those who have fallen asleep. I want you to know again, they are all right. In fact they'll be the privileged ones.' Verse 15 then is an assurance that those Christians who have died prior to the second coming will be advantaged believers, who have their sure and certain place and priority in the coming again of the Lord.

The Return of The Lord (4:16–18)

Concerning His return, Paul says,

It is a personal return (4:16)
It is first of all a personal return, according to prediction and promise: 'The Lord Himself'. The AV started the fashion of inserting the word 'same' in Acts 1:11. It's not in the Greek but it's in the sense of the verse. It's a correct intuition. The men in white said, 'Men of Galilee, why do you stand gazing up into heaven? This same Jesus ...'—the Lord Himself shall descend.

Paul has Acts 1:11 in mind when he says that the Lord will descend from heaven: 'He will come in like manner as you saw Him go.' He went personally, He went up to heaven; He will come personally and He will come down from heaven. We do not have to think of the universe as having heaven 'up there' and hell 'down there'. Is there any other way of going away from the world than going up? Heaven is not 'up there' but 'away', and when Jesus returns He will return from being away; a personal return fulfilling divine prediction and promise.

It is a dramatic, public and unmistakable return (4:16)
'The Lord himself will come down from heaven, with a loud command, with the voice of the archangel and with the trumpet call of God.'

Who gives the command? What does the archangel say? Why will the trumpet sound? We don't know, but we can guess. Who will give the word? Well, who is the only one who knows when it's going to happen? Who else can give the command, except God the Father? He spoke when His Son identified with us in the water of baptism for sinners (Matthew 3:17), He spoke when His Son stood on the Mount of Transfiguration (Matthew 17:5), He spoke in anticipation of Calvary—'I have glorified my name and will glorify it' (John 12:28)—and He will speak finally in that ponderous word of command when He says, 'My beloved Son, go back again.'

The command of the Father; and the voice of the archangel. There's only one archangel mentioned in the Bible, and he is not mentioned very often. The word 'archangel' only occurs again in Jude 9. It refers to the archangel Michael. Michael is mentioned in Revelation 12:7 in the New Testament, and in Daniel 10:13, 21 and 12:1 in the Old Testament. In Daniel he is the great heavenly power who stands up in defence of the purpose of the Messiah and the needs of the people of God. In Revelation he is the great leader of the armies of angels in heaven who defeats the armies of the dragon and casts them down.

So what do you think Michael would say? I think that when the great Michael steps again on to the stage of history and we hear his voice, he will say, 'The victory is won, the kingdoms of this world have become the kingdoms of our God and of His Christ and He will reign for ever and ever.'

And the trumpet of God—why will there be a trumpet? Is it the trumpet of Mount Sinai, which says, 'God is here' (Exod. 19:16)? Of course it is. God is here, our Lord Jesus Christ. Is it the trumpet in Joel 2:1, which says the great and awesome day of the Lord has at last come? Of course it is. Is it the trumpet of Jubilee in Leviticus 25:9, which announces the release of slaves, the remission of debts and the entrance into freedom? Of course it is. That's what it will be like! Is it the trumpet of Matthew 24:31 and of Isaiah 27:12–13, that great trumpet which sounds so that the people of God scattered in the Egypt and Assyria of this world may be brought home to the heavenly Zion? Is it the trumpet which will signal, as Jesus said, the outgoing of the angels of God that gather the elect from the four corners of the earth? Of course it is, of course it is.

The Father will give the command, The voice of the archangel will pronounce the victory. And the trumpet of God will gather His elect from past, present and future, from north, south, east and west, so that the roll may be called up yonder and I'll be there!

There will be resurrection (4:16–17)

Verses 16 and 17 go on to speak about resurrection. 'The Lord himself shall descend . . . the dead in Christ shall rise first: Then we which are alive and remain shall be caught up together with them in the clouds, to meet the Lord in the air' (AV).

The first resurrection is of those who have died. Now, how can those who come with Christ rise to meet Christ? For they do come with Him; they were with Him to begin with and they come with Him. But 'the dead in Christ shall rise'; they are participants of this rising up from the earth. Why? Because when they died they left half of themselves behind. In the Scripture we are not disembodied spirits, and our perfection is not to be a disembodied spirit, however redeemed. We are embodied spirits, we are ensouled bodies, and the body is as much the object of Christ's redemption as the spirit is.

Look forward for example to 5:23, where Paul prays his final prayer for his dear Thessalonians: 'May your whole spirit, soul and body be kept blameless.' There is such a thing as redemption of the body. And Paul teaches in Romans 8:23 that the purposes of God are not complete by the going of the soul to be with Christ, which is far better. There must also be redemption of the body. Only then will creation stop groaning, and we will stop groaning, and the Holy Spirit will stop groaning. So there will be a gathering of the dust of the saints, to meet again the souls which once left them; and there will be a mighty reconstitution of a total redeemed humanity.

We can say a little bit about that redeemed body. Paul says in 1 Corinthians 15 that it's related to our present body as the flower is related to the seed. What a dramatic transformation! In Philippians 3:20–21 he says that on that great day when our expected Saviour from heaven comes, he will change the body that marks our humiliation and make it like the body that marks out His glory. At long last we shall be like Him, because we shall see Him as He is. Those who have died will experience the redemption of the body to match the redemption of the soul.

And likewise those who remain. Verse 17: 'We who are alive and remain shall be caught up together with them in the clouds.'

> Then eyes shall sparkle,
> That brimmed with tears of late.
> Orphans no longer fatherless,
> Nor widows desolate . . .

Together with them, like the ten lepers of Luke 17 who as they went were healed, so we who are still embodied souls and ensouled bodies when He comes again—we'll be healed *en route.* As we are caught up to meet the Lord, so we shall be transformed and enter at last into that inheritance which has been our possession from the start: the full salvation which is ours in Christ Jesus.

Then there's the meeting with the Lord in the air. 'Father,' said Jesus, 'this is my last will and testament, that those whom you have given me be with me where I am, that they may behold my glory' (cf. John 17:24).

'To meet the Lord in the clouds and in the air' If we start by taking those words symbolically they will teach us truth. In the Bible the clouds are the presence of God. He lived among our ancestors of the Exodus in a cloudy, fiery pillar. The cloud said, 'God is here.' When they stood on the Mount of Transfiguration, the cloud overshadowed them; and out of the cloud came the voice that said, 'This is my Son; God is here.' And we are caught up into the clouds, into the very presence of God. And the air is the usurped dominion of Satan, the prince of the power of the air (Ephesians 2:2). We enter into his usurped dominion because he is gone forever. Only Jesus reigns.

But do not think for a moment that there is not reality and objectivity here, as well as symbolism. Symbolism helps; with Jesus we will be caught into the presence of God, with Jesus we will enter into His eternal triumph over Satan. But the objective reality is (and I think this is why it's stated twice) that we will be caught up. We will be snatched, says the Scripture, from the earth. And if we are alive on that day we will be lifted bodily into heaven and stand before Jesus in the fullness of redemption. We will meet Him in the clouds in the air.

'Wherefore comfort one another with these words.'

5: The Church Blameless at the Coming
1 Thessalonians 5:1–28

Chapter 5 has the same shape as the last two passages we studied together. Look back at 4:9, in which Paul spoke 'about brotherly love'. That topic was announced as a command: 'Love one another.' That is Paul's method all through these last sections of 1 Thessalonians. Thus in 4:13 he speaks 'about those who fall asleep', an exactly parallel expression, and relates that to a command in verse 18: 'Therefore encourage one another.'

Today the topic is 'about times and dates' (5:1). He's going to speak to us about the time and date of the return of the Lord Jesus Christ. And he relates that in verse 11 to a command or exhortation to the Thessalonians and so to us: 'Therefore encourage one another and build each other up.' He still has this lovely idea of mutuality, of love between God's dear family members. And how that love is to work out as we love each other, as we comfort each other, as we encourage and build each other up—that's the topic and command.

The topic in particular is the time of the Lord Jesus Christ's return. In these eleven verses Paul deals very faithfully with that topic. It's a section that's full of illustrations. There are in fact nine illustrations in eleven verses: in verse 2 there's the illustration of the thief; in verse 3, the illustration of labour pains that terminate pregnancy; in verses 4–5 the illustrations of darkness and light; in verses

6–7 the illustrations of sleeping and waking; in verses 7–8 the illustrations of drunkenness and sobriety; and in verse 8 the illustration of armour.

But we shall discover that these illustrations are related to very general truths concerning the return of our Lord Jesus Christ, and very general recommendations for our behaviour. At the end of verse 11 we would say to our apostle, 'Yes, we can use these truths to encourage and comfort each other and to build each other up—but please will you tell us, as we wait for the Lord Jesus to come back, what should we actually be *doing*?' And Paul says, 'That's all right; I haven't forgotten. Just read on.'

So there are two sections in today's study.

Waiting for the Day (5:1–11)

Come with me to this event and its significance—the completely undatable coming again of our Lord Jesus Christ. 'You have no need for me to write to you about times and dates ["times and seasons", AV] because you know very well.'

That word 'very well' is the one you would use if you wanted to say, 'At this moment it is twenty-five to twelve *precisely*.' Paul uses the word for precise dating, in order to tell us we don't know the date. You see how he underlines the undatable event? 'The one precise truth about the time of his coming is that we do not know the time.'

He says, 'You have no need for me to write about times and seasons.' I am not sure that we should dwell upon the difference between those words, but there is a difference. Let me illustrate it. 'Time' is August 30th, the date of our wedding; 'a season' is 'our wedding day'. The first refers to chronology, the other to content. Again, 'time' is 'next May', and 'season' is 'when Spring comes'. We cannot locate the coming again of our Lord Jesus Christ either by time or season. We cannot date His coming again at all. It is something that no man knows; not the angels, nor even the Son of God Himself, but only the Father—it is an undatable event.

But we can prepare for that day by recognising certain

truths about it. And the first truth to which Paul introduces us in verse 2 and 3 is,

The day spells disaster (5:2–3)

This is where he starts. He brings us face to face with the solemn truth that the day of the coming again is the day of inescapable divine judgement. He illustrates that with the coming of the thief, which speaks of surprise and unpredictability, bringing harm with it; and with the illustration of pregnancy and of labour pains. Sometimes this illustration is used in the Bible (for example by Jesus in John 16:21) for the onset of hope; but Paul doesn't use it in that way here but simply points to the labour pains themselves as travail and trouble, hurt and pain, which inevitably come once the process has started, and cannot be escaped or evaded. That's why he links the idea of labour pains with that of coming destruction: what will be brought to birth that day is destruction.

Hogg and Vine in their commentary on 1 Thessalonians describe 'destruction' as 'not destruction of being, but destruction of well-being'—not annihilation, but destruction of all comfort and ease. It comes as the inevitable outcome of the day of Christ, as inevitable as labour, the inescapable conclusion of the process of pregnancy. A process is in operation, and the end of it is labour pain, bringing destruction.

Destruction to whom? Paul doesn't say 'to the unbelieving', for there are many who profess belief. He points at the complacent; those who say 'peace and safety', who reject all thought of God bringing history to an end and bringing in a day of judgement, who complacently believe that things will always go on as they have gone on, and that their past will never catch up with them in a destructive judgement from God.

Just as the judgement of God was the first truth to be contradicted, when Satan said in the garden, 'You shall not surely die'; so at the end, people will be clinging complacently to the supposition that there is never a judgement of God. Either they feel they don't deserve it, or they feel He is too nice to do it; so they will live complacently, and judgement will come upon them unawares and there will be no escape.

The day brings fulfilment (5:4–5)

The next two verses tell us, in great contrast, that the day brings fulfilment. Three expressions are used: 'You are not in darkness' (verse 4); 'You are all sons of the light and sons of the day' (verse 5). Of course the sense is 'children', but there is actually a particular force to the word 'sons' as we shall see in a moment. Then at the end of verse 5, 'You do not belong to the night or to the darkness' (the NIV accurately translates the Greek here). So there are three things that we've got to understand.

The *darkness* is of course metaphorical. It means 'ignorance of, estrangement from God' (cf Eph. 4:18), in darkness rather than in light. In Acts 26:18 Paul understood his commission from God as being to bring people from darkness to light, from Satan to God. 'You are not in the darkness.' As Christian believers we have a new habitat, a new environment. We are God's transplants out of that darkness of ignorance and estrangement and have been carried over, as Paul says in Colossians 1:12–14, into the kingdom of the Son of His love, we have a new setting.

Secondly, we are *sons of the light and sons of the day*. The Bible uses that idiom 'sons of' to express a condition in which people are. In the Hebrew of Genesis 12:2 Abraham is said to be 'the son of seventy-five years'. In English it says he was seventy-five years old. 'Son of' is the condition in which a person is. Now, we are sons of light and sons of the day. This is not just our habitat, it is our nature, the new nature that God has given us. It is a light-nature and a day-nature.

The light is the opposite, the end, of the darkness; that is the new nature in its novelty and strength, overcoming, overpowering, banishing the darkness. We are sons of the day. But I hope your translation use the word 'sons' twice, because two separate ideas are involved. We also have a day-nature, because the day is the period when the activity that belongs to the light is carried on. We not only have a new nature bequeathed to us, one with new powers of behaviour built in but also the characteristic life style that goes with day time.

Finally, we are *not of the night.* As the NIV says, we owe it nothing, it cannot command our loyalty, we 'do not belong to the night'.

What a very full and penetrating use of illustrations! We have been brought into a new setting, we have been given a new nature and we have been called to a new commitment. We live already, in our essential Christian nature, in that day into which He will usher us at His coming again. The day is coming; but in reality the day is already here as the sphere in which we live, the powers which we enjoy, and that to which we owe our loyalty.

Therefore when the day comes, beloved brothers and sisters, all that which we have now as potential and enjoy now in part, will blossom into full bloom. The children of the day will be the children of the day indeed. As Paul says in Philippians 3:20–21 'We expect from heaven a Saviour who will change the body that so often humiliates us and make us like the body that glorifies him, according to that mighty working whereby he is able even to subject all things unto himself.' The day is coming and our new nature will come to full bloom.

The day summons us to preparedness (5:6–8)

'So then, let us not be like others who are asleep, but let us be alert and self-controlled'—a better translation is 'clear-headed, thinking clearly'—'because those who sleep, sleep at night, and those who get drunk, get drunk at night.' The night time has its characteristic life-style, sleep; but it also in moral terms has its impermissible behaviour: getting drunk. We must avoid both, because we are day-time people, we are the light. So you mustn't sleep, Paul says to all of us. We must be on the alert and clear-headed, day-time people. Verse 8: We have a characteristic behaviour to go along with our day-time existence; and that characteristic behaviour is a warfare, requiring armour.

To sum up, as the day calls us to preparedness we are to avoid moral and spiritual carelessness and we are to avoid night-time misdemeanours. And we must get into the warfare of living as in the day for our Lord Jesus Christ. We are not in darkness by circumstance or by nature. We have a new position, nature, loyalty—and now a new responsibility, to moral alertness and a consequent warfare, a distinctive way of life.

The verb translated 'to sleep' or 'to be asleep' is not the same verb that has hitherto been translated as sleep, with reference to those who sleep in Jesus, as a metaphor or simile for a believer in death. This is very important. It is a different verb, one used of natural sleep. It is also used of moral laxity, and particularly of moral slackness that would make us unready to meet our returning Lord. The Lord Jesus Himself speaks of it in Mark 13:36, 'Lest [that day] coming suddenly he find you sleeping' (AV). He uses it in the parable of the ten bridesmaids, when He says that they all dropped off to sleep. But the word is never ever used as a metaphor for a dead believer, because a different verb is used in that case. And it I do want you to have this clearly in mind.

We are, by contrast, to be on the alert and clear-headed, so as to live for the day, not morally and spiritually asleep, for Jesus when He comes.

And we are to wear the armour that is our characteristic hallmark as believers. What have we got here but faith, love and hope for the third time in Thessalonians? In 1:3 Paul looked back and saw the genuineness of their experience because he saw faith, hope and love. And do you remember that middle passage, in chapter 3, where we were talking about Satan and temptation? We saw that believers were in the arena, and Paul was almost lifted out of himself with joy because they had survived the temptation. What was the victory? Why, they were standing fast in the Lord. They were people of endurance, stickability, durability. And they were people of faith and love, they were going on with the great Christian basics.

And what now, as we wait and want to be alert for our Lord Jesus' coming again? Why, faith and love and hope. Go on living in the light of a God who is trustworthy. Go on living in the company of believers who are loving. Go on living with your eye fixed upon a Christ who is returning. Go on in faith and love and hope.

The return of our Lord Jesus Christ requires nothing dramatic by way of preparation. We are just to go on with faith and with love and with hope, to go on trusting Him, come what may, and living in the obedience of faith. We must go on loving our fellow-believers and reaching out beyond them in love to the world, and go on with the endurance that hope forgets as we keep our eyes fixed upon Him. And that's our armour. As we go on in these things we are impregnable. We put on a breastplate and a helmet. The Christian going on in faith and love and hope is an armoured believer.

The day can be faced with confidence (5:9–11)

My comments just now about the verb 'to sleep' are about to come home to roost. May I give you my own more literal rendering of verses 9–10? 'God did not appoint us to wrath, but to the personal and full possession of salvation through our Lord Jesus Christ who died for us, so that whether we are awake or asleep we may live together with him.'

Now, what verb does Paul use for 'asleep' in verse 10? Not the verb that means we are dead and living with Jesus, for this verb never means that: this verb alerts us to the possibility of moral and spiritual slackness. And what does 'awake' mean? Well—what has it meant all through these verses, but 'being alert for a coming Lord'?

So what is Paul saying? He is saying something of the most intense and remarkable and glorious comfort.

That day may catch us unawares; it may be one of those days when we are below par and not living as alertly for the Lord Jesus as we might be, when we have fallen short spiritually and dozed a little and our lives are showing some evidence of moral and spiritual slackness. The day before was a Sunday, we were keen as mustard, but the day He chose to come was a Monday and we were having a spiritual day off. So how are we placed, in relation to the coming Lord?

But you see, our great confidence in relation to His coming is not anything that we do or are, but what God in Christ has done for us. And so we are appointed here to God's purpose, His eternal, inflexible council that we are His elect, we are His redeemed:

> The wrath of a sin-hating God
> with us can have nothing to do.

We have been appointed eternally for the personal and full possession of salvation, through our Lord Jesus Christ who died for us. His death covers all our sins, including those sins of slackness which at that moment might unfit us for His coming again. Oh, with what comfort and confidence can we can face the returning Lord! He is the Lord, He is Jesus, He is Christ. And that great fullness of His title is related to His saving work, in which He is God Himself. "Tis mystery all, the immortal dies . . .', 'You killed the prince of life'—in that saving work He was the eternal God, the perfection of humanity, Jesus. And in that saving work He was the Christ, the one anointed, prepared, equipped by God to be the Saviour of sinners. With what confidence we can face His coming again! For the one who comes is that perfect mediator, the one who knew God's requirements and man's needs, and who by His knowledge as 'that righteous one, My servant' has provided righteousness for the many (Isaiah 53:11). And we stand before Him clothed in His righteousness alone, which is His blood-bought donation to us.

So, says Paul, you can face the day with confidence but you must live of course in faith and love and hope. What does that mean in practice?

Living for the Day (5:12–22)

There are fifteen distinct commands here, and some are developed into further commands. It looks like a hopeless jumble. Do you want to know how to live for the day? You are going to learn with a vengeance! But in fact, like the majority of Scripture, this section is a very careful and coherent statement. Let's put down some markers.

Notice in 5:12 the words 'Now we ask you, brothers' (AV, 'We beseech you brethren'). With that word of apostolic appeal, Paul introduces the first three commands: to know, to esteem, to be at peace. Then he separates those commands off into a little section by themselves, by renewing his appeal: Verse 14, 'And we urge [exhort] you'. This is followed by nine commands, which, I shall show you, divide into three groups of three. The first group, in their AV form: warn the unruly; comfort the feeble-minded; support the weak. The second group: be patient towards all; see that none renders evil for evil; follow after that which is good. And the third group: rejoice ever more, pray without ceasing, in everything give thanks.

Notice how Paul rounds the section off: 'This is the will of God for you.' It begins with the apostolic appeal (verse 12) and ends with the will of God (verse 18). This is what the great apostle Paul wants as an apostle, and this is what God wants in his perfect will. How important, then, this series of nine commands is!

I promised you fifteen commands. Here are the last three (verses 19–22). Quench not the Spirit; despise not prophesyings; prove all things. And so that we know how to prove all things or what to do when we have tested them, he adds the related commands 'hold fast to that which is good, abstain from everything that has the nature of evil'—all that is part of testing, so we still have just three commands here.

Do you find that satisfying? It's not a jumble at all. The three initial commands bear on leadership, nine commands in three sections bear on our individual life, and three commands at the end tell us of forces that are working on our behalf. As we move towards the day of which we have been speaking, we have supportive agencies; the leaders in our churches. We have personal obligations, demonstrated by that long middle section with the nine commands. And we have forces working on our behalf, the three commands at the end.

The church has leaders and communal quality (5:12–13)
There is no such thing in the New Testament as a church without leaders, or a church with only one leader. The leaders are usually called 'elders' or 'overseers' or 'deacons'; we don't know what they did, except that there was a distinct emphasis on teaching and ministering the word. But they were the leaders of the church, and Paul's requirement was that elders should be appointed in every church—leaders in the plural.

Paul calls believers firstly to acknowledge the presence of their leaders: 'Know them which labour among you, and are over you in the Lord, and admonish you' (AV). Secondly, to respect them for what they do: 'Esteem them very highly in love for their work's sake'. Thirdly, to respond to the existence of leadership by going all out to create a totally peaceful community: 'Be at peace'. Paul has been appealing for brotherly love, because we are all one in the church. But in case that might distort church life he reminds us that within every church there are leaders. And in case that thought might drive us to argument, dissent and non-acceptance he says, 'You must live at peace.' How easily people leap today to fracture the peace of the church, as though it were a matter of no consequence! 'Be at peace,' says the apostle.

And what is a leader for? A leader is for work. 'They toil', he says. They are to be recognised because they are toilers. They offer Christ-like leadership. They take first place in the Lord, and that means that they do so in the way that the Lord Jesus would. Remember His dramatic words—'Not so among you . . . He that would be great amongst you must be as the least' (cf. Matthew 10:26–27, Mark 10:43–44, Luke 22:26). The minister is a servant and the least of all, because Jesus the great servant came amongst us as one who serves. So leaders do not take first place in spiritual matters, but in a spiritual way, like the Lord Jesus: they are servants living in union with and in the likeness of the Servant Himself.

And they are to 'admonish' you. The word is rather like our expression 'tender loving care'. But to be true to the word, we'd have to drop just a little bit of grit into the idea of tender loving care, for the word also contains the idea of offering direction—tender loving care and pointing the right way; rebuking when necessary, offering direction when necessary, but doing so with tender loving care. That's leadership.

The church has a life style required of all of its members (5:14–17)

Notice that the next nine commands contain seven references to an unqualified obligation: we are all to be like this to everybody, all the time.

Firstly, *we have a ministry to each other.*

Verse 14: 'We exhort you, brethren, to *warn* them that are unruly.' That's the tender loving care word; the leaders exercise it towards those who are led, and the whole body of the church exercises it towards each other. The New Testament isn't much in favour of the idea of leaders who are separate from the people of God. They are in fact to be 'exhibit A' of what a Christian is to be like, and then Christians follow, by the same ministry of tender loving care to those who are unruly: people who step out of line, who are insubordinate, who are lazy, who are disruptive and non-contributory within the fellowship. And it's not to be left to the leaders but to those who are best alongside them, to take them to one side and say, 'I want to exercise tender loving care. If necessary I will rebuke you with tender loving care. If necessary I will redirect you but I want you to come back into line.' We have a ministry of warning.

We have a ministry also of comforting the *feebleminded.* The word actually has a wider meaning than that of mental weakness; it means those who are depressed, who are lacking in gusto, who haven't quite got the energy to deal with life (NIV 'timid').

'Support the *weak*'—the Lord Jesus used the verb 'to support' when He said (Matthew 6:24) that it is impossible to serve two masters. We will give our first loyalty to the one and we'll despise the other. Our ministry in the church, for all of us as Christian brothers and sisters, is to give our first loyalty, our best and first attention to those who are weak.

Secondly, *there are three commands relating to our character.*

We are to be *patient.* If such a word as 'long-tempered'

existed, the opposite of 'short-tempered', it would exactly translate this Greek word. And we are to be *non-retaliatory*; we are to take what people do to us and never answer back or hit back. We are not to render evil for evil, as Jesus commanded we should not. And we are to be people of *unfeigned goodness*, always pursuing that which is good towards others and towards all. That is our character within the fellowship of the church.

Thirdly, *a series of commands to do with our spirituality*—the way we live individually with and before God within the fellowship of the church, rejoicing, praying, giving thanks.

Circumstances are often such that it is impossible to rejoice and impossible to give thanks. They kill our joy and give us nothing to be thankful for. Therefore, please notice that it doesn't say, 'Give thanks for everything.' It says, 'In everything give thanks.' For no matter what the day is like, no matter the circumstances, no matter what distress lies on us, Jesus hasn't changed. Salvation, the Scriptures, heaven, the second coming haven't changed. You see, this is a command calling us to live spiritually, to live in the conscious light of spiritual truth; constantly to fill our minds with Father, Son and Holy Spirit, to refresh our minds in the work of salvation, to renew ourselves in the presence of the Holy Spirit, to rejoice in Holy Scripture, to look at our brothers and sisters and say, 'Isn't it good to belong with them.' It's a call constantly to attend the Lord's Supper and rejoice in the ministry of the things of grace; constantly to look forward to Jesus. It's a great discipline. It's the last thing we want to do when the going is rough! But we are commanded to live spiritually.

Right at the heart of this command to live spiritually is, 'Pray without ceasing'. That is to say, face the whole of life—its infinite variety, all its seemingly impossible demands, our needs and necessities—face the whole of life in the place of prayer—because when we are not able, He is supremely able.

'This is the will of God.' Why, if it were simply Paul's will that would be enough, he is an apostle of Christ. But it's not just Paul; this is the will of God, that within the fellowship of the church we should live in ministry, in character and in spirituality. Ministering to each other, living out a Christ-like character and holding on to God through thick and thin—in rejoicing, prayer and thanksgiving.

The church has power available to it to be what it is meant to be (5:19–22)

We could say, 'It's a tall order to say "Rejoice evermore and in everything give thanks." Paul just doesn't know how we are placed.' But think how Paul was placed. He'd just been flogged in Philippi. He wasn't living in an ivory tower, wrapped in cotton wool. He had the marks on his body. We find it a tall order—doubtless he did too. So what is on our side, as we seek to live out this ministry and this character and this spirituality? What do we have going for us? Paul says two things: the Holy Spirit, and the word of God. 'Quench not the Spirit, despise not prophesyings.'

Let's think about these commands.

The Holy Spirit is here depicted as fire—'Do not put out the fire of the Holy Spirit.' He is spoken of as fire by John the Baptist when he looks forward to Jesus; 'He that cometh after me is mightier than I, whose shoes I am not worthy to bear: he shall baptize you with the Holy Ghost, and with fire . . . he will burn up the chaff with unquenchable fire' (Matt. 3:11–12). The Holy Spirit is the agent of the Lord Jesus' desire to create for Himself a clean, pure and holy people. The fire of the Holy Spirit is the fire that creates holiness.

It was the fire that came upon them on the day of Pentecost. Remember, they did not gather together that day to receive the Holy Spirit, they didn't know He was coming. They gathered to keep the Feast of Pentecost—God's feast for gathering to Himself a people who rest upon His work of salvation and commit themselves to obedience to His law. And the Holy Spirit chose that day to come upon the people of God gathered, resting upon a full and final work of salvation and committing themselves to obedience. He came to endow them to that end, to be the holy people of God.

And of course, He went further. He endowed them with the pentecostal gift of intelligible speech—they spoke and everybody understood—for the communication of the gospel.

The Holy Spirit comes to create us as the holy people of God, with a testimony to the world.

There's something else that's on our side: the word of God is on our side. If we are to understand *prophesyings*, we must think ourselves as completely as we can into the situation Paul was addressing, and then see how it applies to us. Paul's churches did not have the whole word of God. They had that part of it that we call the Old Testament, but it wasn't in everybody's hand. And the New Testament exposition of the person and work of Christ was not yet available. So God used people to prophesy; to bring the word of God to the people of God. As with the Old Testament prophets, that was mostly the word of declaration, but sometimes also it was the word of prediction, so that the people of God might know how to live in the present, because they are aware of the future.

Paul says, 'You are gathering in church at Thessalonica, and the local butcher stands up, and he's going to bring you the word of God. Don't despise the word of God because it comes to you through the local butcher!' Do you see? Don't despise the word of God when it comes to you; listen intently. You see how that applies to us today?

The word of God, however, is now complete. So there is a fundamental sense in which we need no prophecy, because we have the word of God. Even if a prophet were to stand up and say 'I have a word from God for you,' we would still test it by Scripture. We are to be fundamentally Bible people.

Oh, what things we have going for us, beloved, as we set out to minister to each other, to develop Christ-like character, and to rejoice in a true spirituality! The Holy Spirit whose work is to create a holy people; the word of God whose force is to instruct us in the things of God and make us into that image.

We have one more thing going for us, and that is *our own moral commitment*. Test out all things—whether the word of prophecy that comes to you in your church or assembly, or a thought that occurs to you in your quiet time, or a line of conduct that some people propose and you're not sure whether it's right, or whether it's a matter of separation from the world or identification with the world. Whatever has to do with living the life of Christ on earth, do test it. Don't go round with your mouth open and your eyes shut. Be a discerning believer, exercise your God-given faculty of criticism, test everything out, bring it back to the touchstone of Holy Scripture, pray about it, ask the Holy Spirit to illuminate you about it, test all things. But—when you have come to a conclusion as to what is right and what is wrong, then go for it!

Paul's Conclusion (5:23–28)

Let us now come to the final, important truth in this letter. What a wealth of commands have been given to us. And we might well say, 'I'm baffled by this range of requirements, how ever can I live for the coming of the Lord?'

'Now may the God of peace himself sanctify you wholly. May your whole spirit and soul and body be preserved blameless unto the coming of our Lord Jesus Christ' (5:23). Above all things, we have got God Himself on our side. And when we find the task beyond us, if we become somewhat slipshod, even if we have to confess 'I'll never be ready for Jesus when He comes,' I'll tell you something: *the heavenly Father will see to it that there's no single blemish to spoil the day of His Son's return*. Paul says in Philippians 1:6, 'He who began a good work in you will go on putting the finishing touches to it until the day of Christ.' And when the day of Christ comes, the last railing will have been painted, the last picture polished, the last carpet hoovered—everything will be ready for the coming of this mighty guest: the faithful and all-sufficient God.

God Himself will sanctify you. God Himself will preserve you, in an all-embracing, completed holiness that touches every part of your being and covers all that you are. Such are the two words 'sanctify' and 'keep' (NIV) that are used here. He will preserve you in relation to Himself, your 'spirit'; He will preserve you in your personality, your 'soul'. He will preserve you in holy living in your body. He will sanctify and He will preserve. And He will do this in a way that is acceptable for the great day because it is all unto the coming of our Lord Jesus Christ. The faithful and all-sufficient God.

Verse 25, 'Brethren, pray for us.' Paul looks out to the Thessalonian church. He says, 'I want you to be a praying church.' Verse 26: 'Greet all the brethren with an holy kiss'—He says, 'I want you to be a loving church.' Verse 27: 'I charge you by the Lord that this epistle be read unto all the holy brethren'—He says, 'I want you to be a Bible-loving church, living in the light of the whole divine and apostolic Scripture.' Verse 28: 'The grace of our Lord Jesus Christ be with you'—He says, 'I want you to be a church founded upon grace, nourished and kept by grace.'

Prayer, love, Scripture, grace! The Lord be with you.

'The Living Lord and the Living Hope'
Peter's Second Letter

by Dr Roy Clements

1: Confirming Your Reservation
2 Peter 1:1–11

The equivalent to hell on earth has to be Heathrow Airport! There is nothing more soul-destroying than lumbering through the London traffic, staggering up stairs and escalators with a heavy case, only to arrive at the check-in desk to discover that you cannot go where you want to go. The plane's been delayed by fog, there's engine trouble or an air-traffic controllers' strike, or—most tiresome of all—the computer has had a fit of amnesia and for some unaccountable reason your name isn't on the flight list. Next time you see distraught, tear-stained faces outside Heathrow, don't think they are relatives bidding farewell to some loved one. No! They are passengers who never made it, and are therefore condemned to the living hell of the Heathrow departure lounge.

Of course there is only one way to avoid this kind of disappointment. Every experienced air-traveller knows it. *You have to confirm your reservation just before you fly*. They tell you on the tickets, they display reminders at the travel agents. It is so important to make sure. Untold airport misery could be avoided, all for the cost of a phone call. But people don't do it. They forget it, or they neglect it. They assume it will be all right on the day. And so they end up among the weeping, teeth-gnashing brigade in Terminal 3.

This morning I want to talk to you about another kind of journey. It's a journey we will all make sooner or later. They never tell you when your plane is, and they only issue one-way tickets; but it's a very important journey nevertheless. It is the journey from this world to the next one.

And the lesson I want to impress on your mind this morning is this: *Confirm your reservation*. Heathrow for all its terrors is only a taste of the desolation and frustration that will grip the hearts of those who miss out on heaven. Confirm your booking. Don't trust to luck. Don't leave it to chance. Confirm your reservation, so that when your time of departure comes you will have no need for anxiety or uncertainty—you will be sure.

One of the most encouraging things in the first letter of Peter is that it has some advice for us on that very subject. In later studies we shall be looking at the background of the letter. This morning we need only note that like so many other New Testament letters it was written in response to error.

Peter wrote because there were false teachers around. These heretics had invaded the church claiming access to some new superior knowledge, some better revelation. 'We've had mind-blowing experiences which have elevated us to a new spiritual level.' They pretended to be a spiritual élite; the truth, as we shall see in chapter 2, is that they were actually mercenary con-men, trying to gain money and kudos by exploiting the gullibility of the simple-minded.

But they were having a dangerous affect on the church. Was Jesus *really* the unique Son of God? Was he *really* returning one day to remake the universe? Seeds of doubt were being sown in the hearts of the faithful. And the most destructive doubts of all began to appear: 'Am I *really* born again of the Holy Spirit, am I *really* going to heaven?'

Peter's letter is written with the goal of repairing the ailing confidence of the Christians to whom it's addressed. It's a letter about being sure.

Being Sure of Salvation

In the first half of chapter 1 he is concerned that his readers should be sure of their salvation and of heaven. The key verses are 10 and 11. Notice how emphatic they are: 'You will never fall'—in the original, it's a double negative. Peter stresses that it is absolutely out of the question for a Christian to trip up on the way to heaven and fail to reach the destination. He wants his readers to live in that assurance: 'You should be sure that you are going to heaven.'

There is nothing presumptuous or arrogant about such assurance.

This morning we shall study carefully the two paragraphs leading up to verses 10 and 11, to discover together the basis and condition upon which this assurance rests. Peter has two major points. First, we can feel secure about our Christian destiny because it all hinges on God's gracious generosity to us; but second, we must not feel complacent about assurance because assurance also depends to some extent on our voluntary response to God's grace. When you hold these together in the necessary tension, then, says Peter, confidence about your calling and election can be yours. You will never fall.

Power and Promises (1:1–4)

Verse 3 is the key verse for this section: the gracious generosity of God. Here is the fundamental reason a Christian can feel sure; because fundamentally, Christianity isn't self-manufactured. It's a divine gift, not a human achievement. Out of the inexhaustible store of his own omnipotence, God has fully equipped us with all that is necessary to make and keep us Christians. His divine power has given us everything we need for life and godliness.

The experience of this extraordinary generosity of God begins, of course, at our conversion. Peter alludes to that in 1:3 when he says, 'To those who through the righteousness of our God and Saviour Jesus Christ have received a faith as precious as ours.' Notice that word 'received'. Peter doesn't address his letter 'To those who out of the goodness of their hearts have decided to give Jesus a try', but to those who have 'received a faith'. The Greek word means 'to obtain by lot'. The clear implication is that the spiritual response which launches us upon the Christian pathway is itself a divine gift; we don't generate it, still less do we earn it. Indeed, Peter seems to hint that there is a mysterious unpredictability about it—that's the thrust of that word 'lot'. It flows out of the free grace of God.

Peter had a particular personal reason for understanding this. No doubt he could still recall, as vividly as if it had happened yesterday, the time when he first grasped who Jesus was. Do you remember the Gospel account? 'You are the Christ, the Son of the living God' he said. What response did he anticipate from such a remarkable confession, I wonder? Did he expect Jesus to clap? 'Well done, Peter! At last you've worked it out! I've been waiting for weeks for you to say that.' But what he received was not congratulations but a kind of theological education: 'You are blessed, Peter,' He said, 'for flesh and blood have not revealed this to you, but my Father in heaven.'

He says the same to us this morning. Perhaps you feel insecure, unsure of your status in the Christian family. Well; consult your heart. Do you find faith there? All right, it may be a hesitant faith. It may be a weak faith, you may wish you had a great deal more faith than you find. But do you find faith there, a glimmering spark of trust in Jesus? If you do, treasure it. It's a precious, divine gift. No Christian preacher no matter how dynamic, no Christian pastor no matter how sensitive, no Christian friend no matter how concerned, could give you that gift. It lies outside the competence of flesh and blood to bestow it. How did the apostle Paul put it? 'By grace you have been saved through faith, and this is not your own doing, it is the gift of God.'

One important consequence is that the Christian community had at its basis a very strong egalitarianism. Peter himself stresses that: 'You have received a faith as precious as ours'—literally, 'of equal worth to ours'. He uses a word often used in the ancient world for political equality, for sharing the same social status and civil rights. Peter's use of it is very significant, for you will remember that the false teachers, whom Peter is anxious to counteract, presented themselves as superior to others. But right from the start

Peter makes clear that he doesn't look at things that way. Founding father of the Christian church though he is, he refuses to lift himself above the rest of the Christian community to whom he is writing. He even calls himself a servant before he calls himself an apostle.

The gratuitousness of God's grace in this bestowal of faith destroys all élitist pretensions amongst us. Apostles like Peter start where everybody else starts, with a God of impartial justice—of righteousness, as he puts it here—who imparts the same quality to the least as to the greatest. The Christian life begins for everyone at conversion, when they experience God's gracious generosity.

In 1:3 Peter says that it is from that same source of divine generosity that the Christians' ability to persevere in their faith is derived. 'His divine power has given us everything we need for life and godliness through our knowledge of him who called us by his own glory and goodness.' There is an ambiguity in that final phrase. Does Peter mean '*by* His own glory and goodness', or '*to* His own glory and goodness'? I suspect the ambiguity is deliberate; that Peter is implying on one hand that God's calling of us into faith is not the crushing coercion of a tyrant but the irresistible wooing of a lover; that Jesus draws us into a relationship in which we personally know Him not with threats or psychological manipulation but by the magnetic attraction of His own moral beauty. He calls us by His glory and goodness.

But perhaps Peter is also implying that once the personal relationship is sealed, that same alluring moral beauty becomes the goal of our own spiritual progress. The more we know Jesus, the more we long to be like Him. In the depth of our own self-disgust He breaks through to display the kind of person we all wish we could be.

It is said there are two kinds of friend. There are those who drag you down morally, and there are those to know whom is a constant challenge to rise to nobler things. Jesus is the supreme example of the second kind. He calls us not just *by*, but to His glory and goodness. Some of the meagre faith by which we embark upon this path of Christian discipleship flows out of God's generosity, but the incentive which fires our ambition to continue on that pathway also comes from

God's power. His divine power has given us everything we need for life and godliness.

Yet the story of gracious generosity goes a step further, beyond even faith and incentive; to provide also, says Peter, 'promises'—the promises we need in the moral struggle in which we must inevitably engage if we are to live as Christians in a fallen world. Look at 1:4. These are very bold words. Perhaps there are few bolder in the Old Testament, for in Peter's time these were words that were often used by pagans involved in the mystery cults. The Greek world of the first century was fascinated by the idea of escaping from the confines of a corrupt materialistic world, by some kind of union with divinity. It was the quest of the mystery cults of the first century, and it has a lot in common with many mystical, New Age and occult groups today.

Peter is deliberately drawing his vocabulary here from that context. It's as if he wants to say to his contemporaries (as indeed he may want to say to some of us), 'You don't need to go in for esoteric experiences and the occult hocus-pocus which is the stock-in-trade of the mystery cults and New Age cults. You are a Christian: God has already infused divinity into your soul, you are already a participant in the divine nature.' It's an extraordinary statement, but he means it. The Holy Spirit Himself, God, dwells in you. You need not engage in any mystical techniques to acquire Him. He is yours, says Peter, by divine promise—a promise which we have not earned or bought but which has been freely given to us in this gracious generosity of God. He has given us this precious promise so that we may be sure that the Christian life we have begun, we will complete.

Thus, if God's graciousness means there's no room for spiritual élitism in the Christian church, it also means that there's no room for moral defeatism. I believe that one of the commonest causes of lack of assurance in people's Christian lives derives from the spiritual inferiority complex. I've noticed a high incidence of that particular complex at Keswick Conventions. People stare up at mega-saints on the platform and say, 'Oh! If only I could be like that! If only I had his faith, if only I had his holiness! But my problem is, I can never keep it up . . .' Spell-bound in admiration of great saints on the platform, we become psychologically absorbed in our own inabilities and weaknesses and failures and we become demoralised.

Maybe we make excuses for ourselves. Modern psychology and sociology have given us abundant scope to do so. We blame it on our genetics, we blame it on our deprived upbringing, we even blame it on the capitalist system—most of all, perhaps, we blame it on our Freudian complexes. But we blame it on something or anything. A motorist filling in an insurance claim after colliding with a stationary vehicle came to the question, 'Could the other driver have done anything to avoid the accident?' He wrote: 'Yes, he could have parked somewhere else.' That's twentieth-century man all over. Always the victim of circumstances outside his control. There have been few generations more prone to self-pity than ours.

Peter is telling us, 'Whatever truth there may be in all your environmental and genetic explanations for your weaknesses and failure, you are no longer shackled by them. Christianity is about the invasion into this corrupt and fallen world of ours by a sanctifying power; the power of the risen Jesus, the Holy Spirit Himself. God in Christ makes available to us the life that flows out of the very midst of Deity.' That being so, we cannot go on wallowing in moral pessimism about ourselves. When the Bible calls Jesus a Saviour, that's exactly what it means. He rescues us, He saves us from the shackles of our genetic determinism, from the constraints of our environmental conditions—as Peter terms it, 'from the corruption that is in the world'. Jesus opens the door for us to share the very life of heaven itself. 'We've become partakers,' he says, 'in the divine nature.'

So here is the fundamental reason that Christians can be sure. All these things of which we have been speaking depend on God, not on us. He's the source of our saving faith, of our moral motivations and incentives, of our moral strength and ability. His divine power has given us everything we need for life and godliness, says Peter: and when he says 'everything', he means 'everything'. The reason so many of us fail to enjoy a feeling of assurance is that we haven't grasped this central truth of the Bible. We are like the hill-billy farmer I once saw in a film, scratching a precarious living from the scrub land round his home, when all the time he was sitting on top of an oil well. His anxious counting of pennies was completely unnecessary. He only had to dig beneath him to discover wealth beyond his wildest dreams. And yet in his ignorance he lived like a pauper.

How many Christians live on a kind of spiritual subsistence level! You don't have to, says Peter. God's gracious generosity has given you everything you need for life and godliness.

It's all in a single phrase in 1:3. He has 'called us'. That sovereign summons, that divine election which he refers to again in 1:10 ('your calling and election'), provides an unshakeable foundation for your eternal security. When God calls you He doesn't just issue you with an invitation. He gives you a passport, He gives you an air ticket, he gives you your entry visa. It's all there in your hand as you approach the check-in desk. Why should you lack assurance that you're going to set foot on that aeroplane, and make that journey safely?

Faith and Effort (1:5–9)

But there is another side to the story, and it is important to keep both in balance as Peter does in 1:5 onwards: assurance does depend to some extent on our voluntary response to God's grace. Thus in 1:10 Peter draws faith and effort together quite clearly.

Most of us know those invitations that say at the end 'Gentlemen will wear ties', or something of that nature. Well, it's important to understand that entry to heaven is also conditional upon a dress code. God is determined only to have the finest quality of material in His kingdom: He calls it 'holiness'. If you want a fibre analysis, Peter gives us one in verses 5–7: faith, goodness, knowledge, self-control, perseverance, godliness, brotherly kindness, love. Without such qualities of moral character, such holiness, we will not see God.

So how do we obtain those qualities?

Conceivably God could have imposed this necessary holiness upon us like some heavenly computer engineer reprogramming his subservient brains. Or He could have zapped us with holiness; He could have made holiness strike us like lightning while we remained totally passive. Some Christians indeed suggest that is the way God intends it; that on such-and-such a day they were zapped with holiness at the holiness meeting. But I want you to see that that is not the way that Peter seems to describe this business here. Yes, God gives us faith and the incentives of Jesus' glory and goodness; He gives us great promises; and in the granting of all these things we are truly passive. But He does not give us ready-made new personalities. On the contrary, Peter tells us that our holiness is something we are to strive for, in the power of these things He has granted to us.

Remember the man on his oil well. He had to dig for it. God does not want Holy-Spirit-controlled robots. According to the New Testament, what God wants to populate His new world with is a new kind of human being, whose moral character reflects His own.

A human being is a much more subtle and delicate mechanism than a robot. The peculiar matrix of behavioural responses of what I call my human personality is woven, in some deeply mysterious way, into my experience of self-consciousness. I can't separate myself from my behaviour. And self-consciousness—the ego, whatever you want to call it—is precious to God; because it is that self, that person whom He addresses when He calls us: not an 'it' but a 'thou'.

So God's plan to produce holiness in us demands a rather remarkable piece of psychological surgery. He aims to completely revolutionise our lives, to change our behavioural responses fundamentally and to change us from sinners into saints. But He determined to achieve that goal in a way that preserves the integrity of that self-conscious individual within us. It is that person He loves, even while that person is still a sinner. And this surely is why holiness can't be obtained in the purpose of God by anything other than a gradual process of personal moral growth, in which our efforts are wedded together with God's grace. If God were to impress an entire new holy pattern of behaviour on me suddenly, without my co-operation, it is doubtful to what extent I could any longer be the same person. There would be no continuity between the old me and the new me, unless God wilfully destroyed my old self-consciousness. I would be a kind of spiritual schizophrenic, uncertain what identity I really had.

It can't be done like that, by a divine fiat. The old me has to evolve into the new me, along a pathway in which my self-determination and will are fully active.

Now in the middle of that transition, our Christian experience may feel a little schizophrenic. We may feel as if we are being pulled in two directions. Paul speaks about that when he speaks of the spirit struggling with the flesh, the new me struggling with the old me (Rom. 7:7–25). Every Christian who is trying to grow in holiness knows that torture. But the path through it is not in doubt: the New Testament says quite clearly that the secret of victory in this war is to commit my mind and my will to the side of holiness. And that's what Peter is doing here. 'For this very reason', he says, 'make every effort to add to your faith goodness.' Commit your self-determination to the pursuit of those virtues that God wants to cultivate in you, says Peter. Make every effort to add to what I give you, faith, the goodness to which I am calling you in Jesus.

The word translated 'add' in 1:5 is rather interesting. In ancient Greece, in order to keep public spending to the minimum wealthy men were sometimes expected to personally contribute something to public works. They might sponsor a stage production, for example, or build a battleship. This act of lavish co-operation on the part of a rich benefactor was called 'adding'. So Peter is encouraging us to invest our personal resources in this holiness project to which God is calling His church. We're not building ships, we're not putting on stage productions, we are building holy characters, he says. And step by step he lists those qualities which we are required to contribute: faith, virtue, knowledge, self-control, steadfastness, godliness, brotherly kindness, love. This is the ladder of Christian growth, he says.

It begins with faith, where all true holiness must begin.

Any pursuit of holiness which doesn't rest on faith is just moralism, the kind of self-righteousness which Jesus so criticised and hated in the Pharisees. This is where Christian ethics diverges from every form of humanism, because it proceeds from faith in God, not trust in yourself. It proceeds through knowledge, because there is nothing anti-intellectual, nothing obscurantist about this pathway to Christian maturity. The more solidly we grasp God's truth and the more complete our understanding of His person and His purpose, the more equipped we are for holiness. God does not call us slaves, who do not understand His purposes but must cooperate with Him nevertheless. He calls us His sons and daughters. He invites us to have an intelligent participation in His life and plan.

Notice, too, the importance Peter gives to the qualities of self-control and steadfastness. These are words of discipline: the power to resist self-indulgence on the one hand and opposition on the other hand. The person who displays such qualities is certainly not being passive; he or she has passed from mere emotional or intellectual commitment to the pursuit of Christian character in the hard work of God's gymnasia: steadfastness, determination, self-control.

Peter mentions godliness. It was a favourite word among the Greeks. They loved to portray the moral ideal as a golden mean between two extremes, and this word 'godliness' conjures up that idea of balance in the moral life. For in our enthusiasm for holiness it is possible to go a little bit over the top, to become fanatical, to become deranged. You will find in many mental hospitals quite a few people who have obsessions about religion. But, says Peter, true holiness is never morbid, never self-absorbed. It has the effect of integrating the personality, never unhinging it. True holiness is a very sane quality; and it is that moral symmetry and balance that this word 'godliness' expresses.

Finally, notice where this ladder of Christian virtue ends: brotherly affection and love. The highest morality the Greek world could boast was that of the Stoics, but the Stoics never got this far. Endurance they had, self-control they had, but they displayed these things at the expense of all warmth and tenderness in their personalities. The Stoics drained themselves of feeling, steeling themselves against emotion, because that's what they believed religion required of them. 'No,' says Peter. 'God's holiness is not the frigid propriety of a Victorian drawing room. It's not just good manners and respectability. It's love. Love towards my friends, brotherly affection, but more than that: love towards those for whom I entertain no special regard. It is love even for my enemies, agapé, the love which God shares and which it is the supreme work of His Spirit to shed abroad in our hearts.'

So the ladder of Christian virtue begins with faith in God and ends with loving like God. But from first to last, says Peter, God requires our activity in climbing that ladder. 'For this very reason, make every effort . . .' We resemble children who say to their fathers, 'Dad, can you lend me a pound? I want to buy you a birthday present.' We have no power of our own. We depend upon God's generosity for faith, for incentives, for power to do anything for Him. Yet God does want us to do the buying of the present. He'll give us the pound; He requires us to invest it.

His divine power provides all we need to pursue holiness, but nevertheless holiness is something in which one Christian may differ from another. Though faith, incentives and promises are all freely placed at our disposal, we do not all make the use that we should of God's grace. To use a phrase we shall come across in our final study, we do not all grow in grace; some of us are stunted plants, retarded spiritual children. And that is not just unfortunate. It is positively dangerous.

Do you know why some people do not enjoy the assurance of salvation? They could and should do so. But they don't have any title to Christian assurance, not in the state they are in. The Bible only gives security to a Christian whose spiritual life is growing, who's making progress towards holiness. That's why Peter says in 1:8, 'If you possess these qualities in increasing measure'—notice that process of growth—'they will keep you from being ineffective and unproductive in your knowledge of our Lord Jesus Christ.' The person who isn't growing can't expect to feel sure; it's a bit like riding a bicycle; so long as the wheels are going round you will stay upright, but the slower you move, the harder it is to keep your balance. It's the same in our Christian lives; stop growing and you are in danger of a fall.

Calling and Election (1:10–11)

'Therefore, my brothers,' says Peter, 'be all the more eager to make your calling and election sure. For if you do these things, you will never fall.' Is this perhaps a word for somebody who's come to Keswick this week? Is this why, deep down, you are not feeling secure in your relationship with Jesus? You're just not growing, you've stopped making an effort in Christian things. You've started resting on your laurels, you're neglecting the means of grace, maybe your enthusiasm as a young Christian has worn off. When it comes to signs of spiritual life you are always pointing backwards. Whenever you are asked for a testimony it's always ten years out of date. There is nothing in your present experience to witness to that divine nature which you claim to participate in. The sparkle's gone out of your relationship with Christ. To use Peter's words, you have become ineffective and unfruitful in your knowledge of Him.

Well—I am here to tell you it won't do. It simply won't do. You can't expect to enjoy assurance of salvation in that condition. The calling of this first passage of our Bible study at this Keswick is to confirm your reservation, to make sure that that ticket, that passport, that entry visa into heaven, is securely in your hands. How do you do it? By making every effort to add to your faith goodness. If you do these things, says Peter, 'You will never fall, and you will receive a rich welcome into the eternal kingdom of our Lord and Saviour Jesus Christ.'

In the Greek city-states, one way of rewarding a general, or an athlete who had won the Olympic games, was to knock a hole in the city wall to make a special entrance just for them. They called it 'richly providing an entrance'. That's what God does for the victorious Christians says Peter. It's possible, no doubt, to get to heaven by the skin of your teeth. It's possible to squeeze in through the door like a late-comer at a party. But who wants to live with that margin of uncertainty? 'For,' says Peter, 'it's also possible to be received into eternity richly. Seek such an entrance.' It is reserved for those who have made solid progress, who have not received the grace of God in vain but have used what God has given them to furnish themselves with that holy personality which is fit for heaven.

It's said that the film-maker Sam Goldwyn was once approached by an aspiring young starlet for a role in one of his epic motion pictures. 'Can I be in your movie, Mr Goldwyn? Can I?' she said, fluttering her eyelashes and smiling her best Hollywood smile. Sam Goldwyn is reputed to have puffed his cigar, wagged a finger at the young lady and said, 'Darling, I am giving you a definite maybe.'

But Peter can offer us far more than a definite maybe. I want you to be sure, you have got more than that. Ask God this morning for the faith, for the incentives, for the power you need to climb the ladder of Christian fitness. Don't wait for some spiritual experience to zap you, don't sit around contemplating your navel pretending that's spirituality. You can loaf your way to hell; but the kingdom of heaven is taken by force. Make an effort.

2: True Truth
2 Peter 1:12–21

I want to talk to you about doubt; not the kind of doubts about the existence of God that an atheist has, but the kind of doubts about Jesus that a wobbly Christian has. If we are honest, there's no denying that the Christian message that we are gathered here this week to celebrate and affirm has a quite incredible scenario. The Son of God—born as a baby and laid in a manger, walking around Palestine as an ordinary human being, executed under torture on a cross, risen from the dead and ascended beyond our space-time co-ordinates, returning one day to judge and renew the universe—with the best will in the world, it takes a lot to swallow all that! I have to say, I have some sympathy with those who say they have difficulty in doing so. I was an unbeliever myself once upon a time. In fact, looking back on those days I can identify at least three things about the Christian message which made becoming a believer awkward and difficult for me.

The first was *the exclusiveness of Jesus' claims*. In this global village to which we now belong, with so many different faiths pressing on our doorstep, it seems so narrow-minded for Christians to insist that Jesus is the one and only way to God.

The second was *the supernaturals of Jesus' life*. So much of Jesus' story centres around miraculous events like the virgin birth and the resurrection. Miracles by definition are anomalies in the normal pattern of things. People like me who have grown up in a scientific world are, I think, prejudiced against such breaches of the natural order.

The third was *the antiquity of Jesus' story*. It all happened so very long ago—2,000 years. How can we be sure it's not all a tissue of legend and fabrication? Historical evidence is necessarily second-hand; as everybody knows, you can never trust a rumour. So how can I be expected to be sure of what's happened?

For these three reasons I found faith difficult. It's not surprising that those who want to deny Christianity are not short of arguments to justify their scepticism. Indeed, many have felt that if we could only separate Christianity from the embarrassment of its exclusives, its supernaturals and its historical antiquity, it would be vastly more plausible to the average modern man and woman.

That is what underlies the development of so-called liberal theology in the last couple of centuries. Take the notorious former Bishop of Durham, David Jenkins. He caused considerable debate on television and in the newspapers, and much disquiet among Bible-believing Christians. He stated that he didn't really believe that Jesus literally rose from the dead. Why did he say that? Because he thought it was in the interests of Christianity to distance Christianity from the exclusives, the supernaturals and historical roots that are so central to orthodox traditional Christian belief. He knew that twentieth-century people found it difficult to believe in a physical resurrection of the unique Son of God. So he thought he would try to remove that barrier to their acceptance of the Christian message. It would be quite wrong to see him as some kind of deliberate traitor to the Christian cause; he simply wanted to make the Christian faith more credible to modern people.

His was not a new method. Through the centuries the church has had to deal with numerous similar well-meaning attempts by theologians to reinterpret the gospel in such a way that it seems more relevant and plausible to the contemporary world. They have done it by what could be called a policy of tactical surrender to doubt. Indeed, Peter is writing in the face of one such very early assault on the Christian message.

It's important to realise that the Greek-speaking world of the first century, in which Peter was preaching and seeking to evangelise, found just as much difficulty and offensiveness in the exclusiveness and supernaturals and historical elements of Christianity as the twentieth-century world does. Imagine the situation of Christians in those days. Christianity was a tiny sect in a Roman empire that boasted hundreds of religions and philosophies. There was scientific rationalism, Epicurean philosophy, moralistic humanism, stoicism; there was occultism, spiritism, mysticism, dualism, pantheism, animism; star-worship, devil-worship, embryo-worship—it was all there. The Roman empire of the first century was a paradise for the religious dilettante. You could take your pick. Edward Gibbon in his *Decline and Fall of the Roman Empire* comments:

> The various modes of worship which prevailed in the Roman world were all considered by the people as equally true, by the philosophers as equally false, and by the magistrates as equally useful.

How could Christianity expect to be believed in such a welter of competition?

Very early on, smart alecs in the church thought they had found the way. One of the most popular forms of religion in the first century was the mystery cult. These were enormously varied, but were basically a kind of oriental mysticism centring round a piece of ancient mythology. One of the most popular was based on the story of Mithras, a god who came to earth, died and rose again (there's more to his story than that, but that will do for our purposes this morning). The followers of the cult of Mithras believed that by participating in a secret initiation ritual, it was possible for a person to experience the immortal life of Mithras themselves by becoming mystically united in some way with him.

Such cults were very popular in the Greek-speaking first-century world. So if you were a first-century David Jenkins, wanting to make Christianity acceptable and plausible, what could be simpler than to interpret Christianity as a mystery religion—a religion based not on the story of Mithras, but of

Jesus? At a stroke, you've eliminated all those awkward bits. No one seriously believed that Mithras had literally died and rose—and if a few actually did, they didn't need to; it wasn't part of the deal. The important thing about the myths which these mystery religions were built around wasn't the historical accuracy of the story, but the spiritual experience which you could enjoy through mystical initiation into the cult. In the same way, turning Christianity into a mystery religion removed the need to defend the historical accuracy and the supernatural picture of Jesus which the Gospels gave. What actually happened in time and space had become irrelevant. It was the myth that mattered, as that became a vehicle for people who enjoyed a mystical experience of the spirit of Christ.

Moreover by adapting Christianity to the expectations of the Greek religious world you would also have done away with its other offensive element—its exclusiveness. There was nothing unique about mystery religions. You could belong to any number of them if you wanted to. Nobody needed to persecute a Christian because he was a follower of a mystery cult of Jesus. Such things were perfectly respectable.

I mention this because there is abundant evidence that a very early and complex heresy called 'gnosticism' developed in the ancient world precisely along these lines. It represented just such a movement: a capitulation to the mood of the Greek-speaking world. It turned Christianity from a religion of faith and history into a religion of myth and mysticism. And I think it's obvious that Peter, writing close to the end of his life in this second letter, is addressing the very early stages of that gnostic heresy. That's why the word 'knowledge' occurs so often in this book; for the word 'gnostic' comes from the Greek word *gnosis* meaning 'knowledge'.

What I want you to note this morning is the line that the apostle Peter takes in responding to this challenge. If we can identify how Peter replied to first-century gnostics, we shall have a sound basis for identifying how we should respond to the kind of scepticism and reinterpretations which come from wobbly and liberal Christians in the twentieth century.

Our study passage has three paragraphs containing three closely interwoven points. They are all responses to this fundamental scepticism, this fundamental doubt about the importance of the historical roots of the Christian message.

The Apostle's Testimony (1: 12–15)

Clearly, Peter feels he has not got long to live. Jesus predicted that Peter would end his life violently, and obviously he hasn't forgotten. But the prospect of his imminent departure inevitably raised a question in Peter's mind, and no doubt too in the minds of those Christians whom he had led to faith: 'Where is the church going to look for answers to doctrinal questions after you've gone, Peter?' He represented theological authority. He was the one who had taught them Christianity. If he died they would be at the mercy of false teaching. How would they prevent the church from falling into all kinds of heresies? Indeed, they were already beginning to observe such heresies flowering in anticipation of his demise.

For the would-be gnostic theologian this was no problem at all. As far as he was concerned, Christianity was an experience, not a doctrine. The departure of the apostles was neither here nor there. But Peter didn't see it that way at all. It was of the utmost importance to him that the teaching of Christianity which he represented should be preserved without distortion. That's why he speaks of the church as being firmly established in the truth, that truth he's been expounding in the early verses we looked at yesterday. The church knew the truth, had received the truth; but there was always the danger she could forget the truth. So he sees it as his apostolic duty in these closing years of his life to constantly remind them of it: verse 13, 'I think it is right to refresh your memory as long as I live in the tent of this body . . .'

Indeed if you look on to 1:15 you will see that Peter is determined to make sure that after his death they still had access to an authoritative memoir of his apostolic teaching. What is he referring to? There is a very high probability that it is the Gospel of Mark. There's a great deal of early evidence that Peter was Mark's principle source. So it is likely that Peter saw the work on which Mark was engaged, and which might be close to completion as he writes this second letter, as the necessary permanent reminder the church needed of his memoirs of Jesus.

But notice what Peter does *not* say. He doesn't appoint some apostolic successor like Mark to continue to define Christian doctrine with the same authority as he did. Neither does he give liberty to the church to refashion the Christian message after his death, according to the needs and preferences of later generations. The key word of this first paragraph is 'remember'.

For Peter, Christianity was a religion of received truth. He had received it from Christ and he had passed it on to those first-generation Christians, and their duty was to pass it on to others—but always referring back to that original deposit of truth in which the church had originally been established, out of which apostles like Peter were Christ's appointed guardians. This is very close to the point that Jude makes. Jude's is a letter in the New Testament which has many similarities with 2 Peter (you might like to read the two together), and Jude makes this point also in his opening verse.

So there is no room, in this view of Christianity, for gnostic reinterpretation. Undoubtedly authentic apostolic Christianity had a strong element of immediate spiritual experience within it, as we saw yesterday in 1:3–4. Peter could even talk about God's power being in the Christian, he could speak almost like the mystery cults, of the Christian's participation in the divine nature. In that sense, Peter is no enemy of mystic experience in the here-and-now, as part of Christian spirituality. But he was not prepared to see Christianity cut loose from its historical moorings. Christianity is far more than just an experience of the spirit of Christ in the here-and-now. It was received truth, and as such was non-negotiable and immutable.

Now: how had this received truth been received? And where had it come from?

The Divine Testimony (1:16–18)

There are two clues hidden in this paragraph which directly indicate that Peter is engaging, as he writes, with these incipient gnostic false teachers. The first is the word 'stories' in 1:16. Peter is actually using the word for 'myths'—'We did not follow cleverly invented myths when we told you about the power and coming of our Lord Jesus Christ.' I am quite convinced that by so doing Peter is not just rebutting the accusation that the apostles were a pack of liars. He's making a much subtler point and answering a much subtler implication. He's telling us by that phrase that as apostles of Christ they were not purveyors of some mystery cult. He's making it clear to his Greek-speaking audience that Jesus cannot be put in the same category as Mithras, that the historic facts of the gospel story are of critical consequence. 'This is no myth,' he says. 'Jesus really was God in the flesh. Jesus really did die and rise again. He really is coming again in the future. These are not mere metaphors or symbols that mediate some spiritual experience to you; these are concrete historical facts.'

He says, 'I know it because I have the evidence of my own senses to confirm it.' And that's the second clue. The word 'eye-witness' at the end of verse 16 is a translation of a word widely employed by the first-century mystery cults. It was the word they used to describe a person who had reached a higher-than-average level of mystical initiation. So Peter is saying, 'These gnostics make out that their psychedelic experiences of the divine are the real hall-marks of spiritual privilege. Well I'm telling you now that as a Christian apostle, I stood on a Palestinian hillside in the cold light of day; and in full possession of my faculties and with my own eyes I saw Jesus transfigured with the very same divine glory which He will bear again when He comes in judgement. And I heard with my very own physical ears the voice of God Himself identify Jesus as His unique and beloved Son. I was an eye-witness of Deity,' says Peter, 'on that holy mountain, in a way that no mystic guru hiding in the temple of Mithras could ever imagine. And it's for that reason that I cannot allow anybody to pervert Christianity in such a way as to distance themselves from the historical reality of Christ's incarnation or the expectation of His historical future return.'

These are not myths, says Peter. 'These are not old wives' tales that we apostles wove with our fishing nets. This is the testimony of what we as honest men saw with our own eyes. No doubt the world has longed for centuries that God would reveal Himself in such an unambiguous way, and for that reason men have made up many stories. But I am telling you, this time it has happened. Call me a liar if you must, but don't come up with any patronising rubbish about me being like Homer, a brilliant composer of myths. We apostles do not present ourselves to the world as philosophers, authors, poets or bards. We present ourselves to the world as eye-witnesses of Jesus' majesty. And authentic Christianity rests on the authenticity of our testimony.'

It is very hard to exaggerate the importance of this. It is, if you think about it, the answer to those difficulties I spoke about which I had with the Christian message in my early days and which many still have today.

Take the problem of *Jesus' exclusiveness*. If this testimony of Peter is true, how can Christianity be anything but exclusive? God either did speak from heaven and say 'This is my Son', or He didn't. And if He didn't, then there's no point trying to salvage Christianity with talk about it being myths and experience. The whole thing is a hoax and the only thing to do with it is to dispense with it. But if He did thus speak, it surely must follow that this Jesus stands alone. He takes priority over every other person in my life. By definition, this is the Son of God. No more than Peter are we allowed to erect tabernacles to any other prophets. 'This is my Son, listen to Him,' says the voice from heaven.

Take *the supernaturals of Jesus*. If it is true that the Son of God walked this earth, is it surprising that anomalous things happened around Him? Jesus is an anomalous person. If it is true that He really is the Son of God on earth we may have problems, but it is not essentially unexpected that super-natural things should happen to Him and around Him.

Take the question of *historical antiquity*. Of course we can't be absolutely sure of the historical truth of the gospel, if by 'being sure' you mean using some kind of logical truth or laboratory experiment that renders doubt impossible. It just isn't like that. We walk by faith and not by sight. There is no rationalistic truth which can confirm beyond all question that this Christian message has to be believed.

But there are many things in this life that we depend on daily, which can't be proven in that sort of way. In this passage Peter is putting you and me in the position of jurors in a court of law. In a court of law you can't prove scientifically who committed the crime, but you know as well as I do that you can form a reasonable judgement based on the reliability of witnesses. That's what Peter asks us to do here. He can't prove to us in a scientific sense that Jesus was transfigured on that mountain, he can't make it happen again before our very eyes. He can only insist that this is his eye-witness account, and ask us to trust him.

It is possible to exaggerate the difference between the apostolic age and our own. It's perfectly true of course that first-century Christians didn't have our science, our motor cars, our computers. But in one respect first-century Christians like Peter were just the same as we are in the twentieth century. They had eyes in their head in exactly the same place as you and me. Statues prove it! They were not so primitive or unsophisticated as to be unable to testify to what they saw. And that's what Peter is doing here: 'We were eye-witnesses of his majesty . . . we ourselves heard this voice that came from heaven when we were with him on the sacred mountain.'

Do you seriously expect me to believe that apostles like Peter, whose quality of life revolutionised the morality of the ancient world, collaborated to manufacture this monstrous hoax? That aged Peter—who has just been urging on his listeners the necessity of a holy life and knows he is likely to be martyred for his Christian faith—is lying when he writes those words? No. All faith in the Bible is faith in testimony, the testimony of Bible witnesses.

So we do no favours to the gospel when, like David Jenkins, we try to undermine the reliability of those witnesses. On the contrary, far from making Christianity more believable, what we are actually doing is challenging the trustworthiness of the very people upon whose integrity real Christianity pivotally depends; because real Christianity is not based on myths but on memories—the memories of the apostles. That's why at that central feast of our faith, Jesus says to us afresh, 'Remember Me.'

The Biblical Testimony (1:19–21)

Why does Peter go on in 1:19 to talk about the Bible—the Old Testament Scriptures, the words of the prophets? It's all tied up with that word in 1:19, 'interpretation'.

Even if you persuade a wobbly Christian that the apostles have a reasonable claim to be respected as eye-witnesses of real historical events, you have still won only half the battle. For a wobbly Christian as shrewd as David Jenkins or the like will respond, 'Well, the gospel message is events, and maybe I'm prepared to accept these things happened.' But the gospel message is more than just events. The critical thing about the gospel is not the events but the interpretation placed on them.

Take for example the cross, the essential event in our faith. A man dies by public execution under Pontius Pilate, a historical fact witnessed by reliable observers; even David Jenkins doesn't seem to quarrel with that article of the Apostles' Creed. But the apostles said that Jesus was dying for men's sins so that we could be forgiven. There is no way you can see that by physical sight; no eye-witness observation of the cross communicates that meaning to you. It is an interpretation placed on the event.

Our wobbly Christian will say, 'Well, naturally enough, Jews thought in terms of Old Testament sacrifice for sins. And the Greeks thought in terms of some mystery cult like Mithras'. Those were the ideas they were familiar with in their culture, but those interpretations are all relative to that generation. In our twentieth century we must look for new interpretations that speak to modern men and women, based on the presuppositions of our twentieth-century ideas.'

This is the second plank of liberal theology. Even those who may be unwilling to endorse an extreme scepticism regarding the historical accuracy of some New Testament events will still want to say, 'But the Bible's interpretation of those events is cluttered with dispensable mythological ideas.' They would say that the theologian's task is to strip away those outdated mythical frameworks, and to reinterpret the experience of the early Christians in a way more relevant and contemporary for us today.

How will Peter respond to the suggestion that the apostles may not be as reliable interpreters of events as they are observers? He is emphatically positive. Verse 19: 'And we have the word of the prophets to confirm all this'—at least that's what I think he is saying—'and you will do well to pay attention to it, as to a light shining in a dark place . . . you must understand that no prophecy of Scripture came about by the prophet's own interpretation. For prophecy never had its origin in the will of man, but men spoke from God as they were carried along by the Holy Spirit.'

Do you see what Peter is saying? When as an apostle he speaks of the deity of Jesus and of His second coming, he insists they are not merely human deductions from the transfiguration or the resurrection events. These are God-inspired testimony of Scripture. It's the apostle's conviction that God has not just done something in Jesus before many witnesses, but that He has explained what He has done. He has not left us to look at the person of Jesus and the events of His death and resurrection and, as it were, get our own spiritual vibrations from them and make up our own minds what these things mean. He has Himself interpreted those key historical events.

That's what prophecy is all about. The word is much bandied around today, but most people don't know what it means. Some think it has to do with standing up in a meeting and saying 'The Lord has told me . . .', others that it has to do with predicting the future. But a prophet in the Bible is fundamentally a man who has been inspired by the Spirit of God to interpret events God's way. He has been given supernatural insight into what events mean. They may be events of the past, they may be events of the present, maybe events yet to come—but the important thing about the prophet is that he tells you what history means.

Notice particularly how Peter claims that such prophecy is

produced in verses 20–21. He says it negatively and positively. Negatively: 'No prophecy of Scripture came about by the prophet's own interpretation [lit. "of man's own unravelling": the word 'prophet' is not in the Greek text but is supplied, rightly I believe, by the translators].' Many commentators interpreted this to mean that people can't understand the Bible on their own, they need the Holy Spirit or the church to help them. Some find that a tempting interpretation, but I'm quite sure it is wrong. The clue is in the verb: 'No prophecy came into being . . .' Peter is commenting on the origin of Scripture. When a prophet explained the meaning of history he was not giving his own interpretation of these events. He was not an artistic genius, responding to history like a poet responding to nature. He was saying what God said the events meant. Verse 21: 'For prophecy never had its origin in the will of man, but men spoke from God as they were carried along by the Holy Spirit.'

There's a fascinating description here of the interaction of man and God in the giving of Scripture. The production of Scripture, says Peter, means that people were being borne along rather like a boat on the sea, as the Holy Spirit blew upon them. They were not passive instruments, any more than sailors are passive passengers. But they were guided totally by this wind of God—as B. B. Warfield puts it, 'Taken up by the bearer's power and borne to the bearer's goal.'

So, says Peter, the verbal product of this miracle was that they spoke not on their own authority but from God. 'Hear the word of the Lord,' they said. 'This is what God is doing in these events you are experiencing or have heard about.' Scripture is the product of God's creative breath, as that Spirit blew through human hearts and minds and mouths.

You may say, 'I find that as difficult to believe as some of these things you say you believe about Jesus.' If Jesus is supernatural, so is the Bible. There is a strange kind of parallel, actually, between the miracle of the incarnation and the miracle of inspiration. In the incarnation, the Holy Spirit came upon a fallible human woman called Mary and so worked in her that the product of her womb was one hundred percent human and one hundred percent divine

—the Word made flesh. And what happens in inspiration is that that same Holy Spirit works in fallible human prophets so that the words they speak are one hundred percent human but also one hundred percent divine.

The Word of God made Scripture. What does that mean for you and me? What does it mean that God has not just done something utterly unique and supernatural in Jesus, but in the Bible has explained what He has done? It means two things.

First, it means that we in our day and generation must be aware of the trap of trying to make Christianity more relevant to people, by over-emphasising the dimension of present-tense, here-and-now spiritual experience to the neglect of those great foundation historic truths upon which the Christian faith is based. Gnosticism lives again in our day and generation. We live in a time which is very preoccupied with experience, and specifically spiritual experience. There's an immense temptation for us to yield to that secular pressure, to turn Christianity from a religion of faith based on historical events interpreted by Scripture, into a religion of contemporary spiritual experience mediated maybe by the sacraments or maybe by the big group experience.

But the unique claim of Christianity is that God, at a specific place and time in history, has stepped into our world and given us a definitive revelation of Himself before witnesses. And a Christian is first and foremost a person who believes that and is committed to it; who lives his or her life in the light of His coming. Gnostics distort that and turn Christianity into a subjective experience-centred mysticism. I would be the last to deny that Christians have an experience of God. And that experience of God is important. We are participants of the divine nature. But it is a tactical mistake of the first order to try to silence the doubts of wobbly Christians by appeal to such experiences.

What Peter is saying is that as Christians you and I must be, before anything else, Bible students. This is where the wobbly Christian has his or her doubts addressed properly. We can't afford to do away with the Bible and what it speaks of, as David Jenkins does. We certainly cannot afford to read books written by those who do, as a substitute for reading our Bible.

If we want to be sure about Jesus it is to the Bible we must go. Here in a single volume, in Old and New Testaments, God has brought together the eye-witness testimony of the apostles and the divinely inspired interpretation of the prophets. So Peter can say (1:19), 'You do well to pay attention to it, as to a light shining in a dark place, until the day dawns and the morning star rises in your hearts.'

It's a beautiful verse, though a little difficult to fathom. I think what Peter is saying is something like this. The glory of Jesus is veiled again just at the moment. We are in a gloomy dark world, just as the disciples were when they came down from the Mount of Transfiguration. The vision of glory faded and they took the path, the *Via Dolorosa*, to the cross. With them we share the darkness of that first Easter Saturday, between Good Friday and Easter Sunday. We are waiting for the day to dawn, for the glory to be seen again.

Therefore we are called to walk by faith, not by sight. We are remembering till He comes. But our present sense-experience is often one of darkness, not of glory at all. The darkness is inevitably a threatening place where doubts arise and faith is tested. But Peter is convinced that the answer to those doubts lies not with the speculative ideas of the gnostics, but in the true truth of the Bible. Here is God's interpretation, written in God's words, of what Jesus is about. Here is God's answer to those who challenge the credibility of the Christian message. It is a message of received truth, unchanged and unchanging, handed down from those first recipients of it, the apostles. It's a message founded on history, not on mystical experience: it is events confirmed by eye-witness testimony. And it is a message interpreted not by human speculation but by divine revelation through the words of inspired prophets.

That is why John Wesley says,

> I want to know the way to heaven. God has condescended to teach the way, He has written it down in a book. Oh give me that book, at any price give me the book of God, here is knowledge enough for me. Let me be a man of one book.

You will find as you study that book as Wesley did, if you pay attention to it as Peter advises, that the darkness will begin to disappear; the light of dawn will begin to arise.

Many come to Keswick looking for an experience. I sincerely hope you have one! Through the years at this Convention there have been many who have testified to having met the living God in the most remarkable experiential way here. But I tell you, the reason the Keswick Convention is still here helping people, the reason it is still on the track of truth rather than error, has nothing to do with Keswick experience at all. It has everything to do with Bible reading. It has everything to do with the fact that the founding fathers of this movement and those who continue it today are convinced that we must come here to study the Bible together.

Whatever else you do, keep the Bible central. Movements that offer the church spiritual experiences alone will have short-lived success and be perilously vulnerable to error. If you want to find faith, wobbly Christian, here's my advice: get down to reading your place and the morning star dawns in your heart; for it surely will.

3: Liars in the Pulpit
2 Peter 2:1–22

It is commonly assumed that the church's greatest problem today is persuading people to believe. But I suspect the reverse may be the case. In fact people in our late twentieth-century world will believe almost anything, providing it is said with an air of confidence by those who profess to speak with authority on the subject.

On 1 April 1957 the television commentator Richard Dimbleby presented a TV documentary on the spaghetti harvest in Italy. Viewers saw the spaghetti waving in the wind as it grew from the branches of 'the famous Milanese spaghetti trees'. Tens of thousands believed him. Patrick Moore the astronomer scored an even greater triumph on 1 April 1976; in an early morning radio broadcast, he reported that at 9.47 a.m. the planet Pluto would pass behind Jupiter, producing an increased gravitational pull from the heavens. Moore said that at that moment, people would feel lighter. He invited listeners to jump in the air and experience a slight floating sensation. Hundreds swamped the BBC telephone lines to report that the experiment had worked.

It all goes to prove that the principle feature of our modern age is not scepticism but gullibility, and nowhere more obviously than in the numerical success of hundreds of religious sects and cults. Many of them would, one have thought, strained the credulity of Simple Simon by their bizarre and fantastic ideas. But they all have followers.

The most remarkable of all is the extraordinary claim of

Joseph Smith, who claimed that in 1823 he was guided by an angel to some ancient plates hidden near Palmyra in New York State. They were inscribed with Egyptian hieroglyphs which Smith was miraculously able to translate by means of a specially provided pair of celestial spectacles. The translations revealed extraordinary facts about the early history of the American continent, which it seems was not discovered by Christopher Columbus but by a Jewish prophet called Lehi some 600 years before Christ. Of course the gold plates have never been produced, Smith's supernatural translation seems strangely influenced by the King James Version of the Bible, and archaeologists have searched in vain for any evidence of early Jewish settlements in America. In short the whole thing savours of being a monstrous con. But 3,000,000 adherents of the Church of the Latter Day Saints believe it all.

It is not unbelief the church has to worry about, so much as wrong belief: not the doubter, but the deceiver. He is here today, and he was there in Peter's day. Peter was writing, as we have seen, specifically to counter that threat. He perceived a growing menace in the later years of his life. And in chapter 2 he spells out his fears in stern polemic. So severe is his language that some modern commentators complain of his belligerence and intolerance.

But Peter knew how persistent, intractable and dangerous error could be. He had been schooled in the history of the Old Testament people of God. The authentic word of the prophets had repeatedly had to do battle with fraudulent impersonations, the false prophets. Moreover, Peter had it from the mouth of his Master that similar impostors would arise within the Christian community and mislead Christian disciples. That is probably why we detect a certain air of inevitability in Peter's opening sentence: 'But there were also false prophets among the people'—the Old Testament people of God—'just as there will be false teachers among you.'

Error, says Peter, is not just a potential threat to the church. It is absolutely certain that in every age the thesis of God's truth will be challenged by the antithesis of satanic lies, and with a considerable measure of success—'many will follow' (2:2). So clever will this counterfeit be, it will become absorbed all too easily into the church. Peter says, it's like poisonous waste leaking into a city's water supply. These are 'destructive' heresies (2:1). The word has a flavour of ruin and annihilation verging on the nuclear. These false teachers, he says, lay waste the people of God.

So it's vital that the church in every generation identify with certainty the liars in the pulpit. They are always there. Error is dangerous, and failure to label it and repudiate it will result in spiritual havoc. Peter the apostle, in this last letter he has sent to us, wants to help us in that task. He does it in this chapter by outlining some of the characteristics of false teachers and false teaching, so that we can identify it more efficiently.

I am going to give you six characteristics which Peter observed in the false teachers of his day and which I believe are characteristics of false teachers in every generation. If we absorb and learn those characteristics we shall be sharper in spotting false teachings and hopefully less vulnerable to its ravages. All six are put on the agenda in the first three verses, then further amplified and illustrated as the chapter proceeds. So the first three verses of this rather long and formidable chapter contain the essence of what Peter wants to say.

The Message of False Preaching

Notice the word 'heresies' which Peter uses to describe the false teaching. It is more a transliteration than a translation, for our word 'heresy' comes from the Greek word which Peter uses. Interestingly, it originally derives from the verb meaning 'to choose'. A heretic is a person who chooses what he wants to believe. You may say, 'What's wrong with that? Everybody has a right to his own religious opinions, don't they?' But that's the point; according to the Bible, none of us have any right to any religious opinions whatsoever. The Bible says that our opinions on matters of faith must be constrained by what God has revealed of Himself. That's why the second commandment is, 'Thou shalt not make any graven image'. What does the idolater do? He picks up his chisel and piece of wood and says, 'I think God is like this'. He chooses what sort of God he is going to believe in. He has religious opinions and he sanctifies them as an object of worship.

Even without chisel and wood, we can construct mental images of what we think God is like and then choose that God. I well remember a Cambridge undergraduate saying to me, 'My God would never send anyone to hell.' Which was absolutely true; her god wouldn't hurt a fly. But as I tried to explain to her, what basis had she for such confidence that her god had any relevance to the real God who was one day going to judge her? She had chosen what sort of God she wanted to believe in. She had sanctified her own religious opinions.

According to the Bible, the whole point is that God has delivered us from speculation and opinions and has spoken a word of self-disclosure (as we saw yesterday); received truth, truth witnessed both by the eye-witness testimony of the apostles and the inspired testimony of the prophets, truth contained for us in the Old and New Testaments of the Bible.

So Christian theology is not an exercise in creativity or a fine art; it's a science based on biblical data. Preachers may try to be original in various ways, but in one respect they have to be plagiarists; for heresy is, in essence, theological originality. It is the refusal to submit our opinions to God's revealed word. And of course it is a sin. It is a sin of the intellect just as much as much as adultery is a sin of the body. It's an exercise of human choice outside the boundaries of divine permission. I may not do with my body that which God declares to be wrong, and I may not believe with my mind that which God declares to be false. I can no more choose my own creed than I can choose my own moral code. In both, my conscience must submit to the revealed word of God.

The word 'heresy' therefore reminds us that you don't have to be a pagan to be an idolater—just a heretic. You don't have to be a non-Christian, just a liberal Christian, a Christian who will not be bound by the word. Such a so-called Christian is every bit as much a worshipper of graven images as the most primitive animist dancing round his totem pole. The only difference is, the latter does it often out of ignorance, the former out of a pretence of knowledge.

Of course any such false teacher in the church would be bound to betray a certain arrogance, a refusal to submit his ideas to the testing fire of God's revealed truth. And arrogance was certainly a feature of the heretics whom Peter knew, as we see in verses 10–12. They are slightly difficult verses, which may be based upon the Jewish belief that angels are models of tact and discretion. 'Angels', said the Jews, 'never shoot their mouths off.' One tradition even tells how Michael the archangel, in his self-effacement and modesty, refused to rebuke Satan to his face. And that may well be the immediate allusion here, as it certainly is in a parallel verse in the letter of Jude.

But, says Peter, in contrast to the commendable reticence of the angels these false teachers despise authority. They have an unhealthy, familiar attitude to divine mysteries and an audacious contempt for spiritual powers. It is the kind of theological impertinence described in the old proverb, 'Fools rush in where angels fear to tread.' There is no humility in these false teachers, no perception of the fact that they are touching holy things, no disciplined respect and dependence on God's authoritative word; instead (2:18), loud boasts of folly. Like ignorant beasts, he says, without discretion or self-restraint, they blaspheme in matters they don't understand.

Disraeli once said of Gladstone, 'He is a sophisticated rhetorician, inebriated with the exuberance of his own verbosity.' Much the same must have been true of these people. They were arrogant, like ill-bred children who didn't know when to keep their mouths shut, always wanting to push their ideas to the front, and yet so clever with their words that the simple-hearted mistook their bombastic theological insolence for spiritual authority. And listened.

The Method of False Preaching

You will find the seed of Peter's second characteristic again in verse 1, in the word 'secretly'. It suggests that there is a subtlety about the methodology of these false teachers. We are not talking here about some well-defined antagonistic ideology like Islam or Marxism with which the church is in open confrontation. This error is being insinuated into people's minds from within the church, by a clandestine infiltration.

Jesus warned of this. 'Beware of false prophets who come in sheep's clothing, but inwardly are ravenous wolves' (Matt. 7:15). How is this masquerade sustained? Peter tells us in verse 3: 'In their greed these teachers will exploit you with stories they have made up.' A better, more literal translation is: 'They will exploit you with plastic words.' The Greek means 'words specially moulded so as to appeal to the hearer'.

Peter may have meant myths, made-up stories; for we know that the gnostic heretics had a lot of time for myths. But the phrase 'plastic words' probably embraces more. There are many kinds of phoney speech by which a false teacher may insinuate himself into the minds of a simple-minded believer. Flattery is one which is frequently employed by such undercover agents in the church. I've had such flattery offered to me many times. 'Oh we do so admire your lovely church, so full on Sunday! We think you're doing a wonderful job here. We know a very fine minister in such-and-such a place. Have you heard Dr Wobbly? Perhaps you should invite him to preach . . . He's an extremely good communicator; and so clever! Do you know, he has five degrees? An academic congregation like yours would really appreciate his genius. I can't tell you how exciting it is to sit under the ministry of such a learned and articulate man.'

I suspect that there was just such an air of sophistication about these false teachers in Peter's day. It may well have lent credibility to them in the minds of naive Christians, whose pride was perhaps easily pampered by the thought of sharing conversation with such theological avant-garde. Flattery may well be the phoney talk Peter has in mind here.

Alternatively, 'plastic words' could be a reference to the pseudo-orthodoxy of these people. It's another classic ploy of false teachers to select their vocabulary so as to give their ideas an illusion of Christian authenticity. They will speak of

Christ, salvation, reconciliation, mission and so forth—but they will cleverly distort the meanings of those words, so that they are using biblical language but no longer in a biblical way. Thus 'Christ' becomes a label for the cosmic spirit that informs all religions. 'Salvation' becomes the emancipation of the black races. 'Reconciliation' becomes the brotherhood of man expressed in the Labour movement. 'Mission' becomes international harmony. And so on . . .

It can be really hard to penetrate such a wall of falsehood. It means diving beneath the sheep's clothing and trying to identify the wolf. It means going beyond what they affirm, and asking what they deny; going beyond what they say, and enquiring what they really mean. For false teachers are plausible; false teaching is almost invariably propagated by nice, respectable, warm-hearted people. And the devil will do his utmost to make it look as if we are quibbling about words and lacking in charity when we try to expose the falseness of their ideas. This is their message: not an open assault upon the truth, but its subversion.

The Motives of False Preaching

Verse 3: 'In their greed these teachers will exploit you'—or more literally, 'will make a commercial enterprise of you'. The Greek word means 'to manage a shop'. The implication is that money is the driving force behind these false teachers. I am not saying that this is always the case, but experience abundantly confirms that it often is. So often when you look behind the propaganda front of false teaching, you will discover that financial self-interest is really informing the whole show. It is not too cynical to suggest that if you want to identify questionable cults and groups, ask to see their annual accounts—if you can get hold of them at all. See where the money comes from and where it goes. Don't be surprised if you get some nasty shocks, for successful religion is big business and there is a lot of money to be made out of it.

One Old Testament character who was well aware of the profit-making possibilities of being a preacher was Balaam. That is undoubtedly why Peter cites him in verse 15. Notice the phrase 'the wages of wickedness'. Balaam was a prophet who took bribes; for a fee he would invent an oracle or a curse, exploiting people with plastic words, with his stock-in-trade. And as Peter rather sarcastically reminds us in this chapter, the principle reason we remember Balaam's story now is because his donkey proved more reliably inspired by God than he did (2:16). He implies that you are more likely to hear the word of God from the lips of dumb animals than from those who, like Balaam, wander off the path of truth for the sake of thirty pieces of silver.

The Morals of False Preaching

There is another reason, however, why Balaam is a good model for these false teachers. In the book of Numbers we are told that he was not only financially corrupt but was also responsible for a disastrous collapse in sexual propriety among the people of Israel. It was at his instigation that the young women of Moab were sent to entice the young men of Israel into pagan worship of Baal. And that, Peter quite clearly felt, was another tell-tale indicator of erroneous teachers: not just their motives but their morals. They were not just profiteers, they were libertines.

Peter emphasises this point throughout the chapter. In verse 2 he speaks of their 'shameful ways', implying their reckless immorality. In verse 10 he speaks of 'those who follow the corrupt desire of the sinful nature . . .', which may well be a euphemism for sexual perversion. In verse 13 he says 'Their idea of pleasure is to carouse in broad daylight.' There was something brazen about their hedonistic self-indulgent life-style. In verse 14 he describes them as 'never stopping sinning'; they are experts in self-indulgence, they have schooled themselves in forbidden desires. He describes them as having 'eyes full of adultery' (literally 'full of the adulteress')—that is, every woman they look at they size up as a potential consort for their lust. So habitual has this moral corruption become, they are completely obsessed by it. It recalls Milton's acid comment about just such unworthy money-grabbing and immoral shepherds in his poem 'Lycidas'.

Of course not every heretic is as shameless in his undermining of Christian moral standards. But it is a general rule that those who depart from the way of truth intellectually are very likely sooner or later to be found, with their followers, having departed from the way of righteousness morally. The two paths are really one. Intellectual truth and moral truth both find their fount in the One who said, 'I am the truth'. Once we deny Him by our doctrines, we will soon be denying Him also by our actions.

So it is no coincidence that in our own day it is the very same liberal theologians who cast out the deity of Christ, His historical resurrection and other central creedal doctrines of our faith, who are also be found permissive on ethical matters.

Of course, permissive moral talk has its appeal. It panders to our sinful nature, it anaesthetises our conscience with its fake spirituality and theological rationalisations. Peter is under no illusion about how successful this kind of demoralising heresy will be: 'Many will follow their licentiousness.' But this fourth, moral test at least has this advantage: it provides a point of identification which even the most simple-minded, ordinary and perhaps ill-informed Christian can nevertheless use. Sometimes pin-pointing doctrinal error can be extremely difficult. It requires a very thorough knowledge of the Bible, and a great deal of penetration and insight, to put your finger on what it is these people are saying which is false. But when that error works its way through and emerges as moral failure and moral permissiveness in people's lives, everybody can see it. That no doubt is why Jesus said, 'By their fruits you will know them.' If you want to spot false teachers in the church, don't just look at their creed, look at their lives.

Here then are the first four characteristics of false teachers. A religion of opinion not of revelation, insinuated into the church by crafty and sensuous speech; and a religion which is most of all soft on sin and motivated by gain. It's a very solemn, harsh picture. It's one which I suggest to you is as true today as it was then. You will find just such teaching harbouring in the church of Jesus Christ today, quietly poisoning her bloodstream like toadstools that have mistakenly got into the mushroom soup. Error is dangerous. The last two characteristics illustrated that danger.

The Effects of False Preaching

The first effect which Peter describes in 2:2 is that false teaching means that *the church loses its reputation*. 'Many will follow their shameful ways and will bring the way of truth into disrepute.' We were saddened by the scandals involving the American TV evangelists such as Jimmy Swaggart, who were found in serious moral failure despite the millions who watched their TV programmes. That moral collapse undermined years of evangelistic endeavour. People could no longer trust those who purported to be ministers of the Word of God.

Jesus said that His disciples were meant to be salt, counteracting the corruption in the world; but Jesus also said that if that moral salinity is lost, they would be good for nothing except to be trodden underfoot. Once the church loses its moral taste, it opens itself up to the contempt of the world. And that, it has to be said, has frequently been a consequence of false teaching, that which leads into moral licence within the church.

We may call ourselves Christians and boast about our personal relationship with God and so forth. We may claim we have a message that the world needs to hear, and organise Sunday Schools and missionary societies in order to propagate our faith. But what is the world's opinion of Christians? Again and again you hear the jibe: 'The church? Oh the church is full of hypocrites.' Sadly, it is all too often true.

Ministers complain that people won't come to church any more. 'It must be the secularism of our age,' they say. Must it? The people I talk to on the street aren't very secular, not in that sense. I wonder sometimes whether the reluctance of people to identify with the institutional church doesn't have more to do with the fact that people don't want to belong to something so characterised by unctuous humbug. For that is the image the church has succeeded in getting for itself in the world today.

Paul said to the Jews, 'The name of God is blasphemed among the heathen because of you' (Rom. 2:24). Little wonder that Peter calls these false teachers 'blots and blemishes on your love feasts' . The church needs to be known for the purity of its moral code, for the sincerity of its love. But too often these false teachers render it ugly and repellent. They are blots on the Christian landscape, advocates of moral permissiveness that destroy the church's reputation in the world.

A second effect follows closely. *The church is emptied of its spiritual power* (2:17). Peter employs pictures of a dried-up spring and a cloud driven away by the wind. This false teaching promises so much but yields nothing. It frustrates its adherents, leaving them permanently unsatisfied. They've got nothing to offer, they are waterless springs, empty clouds. Oh, their avant-garde ideas may sound very exciting in the lecture hall, but they have nothing to offer the real person in the streets facing real problems in life. After all, he can get all the permissiveness he wants without needing a theological excuse for it.

No. The cruel thing about this false teaching, says Peter, is that it draws nobody truly into the church, but it corrupts those who are on the fringes of Christian experience and ruins them. It is a special danger for young believers, for marginal Christians. Verse 18: 'They entice people who are just escaping from those who live in error.' It is always the immature Christian who is particularly vulnerable to this kind of false teaching.

Notice the word 'seduce' in verse 14 and 'entice' in verse 18. Both are words that come from fishing. Rhetoric is the lure, the seduction. Sensuality is the bait, the enticement. And those who aren't yet spiritually mature enough to distinguish the thrill of animal instinct from that of real spiritual experience are trapped; they are hooked.

Verse 19: they promise them freedom. That's always an appealing word, especially to a young idealist—freedom from psychological inhibition and bourgeois morality, freedom to be spontaneous, to be unfettered by convention. Freedom to be oneself and think for oneself. It's an intoxicating word, freedom. But, says Peter, it's all one big confidence trick as far as these people are concerned. 'They promise them freedom while they themselves are slaves of depravity—for a man is a slave to whatever has mastered him.' The truth is that these very people who preach moral liberation are slaves to their own corruption. They can't stop sinning even if they want to. And what's new about the freedom to sin? We've always had it. It's the freedom to live holy lives we lack; and these people haven't got that. No, they promised freedom, but there is no freedom in sin. Sin is grimly predictable, the most inexorable fate to which human beings can commit themselves. There's only one thing in the world that can deliver a person from that bondage: the knowledge of Jesus Christ as Lord and Saviour. That is why it's such tragic folly when those who are on the edge of Christian experience, just making that great discovery, are sucked back into their old servitude again as a result of this kind of false teaching. But that is so often the way it goes; little wonder Peter announces so grim a destiny for those responsible.

The End of False Preaching

Look finally at the end of these false teachers. Again, the seed of what Peter has to say on this solemn subject is in verse 3: 'Their condemnation has long been hanging over them, and their destruction has not been sleeping.'

In the course of the chapter Peter gives three examples of the way God judged in ancient times: the angels who sinned, Noah's world which perished under the flood, and Sodom and Gomorrah, the cities that were punished in some awful holocaust.

Probably he chose those particular examples for two reasons. First, they were all associated with sensuality and moral anarchy, just like the false teachers. Heaven, it seems, has a particular horror of any teaching which leads to immorality, particularly sexual immorality. That's a warning our particular generation needs to heed! If we dare to twist the gospel of holiness into a message that condones sexual misbehaviour, we had better watch out (2:9–10, where Peter may have had Sodom and Gomorrah in mind).

But the main reason, I suspect, for Peter's choice of

examples is that all three are also examples of the peril of ignored opportunity and abused privilege. The angels enjoyed heaven itself. The ancient world listened to Noah's preaching. Sodom and Gomorrah had righteous Lot as a companion. But in spite of these advantages, they all ignored the claim of God on their minds and their hearts. In the same way, says Peter, there is a streak of gross ingratitude in the behaviour of these latter-day false teachers: they deny the sovereign Lord who bought them (2:2), like slaves purchased in the market place who will not own their master. There is a streak of gross ingratitude in them and as a result they put themselves and their adherents in a perilous position.

Finally, verses 20 and 22, the end of the chapter. I don't know about you, but I find those verses particularly gripping and frightening. Peter is using melodramatic language here; but the reason is surely to press upon us the appalling reality he is describing.

He is telling us in these closing verses that false teaching can bring about a situation in which a person is worse off for having heard the gospel, because of the effects of such false teaching.

In fact, we learn from several parts of Scripture that it's possible for a person to have some partial experience of Christ, some preliminary taste even of the work of the Holy Spirit, and yet to fall away. A person can, like a comet, come into the orbit of Christian teaching and then to fly off again without having been truly been captured to do Christ's will. Jesus Himself warned us of that possibility in His famous parable of the sower. It is the danger of half a blessing. It's not enough for a person to be instructed in Christian truth, we must be delivered from the root of sin which dwells within us. We must be born again, says Jesus. We must be spiritually renewed if we are going to bring forth good fruit. But if a person is merely taken out of the world socially for a while, into the family of the church, without a renewing work of the Holy Spirit in their soul, then, says Peter, he is like a pig that is washed but—because it's still a pig—goes straight back to the mud again when you release it. Jesus similarly warned of the danger of being like a person out of whom a devil was cast, only to return with seven more evil spirits. The last state, He says, is worse than the first (Luke 11:25).

A partial experience is worse than no experience at all. It can inoculate you against the real thing. How much worse punishment, says the writer to the Hebrews, do you think a person will deserve who has spurned the Son of God and profaned the blood of the covenant and outraged the spirit of grace? (cf Heb. 10:29). I don't think we need to read this as a denial of the security of the true believer. Peter himself says in verse 9 quite plainly that the true child of God does not get embroiled again in the depths of sinful bondage that they once knew. But this passage leaves us no room at all for spiritual complacency. God's real people, says Peter, are always identifiable, just as Noah and Lot were identifiable in their world. But the mark of false teaching is that it conforms to this world, it blurs the distinction between the church and the world and between right and wrong, it dresses vice up as virtue, it compromises to the passing fads of contemporary philosophy and ethics. It is an echo of the world.

God's true people, says Peter, are not deceived by it. Jesus Himself said that if it were possible they could deceive even the elect (cf Matt. 24:24)—but by the grace of God that isn't possible. He is able to keep us from falling, He will present us faultless before His presence with exceeding joy (Jude 24)—thank God He is able!—but that promise is only for those who like Noah are preachers of righteousness in an ungodly world, and people like Lot whose heart is vexed within them at the moral anarchy around. The truly renewed person does not return to the mire of his old life. He is repelled by such a thought. If he drifts in that direction, he is pulled back. He spots the toadstool in the pile of mushrooms. He isn't duped by the protagonists of error, by so-called botanists who declare the toadstool harmless.

But woe to the church where the advice of such spiritually discerning and godly people is not heeded. Woe to the church where the apologists of Satan get a hold. And woe to those who are seduced by those false teachers before they have closed their contract with Jesus, for thereafter they are triply difficult to reach. False teaching is dangerous. Please don't underestimate it. I tell you again, the biggest problem the church faces in the late twentieth century is not that people believe nothing, it is that people will believe anything.

What does that mean for you and me? It means we have to be discriminating. Intolerance is not politically correct today, it's the unforgivable sin. But be discriminating! Don't believe something just because you have read it in a book, or been told it by some glib preacher, or have heard it from somebody on your television set. Test everything, for error is dangerous, and never more so than when is published by those who claim to have special knowledge and authority.

I know this from Cambridge. You might think that young people bright enough to go up to university would be the first to recognise error when they saw it. Quite the contrary! There is no group in the entire country more gullible than undergraduates. Because they are told something by some book or some teacher with higher academic qualifications than their own, because they hear that Dr So-and-so is giving a lecture on this or that, they go along and listen with quiet and expectant reverence, with rapt admiration for his complicated sentences and unintelligible vocabulary. Then they go home and say: 'What a wonderful man! Such intellectual penetration, such encyclopaedic knowledge!'

We are all of us far too gullible. Especially we Christians. We are too nice. We never suspected someone could be so nasty as to be deceiving us, especially if they wear an academic gown and have the title 'Reverend Doctor' in front of their name. Yet it happens; it has always happened and it still happens today. There are people who claim special knowledge and special authority in religious matters, and are teaching lethal errors. Some of them are lecturers at universities, some of them are bishops in the church, some of them are ministers of churches which you may be attending. Some of them write highly acclaimed books which get into evangelical book stalls—which I fear these days are not always as discriminating as they should be, either. I simply want to warn you to be aware of them. Don't be duped, don't be so humble that you believe anything and everything you hear. Don't even believe everything I tell you just because I tell you. 'Oh,' you say, 'Dr Clements? From the Keswick Convention platform? He couldn't possibly be telling us anything untrue!' Dear friend, don't you know the Bible says that Satan can transform himself into an angel of light (cf 2 Cor. 11:14)? So a six-foot-five Baptist pastor is well within his repertoire.

What's our answer to this pernicious fungus, this poisonous weed of false teaching in the church?

It is what we talked about yesterday. We must be saturated with the Book, with the received truth. It's no good saying 'Oh I just don't agree with that man.' My opinions on the matter are no more valid than his opinions. If we are reduced to opinions, there is no meaning to be attached to the phrase 'false teaching'. Put this book at the centre of your life and your faith and your church. Be discriminating. For I warn you, if you aren't then the verdict of eternity upon even you could be: 'Their last state was worse than their first.'

4: Living with Eternity in View 2 Peter 3:1–13

Our text is verse 13: 'In keeping with his promise we are looking forward to a new heaven and a new earth, the home of righteousness.'

Creation in Reverse

Man said, 'Let there be power.' And there was power; and man saw that the power looked good. He called those who sought power 'great leaders'. The evening and the morning were the sixth day.

Then man said 'Let there be a division among all peoples and divide those who are for my power from those who are against my power.' And it was so. The hostile people he called 'them' and the friendly people he called 'us'. The evening and the morning were the fifth day.

Then man said, 'Let us gather our power together in one place and create one empire of control, brain-washing and indoctrination to control men's minds, militia and secret police to control men's behaviour, myths and symbols to control men's emotions.' And it was so. The evening and the morning were the fourth day.

Then man said, 'Let there be censorship to divide the propaganda from the truth.' And he made two great bureaux, one to write the news for those at home and the other to write the news for those abroad. And it was so. The evening and morning were the third day.

Then man said, 'Let us make engines of destruction which can exterminate every form of life that moves on the face of the earth and in the sea.' So man made weapons of war, missiles and bombs, lethal germs and chemicals. He called this arsenal

> 'defences and deterrents'. The evening and the morning were the second day.
>
> Then man said, 'Let us make God in our own image and let him take the blame for the suffering we shall cause.' So man made God in his own image, the image of man created he him. Capitalism and socialism created he them. And he said, 'Rampage unfettered and extend your dominion over the whole earth. Shatter the peace, rape the environment, exploit, oppress and kill.' So man saw all that he had made and behold it was very, very bad. There was evening and morning, the last day.[1]

That parody of Genesis 1 was written by a young student. Is that what the future actually holds? Many fear it may be; that we are conspirators in a cosmic suicide act, doomed to self-annihilation. Of course we haven't always felt so gloomy. A century ago the humanists were hailing evolution as the guarantor of Utopia—inexorably the march of change moves forwards and upwards, towards the glorious perfection of the human race. But today such optimistic ideas sound hollow and almost laughable to most ears. Experience has revealed them to be fantasies of an infantile imagination, as far removed from reality as Disneyland is from Hiroshima.

Will we allow the greenhouse effect to melt the ice-cap and drown us all? Will the hole in the ozone layer expand and incinerate us all? Will some Middle-Eastern power obtain enough plutonium to nuke us all? Arthur Clark, the author of the book of the film *2001*, said 'No age has shown more interest in the future than ours; which is ironic, since it may not have one.'

All kinds of predictions and forecasts are being made by government think-tanks and science-fiction authors of all sorts, and the picture is almost always a gloomy one. More and more urgently the question of human destiny is pressing itself upon people's consciousness. Where is this remorseless river of time taking us?

This morning, our Bible passage wants to answer that rising sense of insecurity in our hearts. The key verb is 'looking forward'. It occurs three times, in verses 12, 13 and

1. Quoted in Stephen Travis, *The Jesus Hope* (Inter-Varsity Press, Leicester, 1981).

14. For Peter the Christian life is totally bound up with this experience of anticipation. It's not too much to say that Christianity can only be made sense of in the light of the future, in the light of His coming. In the spectrum of world faiths the Bible gives a unique appreciation to the future: the passage of time is meaningful and directed, we are going somewhere, time has a goal.

Christianity is not just a message about my vertical, here-and-now relationship with God. It's not just a message about having Jesus in your heart, nor even just a message of going to heaven when you die. It's a message about a new heaven and a new earth, which in one shattering future event will replace this old and corrupt world. If we are willing to receive it, it is this promise that makes sense of history's progress without surrendering to some naive evolutionary optimism which is bound to lead to disillusionment. And this final chapter of 2 Peter was written as a solemn reminder of that promise, in the face of certain sceptics who wanted to deny it.

Throughout almost all of this letter Peter is engaging with a group of false teachers. We have learned a lot about their methods and motives yesterday. Today we will see how he spells out one particular element of their theological system. They cast doubt on the Christian doctrine of the future. To use Peter's phrase, they 'scoffed' at the idea of Jesus and His second coming. And that was a denial Peter could not allow to pass unchallenged.

There is room no doubt within the sphere of Christian orthodoxy for a diversity of opinion on a wide range of issues. But the expectation of the personal return of Christ in glory is not one of them. Take away that hope, and you have severed the main artery of Christianity's blood stream and distorted Christianity into something else. If these heretics succeeded in establishing their ideas, no one could prevent the trickling away of the life of the church through this fatal wound in her doctrine. A haemorrhage had to be stopped, and stopped quickly. And Peter in this concluding chapter is applying the necessary tourniquet.

We are going to look at the chapter in three parts today and tomorrow: Why the sceptics doubt; What the sceptics ignore; and How then believers should live. Today we will concentrate on the first two.

Why the Sceptics Doubt (3:3–4)

Superficially the problem of the sceptics is simply one of disillusionment. This much-discussed event, the coming, hadn't happened. Perhaps for Peter's contemporaries, as for some of ours, the phrase 'the end of the world' had become so hackneyed and associated with fanatical eccentrics that it had a comic instead of a sobering effect on the popular imagination. Did they have sandwich-board evangelists in the first century, with lurid warnings about the imminence of apocalyptic doom? It wouldn't surprise me if they did. And so who could blame some of the Christians for beginning to wonder whether it wasn't all a load of nonsense, fit only for the minds of cranks and lunatics. Let's face it: the idea of Christ bursting through the skies to transform this world of ours is not one which any of us can easily accept. And it is perfectly true to say that the years have passed by and that momentous day has not yet arrived.

If it was hard to believe in Peter's day, thirty years after the cross and resurrection of Jesus, it is surely even harder to believe it today when nineteen centuries have come and gone. Practical doubt of that sort is to be expected. No sane person could possibly interact with what the Bible says about the future without experiencing some measure of honest incredulity. And if that was all that was involved in the scepticism Peter refers to, I am quite sure he would have dealt with it rather more sympathetically, more pastorally and gently, than he does in this chapter—perhaps as Jesus dealt with doubting Thomas.

But it's clear that in this case there were more fundamental and unworthy factors at work. There was a sinful error and prejudice. 'Scoffers will come', he says. The word has a rather pejorative tone. It conveys the idea of dismissive mockery. These sceptics weren't just disappointed that Jesus hadn't come again, they were fundamentally contemptuous at the very idea that He *could* come again. It implies that the thought is so ridiculous that it was really quite inconceivable—the subject of derision, rather than debate, among them.

And almost certainly that was the attitude. If you cast your minds back to the first chapter, you may recall that there are good reasons for believing that the false teachers wanted to reinterpret the gospel in a very fundamental way. They wanted to make it more congenial to the Greeks of their day, more like a mystery cult. They were sure they would have a better response to their evangelism if people saturated in Greek ways of thought could only have the Christian message marketed for them with this advertising image. But unfortunately so far as Christianity is concerned the mystery cults had a crippling blind spot. They had no interest in history. Their stock-in-trade was myth—fables representing timeless truths in pseudo-narrative form, but with no real foundation in the world of concrete facts. If Christianity is to be turned into a mystery religion then Jesus has to be turned into a mythological figure. Ideas such as His literal incarnation or resurrection were preposterous to the Greek mind, which found it extremely difficult to believe that immortality could muddle itself up in that crude physical way with this material and corrupt world.

No, Jesus would have to be interpreted mythologically. That was the key to Christianity, so far as these false teachers were concerned; not the historical events of Jesus's life and death; but the mystical experience which the Spirit of Jesus here and now could communicate to you.

Against that background Peter in chapter 1 insisted that we do not follow cleverly invented myths. And I suspect that the same mistake of trying to make Jesus a myth underlies this scoffing attitude about the return of Christ. There was an aversion to real history, and that meant not just the denial of the reality of Jesus' first coming in the past, it also implied an aversion to the history of Jesus's second coming in the future. At the root of both is this intellectual prejudice of the Greek mind-set, about any god who gets himself involved with this material world of ours.

The same kind of prejudice is detectable today among many so-called Christians who are sceptical of the doctrine of Christ's return. One finds a sense of embarrassment with the idea that Jesus could return to this world. Just like the false teachers of the first century they prefer to interpret all these miraculous and eschatological dimensions of the Christian message as myth. The important thing, they tell us, is not history past or history future, but the present-tense experience of the Christian and the church here and now. Indeed, you will find quite a few liberal scholars who would insist that the prophecy about Jesus' coming again was fulfilled on the day of Pentecost. We are not to be looking forward to some future coming, they say, but to be living in the experience of this realised eschatology—Jesus, who has come again in the person of the Holy Spirit.

At the root of this contemporary Christian scepticism about the return of Christ lies exactly the same kind of error and prejudice that we find amongst these false teachers of Peter's day. Christianity as it was presented in the Bible just didn't fit in with their pre-conceived ideas and preferences. Rather than change their minds, they decided to change Christianity.

What was the reason for that mental inflexibility? Why were they so reluctant to change their minds? Peter gives us a clue in verse 3: 'scoffers . . . following their own evil desires.' There was a definite moral component in their sceptical prejudice. It wasn't so much that they couldn't believe in the second coming of Christ, but that they had strong personal reasons for not wanting to believe in it.

In my experience it is rare to find an example of religious doubt which is not coloured to some extent by strong moral overtones of that sort. Often when talking to students in Cambridge I find people who want to kid themselves that their problems with Christianity are purely intellectual. But it doesn't usually require a great deal of psychological penetration to detect that as often as not it isn't intellectual integrity which is determining their unbelief, but interest in sustaining their freedom from the moral constraints of Christianity. Every preacher and pastor soon learns that the battle for faith is not ultimately fought in the mind but in the will. In the last analysis it is not a failure of our Christian apologetics that is responsible for the persistence of the sceptic in our midst, it is the absence of moral surrender. Repentance is hard.

So that is why the sceptic doubts. Superficially, it is disillusionment: 'It's a hard thing to believe, and time is passing.' But underneath that superficial disillusionment there is intellectual and moral error and prejudice. And my judgement is that exactly those same things are responsible for modern scepticism about Jesus's return. And if that is so, then presumably the answer Peter provides will be of equal relevance.

What the Sceptics Ignore (3:5–10)

The first and the most fundamental thing which the sceptics ignore, says Peter, is the Bible. In the first two verses you will see that once again Peter begins his whole discussion of this scepticism in the church by drawing his readers back to that body of received truth of which we spoke about in our second study: 'The word spoken by the holy prophets'—in other words what we call the Old Testament—'and the command given through our Lord and Saviour through your apostles'—in other words what we call the New Testament. The Bible, insists Peter, is unanimous in its testimony on this matter of the expectation of the personal return of God's Messiah and His kingly reign over the universe. It is spoken about in the warp and woof of the whole of the Old and New Testaments. 'I'm not saying anything new,' says Peter. 'I'm just reminding you, expounding what the Scriptures say.'

If you cast your eye down the chapter you will quickly see that that is indeed the case. In verse 5 Peter refers to Genesis 1 and the record of creation, in verse 6 to Genesis 6 and the record of Noah's flood, and in verse 7 to innumerable Old Testament prophecies about the coming judgement of God in fire. In verse 8 he quotes Psalm 90, in verse 10 a Gospel saying of Jesus, recorded both by Matthew and Luke, about His coming as a thief. In verse 13 he refers explicitly to Isaiah 65 with its mention of a new heaven and a new earth. And finally, as we shall see tomorrow, in verses 15–16 he cites the general support of the epistles of Paul quite explicitly, including them within the compendium of inspired Scripture.

Here we have then clear evidence that from very early on,

the canonical unity of the Bible in its Old and New Testaments was well recognised by the new church. The apostles of the New Testament were what the prophets were for the Old Testament; the inspired and authoritative source of God's word on all matters of faith and conduct.

So in countering the scepticism of these scoffers Peter doesn't need any fresh revelation. He merely needs to remind the church of what they have already learned. 'I'm not saying anything new about this,' he says, 'because at the end of the apostolic age there is nothing new to say.' The church has been built on the foundation of the apostles and the prophets; all that is needed for the maintenance of Christian orthodoxy is a constant reference back to that once-for-all deposit of biblical, received truth.

We considered this at length two days ago. Suffice it to say here that where we find theologians and even prominent churchmen denying the second coming of Jesus, they are, just like these first-century false teachers, ignoring the Bible. The question of the return of Christ is simply not open to doubt in the Bible. It is not in the least ambiguous on this subject. From cover to cover the testimony of prophet and apostle is that the world is going somewhere, it had a beginning in time and it will have an ending in time. And that ending will be the coming of God's Messiah in glory to set up an eternal kingdom and a new heaven and a new earth. I don't think any honest person reading the Bible with an open mind could come to any other conclusion than that that is what the Bible expects. So if there are people (be they with theological degrees or holding church office) who say that is not so, they are saying it in the face of the testimony of the prophet and apostle.

Let me make it clear: I don't mind in the least that people should have doubts. I'm all in favour of freedom of thought. But I do object to people, including scholars and churchmen, denying the fundamental affirmations of the Bible in this matter and still wanting to call themselves Christians. I have doubts myself. I doubt the claims of the Church of the Latter Day Saints—but then I don't claim to be a Mormon. I doubt the divine inspiration of the Qur'an—but then I don't claim to be a Muslim. I'm no advocate of mindless gullibility. It's vital people should think critically about their religious and philosophical opinions and the basis of their lives. But I simply cannot allow the meaning of the word Christian to be diluted by those who deny the plain teaching of the Bible on this matter. Where can we look to for a definition of what a Christian is and what a Christian believes, if not to the Bible?

Peter is saying, 'The doctrine of the second coming of Jesus is not a matter of taste. It's not an optional extra for a Christian who likes to think about these last things. This is a fundamental truth, a non-negotiable part of the biblical deposit. If prophet and apostle can't be trusted on this point, how can they be trusted about anything?' If you have learnt nothing else from this series of Bible readings in 2 Peter, I hope you have at least learned why the Bible is so important, and never more so than in days of doubt.

What the Bible says about God's relationship to history

Verses 5–6 refer to Noah's flood. Here, says Peter, is a historical example of God doing just what these sceptics say God can't do: intervening in history to destroy the world.

Notice, he accuses these false teachers of deliberately ignoring this fact. Once again they are shutting their eyes to self-evident truth in the Bible. This is not objective scholarship but downright prejudice; they are casting a blind eye to the biblical evidence, because it doesn't fit with what they want to believe, just as Nelson turned his blind eye to the French fleet.

A physics student once said to David Watson the evangelist, 'I've made up my mind so don't confuse me with facts.' But Peter points out that the Bible witnesses to countless times in which God has intervened in history in judgement. And Noah's flood is a classic example of that. If He has done so once, what is to stop Him intervening again in such a way as to wind up history for good and all? You are just deliberately forgetting that biblical witness, says Peter, in your scepticism about the return of Christ.

What the Bible says about God's relationship to the universe

Verse 7 reveals the second thing that the sceptics deliberately ignore.

A common fallacy, I find, is belief in what I call a 'finger-poking' God, who sits up in heaven and every now and again pokes down a finger and stirs things up a bit. The world calls these occasional interruptions 'luck'; Christians call them 'providence'. But that is not a correct picture at all. According to the Bible the world is not like a machine which runs on its own with some celestial mechanic every now and again throwing a spanner in the works; the universe depends upon God's upholding energy and command continuously. The same word that commanded the world to be, says Peter, sustains that world in being.

A picture I often use when trying to explain this to students is that of a television screen. The action on the screen seems to be going on all on its own; but when you penetrate a little deeper you realise that the picture is being upheld on the screen, projected continuously on to the screen from behind. In the same way, this world of ours which seems to run on its own is actually being continuously projected and upheld in existence by the creational word of God. He didn't stop uttering that word of command on the sixth day.

That's why Paul can say that 'in Christ all things hold together'. In fact contemporary scientists would have no difficulty in understanding that. We are becoming more and more aware of just how delicately balanced the cosmos is, how tiny a disturbance in the fundamental constants that define the fundamental energies of our world would be needed for the whole universe to fall into chaos. To bring this world to an end doesn't require some momentous action on God's part. All He has to do, says Peter, is to cease for one moment that upholding work which He has been performing since the day of creation. For Him it is as simple as changing the channel on your TV set. If only you understood God's relationship to this universe, you would not be quite so complacent about the security of this universe.

What the Bible says about God's relationship to time

Verse 8: 'With the Lord a day is like a thousand years, and a thousand years are like a day.'

Think about it; time can only be measured in an arena where change is taking place. Our cars wear out, our bodies age, rivers flow to the sea. It's by observing such changes that we understand time is passing. Scientists generalise the facts about this direction of change which we observe around us, and call them the laws of thermo-dynamics.

Suppose though that we lived in a world of changelessness, a world in which water could run downhill or uphill or remain locked in suspended animation between heaven and earth. Suppose our eyes could move not only right and left, but backwards and forwards in time so that we could perceive the horizons of history as well as the horizons of our globe. Suppose, in a word, we lived in eternity. Well, says Peter, in such a world a thousand years is like a day and a day like a thousand years. To live in eternity is to see time from a perspective and with an intensity which cannot possibly be imagined by us who are borne along with it. When a person who lives in eternity like that plans to do something, he's planning in time as well as in space. He determines the end as well as the beginning, he leaves nothing to chance because he is thwarted by no unforeseen circumstances. Whether the dimension of his creation in time is five seconds or five millennia, it's no less certain.

This, says Peter, is the God the Bible talks about. He inhabits eternity and therefore He is the alpha and the omega, the beginning and the end, who says, 'I work, and who can hinder it?' (Isa. 43:13). Does it seem perhaps that the events of Jesus's life, the cross and the resurrection are a long long way off because they took place 2,000 years ago? Why, says Peter: to God, 2,000 years ago is as recent as the day before yesterday.

It's even more subtle than that. For the cross never becomes a mere memory to God. It is a permanent event in His eternal vision. That's why when John looks into heaven he sees a lamb who has only just been slain. The wounds of Jesus's suffering are always fresh in the mind of God. That's why He can speak of Him as the lamb slain from the foundation of the world. Don't you see then, that once you realise just a little of God's perspective on time, all our complaints about the apparent delay in Jesus's coming seem childish and ill-conceived?

What the Bible says about God's relationship to us

This is perhaps the most important of all. Verse 9: 'The Lord is not slow in keeping his promise, as some understand slowness. He is patient with you, not wanting anyone to perish, but everyone to come to repentance.'

Two mothers outside a supermarket both have screaming children in their prams. Both seem to be doing absolutely nothing about it. Appearances, however, could be deceptive. You see, one mother is deaf. She can't hear the baby screaming and therefore isn't bothered about it at all. The other mother is patient, she is waiting for the screaming to stop. The two situations are quite dissimilar. Never mistake patience for indifference! Indifference can't be angry, irritated or provoked. Patience is angry but controls the anger; it is irritated but refuses to express the irritation; it is provoked but does not quickly surrender to provocation.

What you must understand about God, says Peter, is that He is being patient with us. He is not indifferent. He could, like an avenging judge, burst in upon this wicked world in righteous wrath and everlasting punishment. Hear now! Don't mistake His inactivity for apathy. But He is patient. He doesn't enjoy the death of the wicked, He wants to see repentance, He wants His enemies to find His grace.

Speaking very personally about this, I am glad the world didn't end in 1960, because I wasn't a Christian in 1960. Don't be too ready with complaints that Jesus is taking a long while coming! He will come when His sheep have all been found, He will not lose one of them. Indeed He'll leave the ninety-and-nine in the wind and the rain in the wilderness until the very last one is safe. Of course it is cold and uncomfortable sometimes, waiting for Christ to bring in His reign of righteousness. But don't complain about it, for there are more people yet to be saved.

What you must *not* do is confuse His patience and long-suffering for indifference. For he says in verse 10, 'But the day of the Lord will come'—there's no doubt about that—'like a thief.' The picture of the thief in the night is of course a common one in the New Testament. In fact, Jesus is the first person to use it, and some have suggested that the analogy speaks of the secrecy of His coming; they have used it to support the idea of a so-called 'secret rapture'. I don't want to argue the pros and cons of that view today, but I do want to say that I don't think this metaphor can validly be used to support it. Whenever the metaphor of the thief is used in the New Testament about Jesus's coming, it is not associated with secrecy but with unexpectedness. In fact Peter here links the idea of Jesus's coming like a thief, with global holocaust. You can hardly say that is a clandestine event.

It is unexpectedness which this picture of the thief communicates to us. When Jesus comes, nobody will be immediately anticipating it. Perhaps that's why we are given so little information about the date of Jesus's coming, and why the Bible is so reluctant to encourage us to speculate on that subject.

There's an old mathematical puzzle which I always think of in connection with the unexpectedness of Jesus's return. A criminal was condemned to death. But in a fit of unusual vindictiveness, the judge added this rider. 'Your execution will take place at 9 am one day next week. But to make your punishment especially severe, you will not be told which day it will be until the day arrives. It will be impossible for you to know which day it will be until that day arrives.'

An hour later the prisoner presented an appeal to the court, claiming that his conviction would have to quashed on the grounds that the sentence was impossible to execute. His argument was as follows. He could not be executed on the seventh day, for if he was still alive by 9.05 am on the sixth day he would know, a day too early, that his execution must be on the seventh day, for that was the only one left. But the sixth day was also ruled out, for by 9.05 am on the fifth day he would know that because the seventh day was not possible, the sixth was the only possibility—but again, he would have had a day's notice, which the sentence forbade. By similar arguments he eliminated the fifth, fourth, third, second and finally the first day; and so he assured the judge the only thing they could possibly do was to execute him immediately. But since he was fully prepared for this, that too failed the judge's requirement that sentence should be carried out unexpectedly. So he applied to be pardoned.

There is a fallacy in that logic, but perhaps it does indicate why the date of Christ's coming has been left so totally unknown. We are not even told 'It will be some time in the next 5,000 years.' We are simply told, with no conditions, no time limit at all, that it will happen; and when it happens, it will be unexpected, like a thief.

I suppose it is inevitable that there will always be those who aren't satisfied with that, who insist on playing those well-known Christian parlour games 'Count the earthquakes . . . Spot the antichrist'. In fact those who are keen to try to decipher some coded clue about the date of Christ's return in the Bible may find 1996 a peculiarly significant year. For there is a very ancient tradition in the church that said that since a thousand years are as one day and there are seven days of creation, perhaps the whole of history from the day of creation till the end of creation will last 7,000 years: 6,000 years of human history, and a final Sabbath 1,000 years of the millennium. If anybody holding to that theory also holds to Archbishop Ussher's 4004 BC date for the creation, then 1996 is going to be a very significant year . . .

The truth is, of course, that all such speculations are not just nonsense, they are anti-biblical nonsense. The Bible does not encourage us to speculate in that way. If Jesus Himself could not calculate the date of His return by careful study of the prophecy of Daniel, I doubt whether you will be able to.

No: what the Bible tells us that there will plenty of people scorning the idea of Jesus's coming, only seconds before He actually comes. So don't be surprised that it is taking longer than you thought. People were expecting Christ's return in the early part of the first century. Now 2,000 years have gone by and many people are not expecting Christ's return. Well—that just makes it all the more likely that it will be today. For when it happens it will be unexpected. Don't let doubt lead you into a state of unpreparedness; don't mistake God's patience for indifference. The day of the Lord will come like a thief.

And that brings us to the final subject for this third chapter.

How Believers Should Live (3:11–17)

Verses 10–11 are, if you like, the final challenge to those scoffers. They came, you remember, following their own evil desires: so of course they scoffed. A person who wants to live without regard to God's moral law will keep all thought of God's coming judgement as far from his mind as possible. There are countless people who scorn the Christian message today, not because they have intellectual doubts and not even because they have honest practical doubts; but simply because if they allowed themselves the tiniest suspicion that this Christ was really coming, they would crumple into terrified despair. They would cry to the mountains and the rocks to fall on them and hide them from the face of him who sits on the throne and from the wrath of the lamb (cf Rev. 6:16).

Peter is here telling us here about the climax of history and the coming of Christ not to satisfy our idle curiosity, but as a challenge to our moral living. What kind of people ought you to be? That's his logic. You and I are going to stand in God's presence, with no material props behind which hide, he says. Our latest-registration cars, pampered complexions, DIY improved homes, university degrees, shares in BT—all these things, he says, will be destroyed with the old order: they will be dissolved. Only one thing will shield us from shame on the day of His coming. What is it? Character, character. What kind of people ought you to be? You ought to live holy and godly lives as you look forward to the day of His coming.

There will be many people on that day who would willingly exchange millions of pounds for just five pence's worth of faith, hope and charity. For those will be the things that abide on that day. They are the currency of heaven.

Doesn't that mean that this Keswick message—ignored no doubt by many, scoffed at no doubt by many—is utterly relevant? To be a Christian is to live with eternity in view. It is to live in the light of His coming. And supremely, that means to live holy lives.

5: Growing in Grace
2 Peter 3:14–18

There's always a special interest in a person's last words. When someone knows they are about to die, almost inevitably they are going to use what little breath remains to them to say something significant. Of course it's not always so. Some people are so incorrigibly flippant they can't be serious even on their deathbed. Oscar Wilde is reputed to have left this earth with the famous ultimatum, 'Either this wallpaper goes or I do.' And of course there are some who die so suddenly they are given no opportunity to say anything weighty with their last words, like the general in the American Civil War who died uttering this immortal sentence: 'They couldn't hit an elephant at this distance.'

Today we come to the closing verses of Peter's final letter. So we should be especially aware that we are reading his last words. He knows his time is short, he told us so back in 1:14. He knows, too, the church is in danger; so you can be sure that he is considering his words carefully as he brings his letter to an end.

Significantly, he introduces no new theme in these closing lines. Instead he chooses to summarise all his previous advice and exhortation in a few brief sentences. He's told us right from the beginning that this whole letter is a reminder of what Christians already ought to know. So, if you like, this closing paragraph is a reminder of the reminder.

I want to look at this closing paragraph under four headings. First,

A Life of Militant Holiness

Of course we must link what we say today with yesterday's study which concluded with 2:11–13, for those verses lead in to verse 14. And my first reaction to Peter's words, 'So then, friends, since you are looking forward to . . . a new heaven and a new earth, the home of righteousness', is to say, 'Are you quite sure, Peter, that that's what these Christians are looking forward to?' Some of us, I'm afraid, are not thinking in terms of a new heaven and a new earth, the home of righteousness at all. I suspect some of us would have to admit we are just waiting to 'go to heaven', which in our rather confused jumble of thoughts probably means flying around like angels, plucking harps of gold, sitting on some ethereal cloud, clothed in some kind of celestial negligée. At least that was my picture of 'going to heaven' in my early days as a Christian. A new heaven and a new earth, the home of righteousness—that sounds far too unspiritual. Didn't we want to get away from earth? Earth is so materialistic . . .

But didn't you know that Christianity is actually a most materialistic religion? Not in the sense of idolising money or possessions, to which Christianity is unutterably opposed. But Christianity is not negative towards material things. To believe that it is, is one of the most pervasive, indeed pernicious, mistakes that people make about Christianity. What did Jesus say in that famously anti-materialistic Sermon on the Mount? 'Don't be anxious, saying "What shall we eat or what shall we drink or what shall we wear?" Seek first God's kingdom, for after all these material things are an encumbrance to your spiritual development'—is that what He said in Matthew 6:31? No. He closed that famous sentence by saying, 'Seek first God's kingdom and all these things shall be yours as well.' That's a very neglected clause. Jesus never belittles the importance of material things. The meek shall inherit—what? Not the second cloud on the right past Mars!

I want you to think very seriously about that aspect of Peter's words here, because I do think it lies behind some very serious mistakes.

One of the complaints people have about 'holiness

teaching' is that it makes people so impractical. You must have heard the jibe, 'He's so heavenly-minded he's no earthly use.' And I think it has to be said that there have been times when evangelical Bible-believing Christians were so focused on 'spiritual' things that they neglected their proper concern for this world and the material welfare of their fellow human beings. It is important to remember that our hope, the thing to which we look forward is *earthy*—a new heavens and a new earth.

Oh, truly this world must be renewed, just as these bodies of ours must be renewed; for the sin of Adam, the fall, has corrupted and permeated everything, even the natural order. As Paul says, it has become subjected to a bondage to decay. There has to be a dissolving of that old order, says Peter. But only in order to remould it into the new order, which is a new heavens and a new earth in which righteousness are at home. Society then will be free not just of personal immorality, but also of social injustice.

That word 'righteousness' at the end of verse 13 always in the Bible embraces both of those. The God of the Bible is concerned for our personal holiness. But holiness embraces more than just that. It embraces also our concern for social justice in the world. If perhaps people understood that better, Christians would be criticised rather less often for being 'no earthly use'.

I'm reminded of George Bernard Shaw's complaint, delivered in his usual pugnacious way: 'Heaven as conventionally conceived is a place so inane, so dull, so useless, so miserable, that nobody has ever ventured to describe a whole day in heaven, though plenty of people have described a day at the seaside.'[1] Of course Shaw was a militant socialist, greatly concerned for human dignity and social justice. Strumming a harp on some cloud had little appeal for him, he'd rather go to Clacton any day. If only someone had mentioned a new earth in which righteousness dwells, maybe he would have been less of a sceptic.

The trouble with many of us is that we have taken the

---

1. From the Preface to *Misalliance* (1910).

hints which the Bible gives about the intermediate state in which Christian believers survive death and wait for the last day, and we've turned that into a permanent and eternal expectation, as if an existence of some kind of disembodied spirit were the best God had for us. It is not so! The Christian doctrine is not the immortality of the soul, it is the resurrection of the body. That's what we are looking forward to; a new world not unlike this one, purged of sin and fallenness, purged of its bondage to decay and suffering—but a new heaven and a new earth nevertheless, in which righteousness will be at home.

Who do you think said this? 'I do not think that in the last forty years I have lived one conscious hour that was not influenced by the thought of our Lord's return.' That was a man who lived in the light of His coming. Do you know who he was? Anthony Ashley Cooper, better known as Lord Shaftesbury; a man who arguably did more to improve the welfare of the poor and the disadvantaged in the nineteenth century than any other single individual. He was a Bible-believing Christian. His concern for social justice wasn't driven by Marxist or Socialist ideology. He tells us what drove it: 'I have not spent one hour which is not influenced by the thought of the Lord's return.' He remembered, you see, what Jesus had said about that great judgement in Matthew 25: 'Inasmuch as you did it not to one of the least of these you did it not to me. Not one cup of water given to the least of these little ones will lose it's reward.' Those of us who, like Shaftesbury, understand the kind of world to which we're looking forward to are concerned not just for personal holiness, but for social justice.

Peter may have this at the back of his mind when he says in verse 12, 'as you look forward to the day of God and speed it's coming'. What does he mean by that, 'speed its coming'? Does Peter believe that the day of the Lord is flexible, that the date is movable? Some people have suggested that. Some people have suggested that we can speed the day of the Lord by our evangelism, for instance, because Jesus said the gospel had to be preached to every nation; the quicker we get through all the nations with our evangelism, the quicker the Lord will come. Others have suggested we can speed the

Lord's coming with our prayers; the more urgently and persistently we pray 'Your kingdom come', the quicker it will come. But it seems to me rather more likely from the evidence of the New Testament that the day of the Lord is actually a fixture. God has appointed a day in which He will judge the world says Paul; fixed it by a divine decree (cf Acts 17:31).

I suspect that what Peter's actually getting at in 3:12 is not that you can actually reschedule the day of the Lord, but that you can reduce the weariness of the wait. How? By being active in the pursuit of God's righteousness. 'A watched pot never boils.' People whose response to the second coming is to go and sit on a mountain top and wait for the Lord to come are possibly going to find the wait rather wearisome. 'No,' says Jesus, 'be busy till I come, be occupied till I come. There's work to be done, talents to be employed, and there are sheep to be found, and there are little ones to be cared for, and there are those in prison to be visited and those who are hungry to be fed. Inasmuch as you did it to these you did it to Me.'

Since you look forward to the day of God and speed its coming, 'You ought to live holy and godly lives,' says Peter. Verse 14: 'Make every effort to be found spotless, blameless and at peace with him.'

We are to live then a life of militant holiness, which is to be understood not simply as a concern for our own personal righteousness as individuals, but a concern also for justice in the community.

A Confidence In the Old and New Testament Scriptures

We have said an awful lot about the importance of received, biblical truth during this week and I hesitate to spend too much time reiterating the point. But Peter does just add one or two things in verses 15–16 which are of interest, not least his commendation of the epistles of Paul.

I don't know why it is, but Paul always seems to get the thick end of the stick whenever people decide to have a go at the Bible. Sceptics always seem to single him out as worthy of special vitriolic treatment. Only a few weeks ago a young lady in Cambridge said to me, 'Oh I love the Gospels and the picture they give of Jesus! But I can't stand Paul. He's so severe, so dogmatic and he's such a male chauvinist,' she said.

I don't understand where this unfavourable impression of the great apostle comes from. I'm quite sure it's unjustified. If you are thinking about ethics, quite frankly the moral standards of Jesus are far more outspokenly stringent than Paul's. It was after all Jesus, not Paul, who made that searching identification between looking lustfully and adultery. If you look at the doctrine of judgement, it is Jesus who uses far more terrorising language in His descriptions of hell than Paul ever does. It was Jesus, after all, who spoke of the everlasting burnings and the worm that never dies. As for His opinion on women—well, I hesitate to get involved in that. But if radical feminists want to have a go at anyone in the Bible, surely it is again Jesus who committed the most conspicuously sexist act when He called twelve apostles and every one of them was male.

In every way it seems to me that Jesus is far more obviously controversial and provocative to our modern world than Paul ever is. And yet it is Paul's words which always get slighted. I feel really sorry for Paul. I think Peter did too. It seems that even in the first century Peter has to come to the defence of his apostolic colleague: 'Our dear brother Paul wrote you with the wisdom that God gave him.'

Notice the warmth of the commendation, 'our dear brother'. There has been a persistent tendency by theologians to drive a wedge between Peter and Paul, to suggest that these two great men were at loggerheads in the early church, Peter defending the Jewish believers and Paul the Gentiles. Suffice it to say that popular as that idea has been, there isn't a whisper of any such antagonism here. But notice too the candour of Peter's assessment of Paul's writings. 'These letters,' he says, 'contain some things that are hard to understand.' I think he may have had his tongue somewhat in his cheek when he wrote that, but of course it's not a criticism of Paul's writing. It's just a statement of fact with which every Bible student can sympathise. The Bible's not an easy book, and the epistles of Paul are particularly difficult. If you have found them difficult don't be discouraged; Peter did too. Don't think there's anything wrong with you. There is an intellectual depth in Paul's letters that challenges the best theological minds we have, so it must not surprise us if sometimes we find ourselves a little stretched in trying to get to grips with his teaching.

But what I particularly want you to notice is the confidence which Peter nevertheless has in the essential clarity of Scripture, including Paul's letters (3:16); clearly Peter feels that though Paul's letters may be difficult to understand, they are not impossible. If people misunderstand the Bible in serious ways, Peter argues, it has more to do with their own ignorance and instability than with any intrinsic opacity in the text.

Peter of course has been dealing throughout his letter with false teachers who had a vested interest in distorting the meaning of the Bible. But Peter is clear that the Bible is intelligible to the regenerate and honest mind, and he doesn't want his readers to lose their confidence in that.

This is very important for us today. If you read at all widely, or think at all, or talk to people who are in touch with culture, you will come across a prevailing mood that says you really can't have any access to what a book like the Bible really means, that whenever you read something you read into it what it means to you. It is quite impossible to read out of it what the author intended. We have no access to the author's intention. All you can do, it is said, is to make up your mind what it means to you.

In Cambridge, where I live, the whole of the University English Department is pervaded by that kind of radical scepticism about the meaning of texts. It is having an extraordinarily destructive effect on the science of Bible interpretation, for it holds that every reading of Scripture is as good as every other reading of Scripture, for all we can do is come to our own subjective conclusion of what it means to us. I even hear people saying it in Bible studies: 'Well, what this means to me is . . .' I understand what people are getting at when they say that. Of course we bring an interest and our own questions and agenda to the Bible whenever we read it. But it is a fundamental mistake, and certainly quite contrary to the Bible's own expectation of itself, to say that we have no access to God's meaning in the text.

Back in the 1970s the great debate was about the *inerrancy* of Scripture: 'Is the Bible infallible, or does it contain mistakes?' In the 1980s the great debate was about the *sufficiency* of Scripture: 'Is the Bible enough on its own, or do we need the supplementary gift of contemporary prophecy in helping us to understand God's will in our lives?' In the 1990s the key issue for thinking Christians is going to be the *clarity* of Scripture—what the Reformers called the 'perspicuity' of Scripture. But I believe that evangelical Christians are going to be even more distinguished in the future by their belief, not in the inerrancy or even the sufficiency of Scripture, but in their belief that we have access to the divine *intention* of Scripture—that we can read our Bibles and have confidence that we are reading out of it the meaning God intends, not just having our own subjective prejudices confirmed.

Now, Peter certainly believes that. Interpreting Paul can be a difficult task, he says, but it's not a hopeless task. And it's a task Christians must engage in if they are not to be seduced by the erroneous and distorted interpretations of the false teachers.

And that brings me to the third reminder.

A Vigilant Resistance to False Teaching

The issue of false teaching has been driving Peter's agenda throughout this letter. We have seen in these studies just how subtle and dangerous the threat of heresy was in the church. As Peter indicates in verse 17, the false teaching he seeks to counteract doesn't just comprise doctrinal aberration but also moral licence; not just error, but the error of lawless men.

In chapter 2 we saw how the two often go together because our belief informs our behaviour. Our conviction shapes our conduct. If somebody starts to deny the truth of Scripture, they will soon start living in a way which is not according to the moral rules of Scripture. What happens, says Peter, is that people get seduced by this false teaching. Paul said his readers would 'lose their assurance' and fall from their secure position. That again points us back to our very first study in chapter 1: 'Make your calling and election sure,' says Peter, 'add to your faith virtue, for if you do these things you will never fall.' Peter was not prepared, any more than the New Testament in general is prepared, to give assurance of salvation to so-called Christians who are compromised in their faith and in their conduct. If you are seduced by these false teachers you share their error and lawlessness; you will fall from your secure position and you will no longer enjoy the assurance you ought to have as Christians.

This is perhaps particularly relevant to us, for we live in a day when assurance about almost anything is in short supply. I remember drinking coffee in one of the Common Rooms at Cambridge, having just given an evangelistic address. I asked somebody if he disagreed with anything I'd said. He replied, 'Oh well—it's all relative, isn't it.'

I wish I had a pound for every time somebody had said that to me in the last ten years. 'It's all relative, isn't it.' What do people mean by it? If they think about it at all, they mean, 'Don't ask questions about truth. Don't ask me whether I agree with something, it doesn't really matter, does it.' Modern men and women have lost confidence in truth. All we have are our subjective feelings and cultural conditioning. Anything pretending to be more than that is simply illusion and fantasy; it's all relative. You see it in our approach to ethics. We can no longer talk about morality being superior or inferior. All we can talk about is moralities which are *different*, for according to our contemporary world-view everyone's entitled to invent their own moral values where nobody has any right to criticise. It's not a question of being right or wrong, but of being honest, just as we saw earlier in respect to literature: accurate understanding of the author's intention is irrelevant, it's not a question of being right or wrong but of being imaginative. We see it most of all in the field of religion. No longer is it politically correct to talk about 'revealed truth' as opposed to heresy and falsehood. All religious opinions are equally valid insights into the amorphous ocean of spiritual experience which we all have in common. It's not a question of being right or wrong but of being tolerant; for it's all relative.

Words like right and wrong, true and false, good and bad have lost their meaning for modern men and women, except as indicators of personal preference or cultural prejudice. We live in a world without signposts or compass bearings, in which all opinions are as valid as one another, and a world therefore in which any expression of certainty about anything is at best foolishly quixotic and at worst ideologically oppressive. The philosopher Karl Popper went so far as to argue that anybody who claims he has the Truth with a capital 'T' is a potential tyrant. In his view it was only a short step then to add, 'Therefore I must be obeyed.' The only way to preserve democracy is for everyone to agree that it's all ultimately relative. Nobody has any access to absolute truth. Certainty will always therefore elude us. We have our provisional hypotheses and theories and opinions which we may test and talk about, but we cannot affirm them with absolute confidence. It's now politically incorrect to say you're sure of anything.

If you don't believe me, go into any pub or coffee bar and start talking to a non-Christian. Express your certainty about the Christian faith. It won't be long before they say, 'Oh, but surely it's all relative, isn't it?' And in such a world as that, of course it is increasingly difficult to stand as a Christian. Morally it's much more congenial to live as you please, without the guilt-inducing strictures of Christian ethics to bind you. Socially it's much more congenial to affirm that everybody's religion is true, without the embarrassing exclusivity of Christian doctrine. And intellectually it's much more congenial to speculate and hypothesise without the constraining discipline of a Christian revelation always around. We live in a world today where ignorance is bliss, and where consequently it is folly to be wise.

In such a deliberately uncertain agnostic world I say it is very hard to be a Christian, holding your position as one who believes in true truth, the truth of the gospel. It's uncomfortable. New Age mysticism, religious pluralism—these are the fashionable things. The temptation to cut the anchor loose and go with the tide of popular opinion in this matter is very strong. Indeed, it's already proving too strong for many.

I received a couple of letters not long ago from ex-Cambridge students who once attended my church and were key members of the Christian Union in the University of Cambridge. Each of them was writing to tell me why they felt unable any longer to call themselves evangelical Christians. Although they had come to this conclusion by different routes, the ultimate reason behind their abdication of faith was the same in each case; they both found evangelical Christianity 'too self-assured'—too reluctant to accommodate other people's ideas, too narrow-minded, too dogmatic; too unfashionably certain, in other words, in this uncertain world.

I don't want to be misunderstood on this point. I am by temperament a very open-minded non-judgemental kind of person. I can sympathise considerably with the disillusionment both these students had experienced at the hands of what was, I think, an excessively defensive and rigidly doctrinaire evangelicalism in the churches which each of them had been attending since leaving Cambridge. I confess to you frankly that I often find myself embarrassed and frustrated by the bigotry and obscurantism of some of my evangelical colleagues who use the phrase 'the Bible says', often in an irresponsible way, to support completely unwarranted authoritarianism in matters which really ought to be left to the conscience of the individual believer. In my observation, there are far more claims to infallibility in evangelical churches than there have ever been in the Vatican.

But—and it's a very big 'but'—there are certain things that are non-negotiable in the Christian faith, certain affirmations which are not optional extras, certain convictions which a person must have or else forfeit the very name 'Christian'. These are the things that no reasonable and honest person could deny are shouting at you from the pages of Scripture, congenial though it would be to echo the platitudes of our relativistic, pluralistic world which tell us that 'Really you can believe what you like—it doesn't matter as long as you are sincere.' Convenient as it would be to echo that kind of attitude, the Bible won't allow us to. Jesus won't allow us to. For our faith is a faith of revelation; it admits of no hybridisations, improvements, modifications or adaptations. It is a word from on high which we take or we leave. As Elijah said to those wobbly Jews, 'If the Lord is God follow Him, if Baal follow him. Whatever you do, don't go on wavering between different opinions. Biblical truth will not allow you to sit on the fence that way' (cf 1 Ki. 18:21).

So that is why Peter summons us in this letter to vigilant resistance against false teaching. If we succumb to the relativistic mood of our age, then just as if his readers here had succumbed to the gnosticising vagaries of his day, we too will lose our assurance and fall from our secure position. And in this uncertain, relativistic agnostic world of ours, security is very hard to find.

And that brings me to the last of the quartet of reminders in which Peter draws together the threads of his whole letter for us in his closing words.

A Commitment to Spiritual Maturity

Look at the very last word of all. 'But grow in the grace and knowledge of our Lord and Saviour Jesus Christ. To him be glory both now and for ever!'

Having never had to participate in armed conflict for my country, I think the most courageous thing I've ever done was to allow my wife to teach me to drive. She wasn't my wife then—in fact we'd only known one another a short while. And I, poor fool, thought that allowing her to teach me to drive would be a fine way of cementing our relationship. 'It's easy' she said, 'you just engage first gear, put one foot on the accelerator and take your other foot off the clutch simultaneously.' So I did. The next few moments are largely blotted from my memory by shock. The car seemed to rear up on its back wheels like a wild horse, lurch forward at about fifty miles an hour like a drunken kangaroo and then stop suddenly like a recalcitrant donkey. And as my mind cleared from this succession of zoological jerks, I heard Jane in the seat beside me saying, 'Well I meant to tell you to do it slowly.' It was very nearly the end of a beautiful friendship.

For many people, beginning the Christian life is rather like my first efforts to drive. Many relationships with Jesus Christ end in disillusionment simply because converts haven't been taught properly how to make normal progress along the Christian highway. Instead of a smooth transition through the gears into full Christian experience, their spiritual life is characterised by kangaroo jumps—an initial spasm of violent enthusiasm, followed by uncontrolled inertia and finally a stalled engine. Yet for some Christians this isn't just an initial experience. Their whole Christian life is comprised of such fits and starts. They lurch from one decision to the next, one reconsecration to the next, one filling of the Spirit to the next. I call them 'Christian kangaroos'. Years after their first commitment to the Christian way, these undisciplined hops have taken them very little further along the road to Christian maturity.

When you turn to the teaching of the apostles in the New Testament, you discover a very important emphasis. The apostles hardly say a word to the young churches about growing numerically. What often seems to me to be the sum total of our interest, the numerical increase of our congregations, seems to be for them a matter of comparatively little concern. Quantity considerations were never paramount in their thinking, certainly not in the teaching of the apostles. The interesting thing is that when you look into the New Testament it was spiritual growth, moral growth, growth in grace and knowledge of our Lord Jesus Christ that they were most concerned to generate among their believers. For the real strength of the kingdom of God has never been measured by numbers alone, but by the quality of discipleship displayed by its members.

There have been times, indeed there are places in this world today, where the church is numerically very strong but is still a weak church, for there is no maturity there. The trouble with Christian kangaroos is that when they reproduce, all they produce is more kangaroos. Maybe that's why some churches are more like zoos than temples of the Holy Spirit. Just imagine what this town would be like if it were full of learner drivers having their first lesson! There would be collisions, arguments and a complete breakdown of social activity. That's what happens to churches when the learner-driver kangaroo-jump mentality becomes the norm. It's very hard for such a fellowship to break out of its immaturity, because there's nobody there to model a better way. Such churches become superficial and very vulnerable to heresy.

I am sure that is why the apostles repeatedly emphasise Christian maturity and why Peter here chose this sentence as the last he was to utter this church he cared about so much: 'But grow in the grace and knowledge of our Lord and Saviour Jesus Christ. To him be glory both now and for ever!'

That word 'grow' speaks of a gradual progression. I have to confess, though I am not getting at anybody, that I am a little concerned at the popularity of what's becoming called 'deliverance ministry' in our day. There's a certain mind-set which says if you've got a problem as a Christian, the way to get rid of it is to be prayed for by somebody and instantaneously it will disappear and you will be delivered. I'm not disputing there are certain kinds of spiritual and moral bondage in which the approach of the exorcist is a necessary one and in which supernatural deliverance is the only hope. But I'm equally sure that Christian sanctification generally speaking is not obtained that way but rather by a process of growth. Longfellow says in one of his poems,

> The heights by great men reached and kept
> Were not attained by sudden flight,
> But they, while their companions slept,
> Were toiling upward in the night.[2]

Do you want to climb one of these hills around Keswick? It's going to take effort. Of course it's possible to imagine a helicopter picking you up at the bottom and lifting you immediately to the top. But the way most of us have to get to the top of those mountains is gradually, by dint of effort. In the same way, if you really want to have a character which is

2. From 'The Ladder of St Augustine'

fit for the return of Christ you are going to have to grow it; you are going to have to climb that mountain.

Notice Peter says grow 'in grace'. That word 'grace' of course reminds us that the resources whereby we undergo that growth are not our own but God's. As Peter told us back in chapter 1, 'His divine power has given us everything we need for life and godliness.' But growth nevertheless is something we must engage in, in constant dependence on God. As he puts it earlier, 'Make every effort to be found spotless, blameless and at peace with him.'

Notice too he says 'grow in grace and knowledge.' That word 'knowledge' is a reminder that this growth he is talking about is not growth in some kind of legalistic rule book. Neither—as the gnostic false teachers might have suggested—is it the acquiring of some kind of esoteric experience, corresponding perhaps to some kind of spiritual kangaroo jump. Peter is talking about the knowledge of our Lord and Saviour Jesus Christ.

When a Christian uses the word *gnosis* (knowledge) he is speaking about a personal relationship: knowing Jesus. It may be a tough hill to climb, but we do not climb it alone, we have God's grace to strengthen our hearts, and we have Jesus Himself as our companion on the journey. I like to think of my Christian life as waking up every morning and saying, 'Well Jesus, what are we going to do together today?' That's what it ought to feel like to us, not a burdensome, wearisome kind of a bondage to religious ritual or rules, nor the frantic quest for some kind of magical spiritual leap into the heavenlies. 'Grow in grace and the knowledge of Jesus Christ.'

People sometimes ask me, 'What has been the greatest influence on your Christian life?' I think they usually expect me to quote some very famous book by Jim Packer, or maybe a sermon I heard from John Stott. But I can honestly tell you that I think the greatest single influence on my Christian life was a dear Christian woman who died some years ago in her eighties. She was my Bible class teacher when I was first converted. That woman never experienced conversion as some of us mean the word and certainly as I experienced it coming from atheism to faith. Faith had been planted in her heart while she was still a child through the ministry of a Christian family; she had never had to make a conscious decision at a rally, she had never sought a 'second blessing'. And yet I tell you I have never met a person more fit to be called a saint.

She just kept on growing.

That's the testimony I covet for you. You don't need to be a Christian kangaroo. You're not meant to be a Christian kangaroo. There is such a thing as Christian stability, and it is for those who are progressing, making growth. Do you remember those famous words of John Newton? 'I am not what I ought to be. I am not what I want to be. I am not what I hope to be. But I can truly say I am not what I once was. By the grace of God, I am what I am.'

That's the foundation for authentic Christian assurance. I am not asking you this morning whether you are perfect. I don't ask you whether you have arrived. We are not perfect, we have never arrived, none of us have. But—are you moving? Are you growing? For if you are growing in the grace and knowledge of our Lord and Saviour, the glory will certainly be His, now and for ever.

THE ADDRESSES

‘The Lord Is Not Slow’

by Rev. Philip Hacking

2 Peter 3:8–13

Have you ever received one of these letters marked ‘First-Class—Private and Confidential’? Your fingers twitch at the prospect of what might be inside; normally it’s something like a complaint about your tax return! I want to say as we look at 2 Peter 3 that it contains much of the private and confidential things of God. There are some things that remain uncertain. What will the ‘new heaven’ and ‘new earth’ be like? How can we have a new earth that is eternal? How do we know the answers? I think the answer is that we don’t, any more than we know the date of our Lord’s return.

That is why you should mark in red ink in your Bibles Deuteronomy 29:29—‘The secret things belong to the Lord our God.’ I always mentally add a little phrase which isn’t in the original: ‘ . . . leave them there!’. But the passage goes on to say that the things that are revealed belong to us and our children, so that we may do them. Somebody said to me the other day, ‘You know, Philip, I find such difficulty in the bits of the Bible I don’t understand.’ I replied, ‘I find great difficulty in the bits of the Bible I do understand! They’re the problem, because I’ve got to do them and obey them. At least with the bits I don’t understand, I can leave them there.’ I suggest to you, that’s the right thing to do.

But the challenges of these verses are there very clearly and it’s my privilege to share them with you; and, at the beginning of this week that has the theme of ‘The light of His coming’—a terribly neglected theme—to remind you from these last words of the apostle Peter about some great truths that follow.

Notice first of all that it all depends upon the final authority of the word of God. In verse 8 Peter says, 'Do not forget this one thing, dear friends,' and then quotes from Psalm 90:4. In verse 10 he writes, 'But the day of the Lord will come like a thief.' Where does that come from? The lips of Jesus Himself in sacred Scripture. I want to underline this, for we live in an age when the Bible is neglected and its authority eroded. And we need to be on the alert. I remember that back in the 1981 Keswick Convention, Dick Lucas expounded the book of Jude—a book very similar to the second letter of Peter. With prophetic vision, he reminded us that there are two ways to destroy a building. You can blow it up with semtex, or you can quietly remove bricks from the foundation, one by one, until the building falls. 'That,' said Dick, 'is exactly what is happening in the churches these days.' Did we listen? The bricks are being steadily removed and the thing is tottering, and I am not speaking of any one denomination. Once you begin to say, 'Well of course, you can't trust the Bible on this that or the other, because it doesn't speak today,' very soon you will say, 'Why do you believe in the second coming?'

'Well, because the Scripture says so.'

'But wait a minute, we didn't believe the Scripture about this that or the other, sexuality morality and all the rest—so why should we believe when it talks about the second coming, the resurrection, the virgin birth?'

Everything I want to say this morning is based on this. If Scripture is proved wrong then everything collapses around us. And in a world which is hope-less, we are talking about a great Christian hope. Let's not be ashamed of it. Let's believe in it. And let us be sure of it.

We live in an age when the language of verses 10 and 12—the heavens disappearing with a roar, the elements being destroyed by fire—could very easily be literally fulfilled. But we have something positive to say about a Christian hope. We don't know when it will happen, we don't fully know how it will happen, but we have something positive to say about it and we are living today in the light of it. And I believe because the world out there doesn't have a hope, we have a unique opportunity for witness and evangelism.

Let me share with you a lovely phrase which I was very excited to find in a commentary: 'Always in Scripture the moral imperative follows the eschatological indicative'. You should be saying 'Amen!' to that. Did you wake up this morning and say 'Thank you Lord that the moral imperative always follows the eschatological indicative'? Well, I don't blame you if you didn't, if you don't understand it! But let me tell you what it means, and then you'll think 'Amen' even if you don't say it. The *eschatological indicative* is the truth or statement about the Lord's coming. The *moral imperative* is the command that we do something about it. And the rest of what I want to say this morning concerns three future certainties, three eschatological indicatives; and two present attitudes, which are the moral imperatives.

Three Future Certainties (Verses 8–13)

The future certainties are to be found in verses 8–10.

The word of the Lord (verse 8)

I have already mentioned Peter's quotation from Psalm 90:4 in verse 8. By this quotation he is really saying, 'Look, when you put time into the perspective of eternity, what is a thousand years?'

Now of course we are all going to get excited about the next millennium. Some strange extreme Christian groups are getting excited because they are saying, 'This must be it, the Lord is coming back then!' I would want to say: Please don't be so foolish; our Lord said that nobody knows the hour, not even the Son. Don't you realise, the moment you start doing that you are actually being counter-productive? You are playing into the hands of the enemy, encouraging sceptics and those who deride us: 'Look at these foolish people! Time after time you have announced it and time after time you have been proved wrong.' I guess if you go on guessing somebody is bound to get it right, one day. But don't you see how we dishonour the gospel?

No, no. If you look in the light of eternity, what is a thousand years? Look at Psalm 90. It speaks of three-score years and ten. If you've managed to get to 80, it's all hard work. Some 80-year olds look fine; some live beyond 80; we push the barriers on. But the Psalmist is telling us a very important truth in Psalm 90. He's contrasting the eternity of God with the brevity of human life. Do you stop and think of that sometimes, however old you are? How quickly it all goes! And therefore—this is the point—how important every single day is! Don't wish time away. Use time positively, prayerfully, watchfully every day. Because when I see how Peter uses that verse from the word of the Lord in verse 8, he's actually contrasting man's impatience with God's patience.

That's the point of verses 8 and 9. The Lord is not slow but patient. Don't be impatient with Him. Don't expect God to work according to your timetable. We live in an instant age, the age of the Internet; everything happens at once, suddenly, instantly. Fine! But may I say humbly, God's not on Internet so far as I know. He's not in a hurry. He is patient.

And the whole point of the exercise is to remind us that every day counts. Time matters. God entered time in Christ once, He enters time again when Jesus returns. Therefore every day may be the last day. So we live always with the assurance that the end is round the corner. The word of the Lord, which never changes—'Do not be ignorant of, don't forget, this one thing.'

The character of the Lord (verse 9)

The Lord never changes. And with a very vivid picture Peter reminds us that the Lord is patient; the Bible insists that we should be patient because we've got a patient God. That patience of God is mentioned by Peter in 1 Peter 3:20: in the days of the flood God, instead of bringing judgement, was patient. Don't you think God's very patient with this land of ours? I marvel at His patience. We deserve judgement, and yet He is patient, wanting people to repent.

Note that verse 9 does *not* suggest that everybody will

repent, which would be nonsense because of verse 7, 'the day of . . . the destruction of ungodly men.' There is a final day of awesome division, so I cannot lightly say that I'm eagerly anticipating the return of Christ. For my own part I am looking forward to that day, but can I say that lightly when I know that for thousands of people—some close to me—who do not know Christ, the final day will only bring the awesome judgement of eternal separation from God? So in a sense I want God to keep on being patient, so that they might come to Christ. And if that be so, then I will go on preaching the gospel. Thank God for men like Billy Graham, who is determined that he's going to go on preaching the gospel as long as there's breath in his body! And grant that each one of us according to our abilities may have that same concern, because there's a wrath to come.

Paul reminded the Athenians that God has appointed a day when He's going to judge the world in righteousness. He's overlooked the ignorance of the past, but now He's appointed that day and He calls all men everywhere to repent (cf Acts 17:22–31). You cannot get away from the fact that God is a God of justice. There will be that awesome moment when all will appear before the judgement seat of Christ.

The day of the Lord (verse 10)

The image of the thief is an Old Testament picture. In Amos' day the Jews were looking forward to the day of the Lord. It was going to be their big day when the Jewish people would be the top dog, and everybody would acknowledge the suffering people. But Amos said 'Look, the day of the Lord is not light but darkness' (cf Am. 5:20). He uses the vivid metaphor of a man who ran away from a lion only to meet a bear, managed to escape the bear and, leaning on the wall in his own house, was bitten by a serpent.

Why did Amos use such a picture? Because people in his day were putting their weight on something that would ultimately bite them. They were building their house on a foundation that would not stand. And that's why the day of the Lord will come like a thief. It was obviously a very significant metaphor in the early church. Paul picks it up, as you will find in this week's Bible Readings in 1 Thessalonians. It's picked up again more than once in the book of the Revelation.

Margaret and I have been burgled twice. It's not a very pleasant experience. They didn't send us a card beforehand saying, 'We expect to burgle your house at three o'clock next week, please make sure you are out.' They came suddenly. And the day of the Lord will come like a thief says Scripture. The same picture is used in Revelation 3:3 in the letter to the church in Sardis. Sardis has a very interesting history. It stood on an impregnable cliff, which the citizens didn't bother defending. They deployed their armour in other directions. Nobody would ever climb the cliff! But on two occasions somebody did, and they were caught unawares. Somebody came in at the point that they never bothered to protect.

Sometimes what we should be concerned about is not our weak points but our strong points. We pray about our weak points. We are very conscious of them. The church is aware of its weak points. But we are confident of our strengths. Sardis thought they had strengths and they were invaded. And the word to Sardis is, 'Waken up while there is time, awaken and repent. Otherwise I will come like a thief.'

The reminder is that it will happen suddenly, we know not when. One day there will be the day of the Lord. May I say, there could be somebody here who doesn't yet know Jesus in a personal way. You may have come to the Keswick Convention reluctantly, with family or friends, perhaps for a holiday. Or maybe you are a religious person who goes to church, but deep-down you've never made a personal commitment to Jesus. If this were to be the day on which the Lord came like a thief—would He take you with Him? On what grounds? How sure are you that He would know you?

For those of us who do know Jesus personally, this passage is a reminder that we live day by day in the light of the awesome truth of verse 10: the heavens disappearing with a roar, the elements destroyed by fire. All the things that the world calls dear and Christians hold dear, will go.

Remember the Old Testament. When Abraham, Isaac and Jacob moved on, they pitched their tent and they built their altar. The home was impermanent; they just moved the tent on. The thing that remained was the altar, their worship. Most of us live in an age when we have so many possessions. They won't last; they will go, they will be destroyed. Sometimes in a strange work of providence God actually destroys them in front of us, just to remind us that they are only passing.

I trust that we are ready for that day, the day of the Lord.

Two Present Attitudes (Verses 11–14)

What about present attitudes, what are these ethical demands?

It is only if we look forward that we are challenged to live now. What you believe about the future affects the way you live now. Your belief will always affect your behaviour; your creed will always affect your conduct. If you minimise the creed, it affects people's conduct. Take away the belief, and it affects people's behaviour.

And here's the challenge. Three times in verses 11–14 comes the phrase 'looking forward'. Some people feel they've nothing to look forward to. I meet people in my pastoral ministry who are bereft; they've nothing to look forward to, retirement has come. Some people do look forward to retirement, though I confess I'm not looking forward to my own retirement from the ministry in 1997. You'd understand if you knew my hatred of gardening! But for many people there really is nothing left to look forward to. The children have left home. Maybe you're redundant in middle age. Perhaps you have lost your partner.

Well, the Christian always has something.

William Barclay gives three superb examples, taken from heathen tombs, of what happens when the belief that creation has a goal and a climax—one of the main themes of the doctrine of the second advent—is lost. When people reject that view, says William Barclay, they lose their purpose for living. He quotes from three tombs, as follows.

It can lead to hedonism ('Have a good time, it's all going to end one day'). On a tomb in the Middle East is written, 'I was nothing: I am nothing. So thou who art still alive, eat, drink and be merry.'

It can lead to apathy. Here's another tomb: 'Once I had an existence; now I have none. I am not aware of it. It does not concern me.'

It can lead to despair. Here's the final quote: 'Charidas, what is below?'—'Deep darkness.'—'But what of the paths upward?'—'All a lie.' . . . 'Then we're lost.'[1]

That is the philosophy of so many people. Whenever I hear of people who take their life or are similarly in despair because they can't face life any more, I want to say, 'Thank God we have something to look forward to.'

Look forward in hope (verses 12b–13)

To what do we look forward in hope? Not the melting of the heavens and so on, though that's part of it. But one day, out of that melting will come a new heaven and a new earth.

Note the phrase, 'the home of righteousness'. I really don't know what that new heaven and new earth will be like. That's quite exciting, isn't it? What a dull thing it would be in eternity if we all had a preview of what it was going to be like beforehand! But what I do know is that it will be the home of righteousness. And that says a lot to me. I look forward in hope to a day when there'll be no more suffering, there'll be no more sin, there'll be no more parting, and Christ will be all and in all. What a glorious day, when what I now know by faith will be then mine in reality!

I know, too, that there will be nothing that will defile. The book of the Revelation says that there are certain ways of life that are outside. Only those that are written in the Lamb's Book of Life—which should give me a deep concern to reach more people, so that they may be in that Book. And all those things which will not be in heaven, I should not play around with on earth. If you believe in a home of righteousness, then you'll be concerned about a life of righteousness now.

Look forward in holiness (verse 11, 12a, 14)

What kind of people ought you to be? The answer is, 'You ought to live holy and godly lives as you look forward to the

---

1. Illustration taken from William Barclay, *Daily Study Bible* (2nd rev. edn, 1978), p.346.

day of God and speed its coming.' Again in verse 14, 'since you are looking forward to this, make every effort to be found spotless, blameless and at peace with him.' I have just two or three very simple things to say before I finish.

Since we are *looking forward* to that great day, our deepest concern must be to live a life of which, that if the Lord met me today, I would be unashamed. When I became a Christian, life was all very simple. One of the simple rules was to ask—in answer to the dilemma: 'Should I do this and go there or not do this or go there?'—the question: 'Would you be happy for the Lord to find you there if He came again?' It was a bit simplistic, but it had merit in it. Because if the Lord is going to come again, then the kind of life I ought to live should be a holy and godly one.

But we are also *speeding its coming*. That is evangelism. I don't fully understand it, but our Lord says, 'The gospel must first be preached to all nations, then the end will come' (cf Matt. 24:18). So I speed the coming by effective, faithful evangelism. And out from Keswick ought to go a lot of people, this year particularly, to buy up the time in order to win people for Christ.

The final phrase is in verse 14, *Make every effort*. Holiness is God's activity, but we have to respond. To me one of the joys of Keswick is that we unashamedly major on this great theme of holiness. Oh yes, we look at it from different angles, oh yes we enjoy our worship and our praise, and it's great—you really do sing well! But at the end of the day, what we are about, and what is unchangeable about this great Convention, is that we major on holiness, and all the more in the light of His return.

Christians play around with many things that seem to be of so little significance, so peripheral and trivial. And when our Lord returns what He wants to find is you and me engaged in evangelism and living the kind of life that is worthy of Him. So, 'make every effort to be found spotless'. Just one last thing about that. Do the words 'spotless' and 'blameless' ring a bell? In 1 Peter 1:19, Peter says that we are redeemed by a lamb who was spotless and blameless, the sacrificial lamb. And isn't Peter saying that our great desire is that we should become more and more like Jesus?

When Peter says '*at peace*', it doesn't actually say in the Greek 'at peace with Him.' It simply says, 'At peace.' With Him, yes; with one another, yes. If we believe in that great day, what we should be doing today is seeking to be, by God's grace, more and more like Jesus. And so, having received salvation, I'm actually at peace. So if He came at two o'clock this afternoon, I'm ready. If I live all my life out and I have to wait, if I've already gone from this world, I'm ready, it doesn't matter. I'm at peace.

Of course there is a wrong way of being at peace. In a world of such need, with such tragedies as Bosnia happening, it is difficult to be easily at peace. But I can be at peace in my soul, and ready for that great day.

Let me end by quoting the words of Jude:

> But you, dear friends, build yourselves up in your most holy faith and pray in the Holy Spirit. Keep yourselves in God's love as you wait for the mercy of our Lord Jesus Christ to bring you to eternal life. Be merciful to those who doubt; snatch others from the fire and save them; to others show mercy, mixed with fear—hating even the clothing stained by corrupted flesh. (Jude 20–23)

Friends, if you don't care about holiness, you are not ready for the day of our Lord's return. Maybe some of us have got to put things right this week, to be ready for that great day, when finally we shall be changed from glory into glory.

'From Fear to Glory'

By Rev. Robert Amess

Romans 8:1–17

Last September I had the privilege of speaking at the East Anglian Convention in Lowestoft, where on six occasions I preached on the verses that we are looking at now. I had almost limitless time then, and felt frustrated that I did not have more. So you might think it rather a masochistic exercise to return to the passage this afternoon. But I had a desire that we might have an overview of these verses, which was confirmed when I discovered that Philip this evening, quite independently, is taking us on from verse 18 onwards.

Romans 8 is a keystone within a systematic argument. There are various theories proposed as to why the Holy Spirit of God inspired Paul to write to the Romans, but most people will agree that it was a letter of preparation. It was a systematic statement of Paul's conviction and belief, sent to the ever-increasingly important church in Rome as a preparation for his hoped-for coming to them. What of course Paul did not realise at this point is that indeed he would go to Rome, but in chains.

So this letter addresses hardly any specific issue; it addresses no specific problem. It is simply a statement of the gospel of our Lord Jesus Christ, into which we are inevitably breaking in mid-flow, by entering at chapter 8.

One of the striking things about Romans 8 is that because we know the key verses we assume that we know the chapter. But in it is one of the most difficult chapters in the New Testament. Yes, verses such as 8:1 are great verses; we long to hear verse 18 again and again; we love to hear verse 28 (though it's a verse to be used with great care); I've known verse 31 all my life; look at verse 37—I have demonstrated to you that this is a chapter with glorious high water marks. But nevertheless, the sections in between are often complex, dense in their argument, and difficult to grasp.

And the key word is 'Spirit', the Holy Spirit of our Lord Jesus Christ. It is used frequently in this chapter, which is why I have been drawn to it today. The Holy Spirit of Christ, speaking not only of joy and victory, but of sorrow and defeat and groaning. And what we are going to do this afternoon is to break in to the argument, flying through but touching down at one or two specific points.

A few years ago I was invited to preach at the Christian Union at Edinburgh University. The journey from my home in St Ives is one of the longest train journeys in the British Isles. The line west of Penzance wanders through the Cornish countryside, then skirts Dartmoor and for ten lovely minutes runs along the coast between Dawlish and Teignmouth. Then it goes north and becomes less beautiful as it passes through the industrial towns. Eventually after Newcastle it becomes very beautiful again, you travel through the southern uplands and finally you arrive at Princes Street Station, Edinburgh.

That is the picture we have in chapter 8. It begins with condemnation in verse 1 and ends with glory at verse 17. In between, we go through beauty and darkness, we hear of victory and of defeat.

No Condemnation

Can we ever hear verse 1 often enough? Sin there may be; sin there most certainly is, for 'if we claim to be without sin, we deceive ourselves and the truth is not in us' (1 John 1:8)—but 'no condemnation'. Matthew Henry in his commentary observes that the writer does not say that there is no charge against them, for there is; but the charge is thrown out and the indictment is quashed. He does not say that there is nothing in them that deserves judgement. There is, and we see it and we know it and we condemn ourselves for it. But 'there is no condemnation for those who are in Christ Jesus.'

He does not say there will be no heartache, tears or pain, for inevitably the truth of the matter is that there will probably be all those. But there is no condemnation for those who are in Christ Jesus. There may be correction, discipline, rebuke; but for those of us who are in Christ, Paul's shorthand for the whole work of the gospel is: there is no condemnation.

The reason is this: 'Christ redeemed us from the curse of the law by becoming a curse for us' (Gal. 3:13). He died on our behalf.

> Bearing shame and scoffing rude,
> In my place condemned He stood.
> Sealed my pardon with His blood,
> Hallelujah! What a Saviour.

No condemnation!

Let me give you three biblical illustrations. First, do you remember how in Genesis 27 Jacob was dressed in the clothes of Esau, so that when he appeared before the almost blind Isaac, Isaac saw not Jacob but Esau; and seeing Esau blessed him? The second illustration is the cities of refuge mentioned in Joshua 20. They were a means of grace, a place of escape. The law said, 'An eye for and eye, a tooth for a tooth'. If you killed someone accidentally, their family had the right to kill you unless you could escape. You could come to this place of refuge and escape from the condemning law. Within those walls, surrounded by those parapets you were safe. And the third illustration is Noah in the ark. The rain is above, the floods are beneath, but not a drop of rain gets in. Within that ark there is a place of security: no condemnation.

Now: Jacob was a cheat. Manslaughter may have been careless. Noah was far from perfect. But in each case they found a place of refuge, clothed around by another, secure and safe in the grace that had been provided. For those of us who are in Christ there is no condemnation. My God sees Him and is satisfied. Remember that glorious hymn:

Jesus Thy blood and righteousness,
My beauty are, my glorious dress.
Bold shall I stand in that great day,
For who ought to my charge shall lay,
Fully absolved through Thee I am,
From sin and fear and death and shame.
No condemnation now I dread.
Jesus and all in Him is mine,
Alive in Him my living head,
And clothed in righteousness divine.
Bold I approach the eternal throne,
And claim the crown through Christ my own.

That is how it is for the one who is in Christ.

But the truth has to be understood. No, the truth has to be appropriated. We have to live in it and stand upon it—now, through what Christ has done; and not only what Christ has done, but what Christ will do; not only our past spiritual experience but our glorious future. So at the end of our passage, 'Now if we are children, then we are heirs [of the future]—heirs of God and co-heirs with Christ, if indeed we share in his sufferings in order that we may also share in his glory' (verse 17). That is what God has done for us in Christ, and will do for us in Christ. It starts in Penzance and it ends in Princes Street in Edinburgh. But I will tell you, in between there are some hard, difficult places, and we haven't time to look at it all this afternoon.

The Sinful Nature, and the Holy Spirit

We begin to move into the 'industrial regions' with the phrase 'sinful nature'. Look at verse 3, 'it was weakened by the sinful nature', at verse 4, 'who do not live according to the sinful nature', and at verse 5, 'those who live according to the sinful nature'. What does this mean? In Paul's discussion in chapter 6, the Authorised Version speaks in 6:6 of 'the old man', which used to fascinate me as a child: where was he? I tell you, I keep meeting him all the time these days, for he seems to be very much with us, with me.

There is an ongoing debate over the meaning of the word *sarx*, which literally means 'flesh' and is translated here 'sinful nature'. It is the same word that is used in John 1:14—the Lord Jesus Christ 'became flesh', but was without sin. In the present context it speaks of that which drags us down and makes us vulnerable. It speaks of those things which make us indeed groan, 'Oh God!' It speaks of that part of me which as yet has not been changed from one degree of glory to another—that constant reminder that it does not yet appear what I will be.

The other key word in our passage is *pneuma*, 'spirit'. (In the Hebrew it is *ruach*; both words mean exactly the same thing.) It speaks of spirit, of soul, of wind: it speaks of power. Yet for the child of Christ there is this indwelling power, the Spirit of God, the Holy Spirit of God, the One argued over, abused, claimed as the authority for so much that is extreme and bizarre—that Holy Spirit, the third person of the Trinity, part of the Godhead Himself.

Oh my friend, when you lay claim to the Holy Spirit, be careful! When you take the Holy Spirit to endorse your attitude, your mind, your hope, your ambition—be careful. I plead with you by the mercies of Christ, before you say 'The Holy Spirit has told me', be careful. I do not deny any of these things to you or to me, I just plead with you to be careful. Remember who He is, and that familiarity has a tendency to breed contempt.

How many of us understand the Holy Spirit, the third person of God? A blind man was flying a kite: somebody asked him what was the point, as he couldn't see the kite. 'Ah,' said the man, 'I can feel the tug on the string.' That indwelling Holy Spirit of God; that appetite that we have been given, that pull that we have received; that holy ambition that has been inoculated into our hearts so that we might know the glory that is Christ and the glory that is to be revealed to us in the perfect work of Christ. This power that is available by the Holy Spirit to bring us to glory.

The law is powerless, says the Scripture. Verse 3: 'For what the law was powerless to do in that it was weakened by the sinful nature, God did by sending his own Son'—and His Holy Spirit. That glorious phrase! 'God did.'

Notice that in verse 5 Paul mentions two groups of people: 'Those who live according to the sinful nature', and 'Those who live in accordance with the Spirit.' Dare I say it, those two groups are represented here this afternoon, and within the sound of my voice. Those whose appetites are fleshly, those whose ambitions are set in the things of this world; and those whose hearts and minds are set upon the things which are above, by the grace of God, through His Holy Spirit.

I am computer illiterate, but I have a computer on which I am increasingly dependant. When I do something wrong it beeps at me. So I press another button and it beeps again, and another and it beeps again . . . eventually one wants to smash the thing. I've discovered that sometimes the only way to get rid of the beep is to switch the whole thing off and start all over again.

We do this and it's wrong, we do that and it's wrong, we touch that and it's spoiled, we minister this and we influence that and it's all wrong somehow. Beep, beep, beep. Notice the phrase that Paul uses, 'have their minds set'. What does it mean? It means being unable to break out of certain thought forms, having set minds, being unable to transcend oneself. It is impossible for anybody to transcend themselves. Beep, beep, beep. 'I know myself so well,' says Paul in the previous chapter, 'what a wretched man I am!'

There was a monkey that could play the piano. The wonder wasn't that it played the piano badly, it was that it played the piano at all. It had transcended itself. But that is just a humorous story. In reality we do not transcend ourselves: beep, beep, beep. 'But those who live according to the Spirit'—if you however have the mind, purpose, will and power of God in your heart and soul and being, then, by the Spirit of Christ who is in you, you will live increasingly, gloriously, more and more and more, until we see Him.

It's brought about by the Spirit of God. Notice the titles here: 'the Spirit of God', 'the Spirit of Christ'. From verse 9 onwards the emphasis is there. Verse 9, 'the Spirit of God lives in you.' Verse 10, 'But if Christ is in you.' It's synonymous with the same thing in verse 11, 'And if the Spirit of him who raised Jesus from the dead'—that mighty, powerful, glorious, earth-shattering event—'is living in you,'—that same holy, mighty Spirit—'he who raised Christ from the dead will also give life to your mortal bodies.' And for emphasis again, 'through his Spirit, who lives in you.' It's God's work and for His glory.

So that's all right then; over to Him; let go and let God . . . Not so! This, of course, is where these verses have been misunderstood and misapplied.

Look at verse 12, 'Therefore, brothers [and sisters], we have an obligation.' We have been looking at the elect of Thessalonica this week, and we stand on that mighty, mysterious doctrine of election. But there is no one here elect to be second-rate in the things of Christ. There is no one here predestined to be mucky in the things of the gospel. There is no one here chosen of God to be tawdry and cheap in the things of the Spirit. We have an obligation, a responsibility. 'But it is not to the sinful nature,' says Paul. 'We owe that nothing.' Verse 9: 'If anyone does not have the Spirit of Christ, he does not belong to Christ'. But those who have been born again by the Holy Spirit of God, we are those who have an obligation.

'Well,' you say, 'this Holy Spirit talk makes me frightened. There's so much argument today. So many strange things going on. Where will it end?' A few years ago I was asked to preach, and the church inviting me wrote, 'Robert, we are so looking forward to you coming. But you won't preach about the Holy Spirit, will you? Because our church is so split about the Holy Spirit.' What an indictment upon the age in which we live, what an indictment upon modern evangelicalism! May God have mercy upon us.

Look at verses 13–14, 'For if you live according to the sinful nature, you will die; but if by the Spirit you put to death the misdeeds of the body, you will live, because those who are led by the Spirit of God are sons and daughters of God.' Octavius Winslow said one or two things about this leading of the Holy Spirit. He said it was strange and mysterious and frightening. But leave it alone? No.

The Leading of the Holy Spirit

To paraphrase Winslow, 'Those who are led by the Holy Spirit are led to Christ.' Where else would you want to be led? Jesus said concerning the Holy Spirit, 'He shall glorify me, for He shall receive of mine and show it to you' (John 16:14, AV). The Holy Spirit is our comforter, but Jesus is our comforter; and it is to Him that the Spirit leads. Men and women led by the Spirit, people open to the Spirit, are people who are thrilled and excited by the Saviour.

I'll tell you a demonstration of the Spirit's work. It is those who say,

> Thou, O Christ, art all I want;
> More than all in Thee I find.

Secondly, the Holy Spirit leads to truth, as the Saviour Himself said (John 16:13). Understand this, and understand it well; when professing Christians have been led into error, they could not have been led there by the Spirit. The Spirit is truth and reveals nothing but the truth.

Thirdly, He leads to power. Again it was the Saviour who said, 'You shall receive power after the Holy Spirit falls upon you' (cf Luke 24:49). We sing sometimes in church,

> His touch has still its ancient power,
> No word from Him can fruitless fall.

Weak churches, weak believers, our church programmes that would go on exactly the same if the Holy Spirit were removed! God have mercy on us. The Holy Spirit is power, power to be an overcomer, power for victory, power to enthrone Christ, power for service.

Fourthly—this is a very forgotten truth in modern evangelicalism—the Holy Spirit leads to holiness, to men and women being made like Christ. Winslow says at this point, 'It is the Holy Spirit's aim to deepen the impress of the restored image of God in the soul, and to increase our happiness by making us more holy, and to advance our holiness by making us more like God.' The Holy Spirit leads to nothing that is not sanctifying. And in a morally confused age, He will lead. And every virtue we possess, every victory won and every thought of holiness is His and His alone.

Fifthly, He leads to comfort. It is His very name. How many of us need a comforter! Here is the mighty provision of our God in Christ through His Spirit, that the third person of the Trinity bears the name 'Comforter'. The work of the Holy Spirit is to dry tears, to instruct the penitent, to heal the wounded, to console the bereaved.

And lastly, He leads to glory. It's the theme of the chapter; it's the theme of our week together. It is the key to the message in the context of the theme of the week.

Let me read to you the Scripture again, and let it stand for itself.

> For you did not receive a spirit that makes you a slave again to fear, but you received the Spirit of sonship. And by him we cry, '*Abba*, Father'. The Spirit himself testifies with our spirit that we are God's children. Now if we are children, then we are heirs—heirs of God and co-heirs with Christ, if indeed we share in his sufferings in order that we may also share in his glory.

Precious work of the Holy Spirit, to bring me home. Did you hear the love in the passage, the wonder of it all? 'Abba, Father', to bring us to glory. 'Did not the Christ have to suffer these things and then enter into His glory?' (Luke 24:26). Peter—'a witness of Christ's sufferings and one who will share in the glory to be revealed (1 Pet. 5:1).

> The head that once was crowned with thorns
> Is crowned with glory now . . .

The Holy Spirit, to bring us to glory. Resurrection, completeness, wholeness, in future at the Lord's appearing. James puts it like this, 'Listen, my dear brothers [and sisters], has not God chosen those who are poor in the eyes of the world to be rich in faith and to inherit the kingdom he promised those who love him?' (Jas 2:5).

The Lord Jesus Christ Himself, praying intently. Who for? For you and me. 'Father, I want those you have given me to be with me where I am, and to see my glory' (John 17:24).

'Heirs of God and co-heirs with Christ, if indeed we share in his sufferings so that we may also share in his glory.'

World View Meeting

by Mr Nigel Lee

1 Chronicles 4:9

The Challenge of Jabez

In 1 Chronicles 4 we find a long list of ancient Jews. And suddenly in the middle of a list of the descendants of Judah one man, called Jabez, stands out from the midst of what to us is the general obscurity. Verse 9: 'Jabez was more honourable than his brothers. His mother had named Jabez saying, "I gave birth to him in pain." Jabez'—presumably when he grew up—'cried out to the God of Israel, "Oh that you would bless me and enlarge my territory! Let your hand be with me, and keep me from harm so that I will be free from pain." And God granted his request.'

Then it returns to the list: 'Kelub, Shuhah's brother, was the father of Mehir, who was the father of Eshton . . .', and so on, on it goes. It is just as if, as we were going through the telephone directory, we found that the Holy Spirit had caused to be written in red alongside this man's name, 'Give him a ring, he'll do you good.'

Jabez's background, such as we know of it from this verse or two, was somewhat disabling. His mother had had a particularly hard time in bringing him into the world, so, perhaps in a fit of pique, she had named him Jabez, which is a pun on the Hebrew word for 'pain', or 'painful'. Can you imagine going through life with a name like Painful? Being called in to tea as a little lad from playing with the other boys—'Come on, Painful!' Can you imagine your first day at school? You sit down, the teacher goes through the register —'Brown, Hacking, Weston, Motyer, Jones, Lee, Painful'

—everybody's sniggering away. It was an odd way, wasn't it, for her to get her own back?

People do give their children some strange names sometimes. My daughter spent six months in Zambia. She worked in a hospital where her job included weighing babies. She asked one lady what the name of her baby was, and it was 'Tedious'. She asked another; the baby was called 'Porridge'. Can you imagine her on her wedding day? 'I, Porridge, take thee Tedious . . .'

Poor Jabez, having to grow up with a name like that!

Sometimes I think our backgrounds, and the way our parents used to speak to us, and some of the expectations of us when we very young, some of the hurts and the pain that we experienced then, can have an extraordinary limiting, cramping effect upon our understanding of ourselves and our vision of God and our sense of how God answers prayer. They may be experiences from decades ago. Maybe you've come to this Keswick Convention and around your spirit, your heart, these days, this week, is a great big label and it says the same: 'in pain'.

Are there any here who've come in pain? Maybe ministers who've been running on 'Empty' for too long. Or some of you have come and your partner has left you, maybe heartlessly just abandoned you, and you feel so rejected, you've come in pain. Or maybe others of you are here and though your marriage hasn't broken, it's hard, it's hard. You too are in pain. Tonight we come tonight to the World View Meeting. Huh! You're thinking, 'I'm having difficulty even holding myself together, I'm not even ready this Wednesday night to go back at the end of the week home to what I'm facing. I can hardly take on board anything more about the world tonight. I'm in pain, I can't hear any more.'

Jabez stands out from the general obscurity of these chapters of 1 Chronicles. God Himself draws attention to Jabez, because of one prayer. Probably he prayed it repeatedly, but he must have prayed it one day for the first time. It consists of just two sentences. He gathered up his courage and he prayed this prayer, and God was pleased to answer it. Out of all the mass of unrecorded prayer that there has been since the beginning of time, the almighty God has caused the record of this prayer to go into His holy and eternal word, for our encouragement, for our learning tonight.

He asked for God's blessing, 'Bless me,' he said, 'touch me, look on me, change me. I want my life to count. Oh God, rescue me from sameness, greyness, mediocrity and pain.' He prayed it, and God answered. We don't know really the details of how, we are just told that God answered that cry.

I can remember ages ago reading the following in a novel:

> 'Osborne,' said the duchess to a household employee, 'how long have you been with us? According to my records you were employed to look after the dog.'
>
> 'Yes Madam.'
>
> 'Mrs Bellamy tells me that the dog died twenty-seven years ago.'
>
> 'Yes, Madam. What would like me to do now?'

Twenty-seven years, with nothing to show for it! Jabez cries out, 'Oh God, do something different with me, bless me.' He has perhaps three things that he's asking of God in this rescue, this new start.

He prays first of all for God's *enlargement*. 'Would you enlarge my territory, increase me, in what you can entrust to me, in the responsibility that you will commit into my hands? Lord, is there anything more I can do for you? Any more impact that I can have? Lord, is there someone else that you would lay on my heart that I can pray for, pray for, pray for, until we see them turn and respond? Something else that you would put in my pathway for me to attend to, some missionary that you'd want me to really get behind and pray for until my last breath is done?'

Sisters and brothers, please don't think ever, that world vision is only for the young. Let's nail that lie of the devil right now. It is not so! We are all involved.

The one clearest memory I shall have in going back from this Keswick is something that happened to me on either the first or the second night I was here. A lady came to me and said something to me that deeply touched my heart. She said,

'I heard you when you were here two years ago. I have been praying for you regularly ever since.' I need that. Sometimes for some of us our lives are so busy, there are so many phone calls and faxes and pressures, we desperately depend upon others who can pray for us daily at the throne of Grace.

A couple of nights ago I was sitting having a cup of tea late at night with Alec Motyer. He began to ask me about the big distribution of Luke's Gospel that I had mentioned earlier in the week. He said, 'You know, as soon as I heard about that, I stuck a picture of William Tyndale on my study wall at home, and I resolved to pray regularly for this initiative.' He was getting behind us in the work that God has given us to do. Will you pray tonight for God's enlargement of your ministry, your impact, of those that the Lord would lay on your heart, that you can carry faithfully in prayer?

Secondly Jabez prayed for God's *enabling.* He said, 'Let your hand be with me, or be upon me.' It's no good asking the first without the second. It's a strange expression to us in Britain, but it comes quite a lot in the book of Ezra, for example in 7:6. Ezra has just asked for various things from the king of Babylon. And the king of Babylon grants Ezra everything he asked for, 'for,' says Scripture, 'the hand of the Lord . . . was on him.' Doors swung open because of the hand of God. In verse 9, Ezra had a safe journey from Babylon all the way to Jerusalem, 'for the gracious hand of his God was on him,' says Scripture. In verse 28, leading men of Israel start to gather around Ezra in order to support him and join with him in what God had given him to do; because, says verse 28, 'the hand of the Lord my God was on me.' He says the same in 8:18 and so on through the book.

Will you ask the hand of the Lord to be freshly on you?. The hand of the Lord. Imagine—the hand that broke the loaves and multiplied them, the hand that reached out to Peter as he was sinking below the waves and pulled him up, the hand that reached out and lifted Jairus' daughter back to life; that hand. Ask for it to be upon you.

The third thing that Jabez asked was for God's *turning-point* in his life and in his experience, so that he might escape from the conditioning, the limiting effect of his background, and become instead a picture of God's grace. 'My name is

Jabez, I can't change it, I'm stuck with it. But Lord, would you so bless me that actually the testimony of my life goes way beyond the conditioning and the effect of my background? May the reality of blessing, hope and freedom be mine.' That's what he says: 'Let your hand be with me, and keep me from harm so that I will be free from pain.'

That's the challenge tonight; that as you listen to what you've been hearing, the Lord will press on your heart some new steps of faith, commitment or obedience. Cry for the Lord's blessing, His enlargement and enabling, and that He will make your story something that shines with God's grace for other people to see.

We've been thinking all week about the return of the Lord Jesus, and we've sung almost every song in the book that refers to it. The Lord Himself said, in Mark 13, that He was going to come back, and pointed to a number of signs that His coming was drawing closer. There will be an increase of false messiahs and gurus; people like David Koresh, Sun Myung Moon, Sai Baba, and so on. He said there will be an increase of wars and rumours of wars; and I defy you to look in the newspaper today without seeing just that. He talked of upheavals would come in the natural world; earthquakes, famines and so on.

He talked about the rising persecution of believers there would be as we move towards the end. Do you have any idea how many people are martyred every year for Christ? It is utterly astonishing. The average number of Christians who have been put to death for their faith over the last forty years has been 150,000 every year. And, Jesus said, that number would increase. So what does He say in Mark 13? 'Don't be deceived. Don't be alarmed. Don't get the timing wrong, the end is not yet, even though you see these things happening. Don't let your guard down.' And in verse 9 he says, 'There is one thing that you are to do. Bend every effort to preach the gospel. The gospel is to be preached to the ends of the earth and then the end will come.' That is what is to happen. 'And then the Lord will return.'

How are we doing? Tonight I want to be the bringer of good news. God is fulfilling His word. He is fulfilling His promises to Abraham. Do you remember that mind-blowing promise that was given to Abraham? 'Every people group on earth, every single one, will be blessed through you.' What an astonishing thing to say to that man who was His friend! 'Every single people group on earth, not one missing, will be blessed through you.'

People are great at counting up statistics, and I like to remember some of them. Apparently in the year AD 100 there were approximately 360 non-Christians to every Christian. By the year 1900, there 27 non-Christians for every Christian. By the year 1988 there were 11, and in 1992 (the last year for which I have figures) there were 6.8 non-Christians for every Christian. I don't what .8 of a non-Christian is, but it sounds easier to evangelise than a whole one . . .

I'm not sure what definition of 'Christian' is used in those statistics, but you can see that there is a change going on. God is keeping His word. By the year 2000, fifty-two percent of world population will at least call themselves Christians. We know that some of that will be nominal Christianity, but at least it means that they know the name of Christ and there is an entrance there for the gospel. Two hundred years ago, world evangelicalism was confined to Europe, the east coast of North America and the tips perhaps of India and South Africa. Nowadays there are more evangelicals outside Europe than there are inside. God is keeping His promise to Abraham.

I want to encourage you tonight. We face some huge challenges, but it's not all gloom and despair. God is at work, prayer is being answered. The challenge has gone out from this platform year after year after year, and we are getting very close to the end. We could be the generation.

Ten Reasons for Excitement

Let me give you ten reasons why I'm excited.

1. Most of the task that the Lord Jesus left to His church has already been done. By the year 2000, ninety-five percent of the population of the world will at least have access to the gospel through translated Scripture, radio, the Jesus films or a preacher in their own language—possibly all four. I am told that there are about 12,000 known ethno-linguistic groups in the world. Ten thousand of them have, at least embryonically, a church planting movement in them. Only 2,000 groups have nothing at all. We have seen substantial progress over the last two hundred years, beginning to rapidly speed up in the last thirty years.

You may have heard of the '10/40 Window'. It is a geographical 'box' between ten and forty degrees north of the Equator. It contains 62 countries and is the home of eight out of ten of the world's poorest poor. The world's Islamic and Hindu populations live predominantly in the countries in that box. All fifty of the fifty least evangelised mega-cities of the world are in it. And yet, and here's the second reason I'm excited,

2. There is a growing prayer movement beginning to circulate around the globe among Christians. I am confident that many of you are part of it. In October 1993 millions spent time in prayer, and in some cases fasting, for world evangelism. In October 1995 it's estimated that up to thirty million Christians will be spending October in concentrated prayer for world evangelism. Edwin Orr said when God is about to do something, He sets His people praying. And if God stirs you at all tonight to recommit yourself to prayer, it is because I believe God is moving towards the fulfilment of those promises to Abraham, as things prophesied by the Lord Himself.

3. The impact of television. In a single day this year, Billy Graham preached via satellite TV to over one billion people in 165 countries. Can you imagine it? Paul would probably have given his other eye to have been able to do that. We need to harness the impact of technology.

4. The use of English. English is gradually becoming the world's international language. How does a Korean pilot talk to Egyptian traffic control? In English. How does a Brazilian telephone operator make a connection with Tunisia? In English. God has already started equipping you towards world evangelism. He's getting the rest of the world to learn to speak your language.

5. The extraordinary dispersion now of people around the globe because of educational and business opportunities and high-speed travel. I was with my wife Tricia in a meeting in Warwick University about ten months ago. After I'd finished talking she got into conversation with three fellows standing at the back who'd been listening to the talk. They came from Kazakhstan, previously a completely closed country. And she was able to engage them in conversation about the Lord Jesus. There are Mongolians studying in Leeds. There are people from Red China studying all over Britain. I was preaching in Cambridge in a mission in February, and every single night there was a complete row of people from the Republic of China. One night one of them wanted to write something down, but they had no paper. In the end he wrote it on a ten pound note. Would you?

We have unparalleled opportunities in this country.

6. Literature, especially the Scriptures. By the year 2000, eight out of ten people will have at least access to the entire Bible. Nine out of ten in the world will have access to the New Testament. Through the technology we have, the pace of Bible translation is speeding up. It's exciting! Some of you have been praying for things like that for so long.

7. The existence of groups of God-fearers in almost every society. I was recently told of a Christian book shop in a country not far from Saudi Arabia. Night after night a big car draws up and a group of Arabs get out. They don't say anything; they come into this Christian book shop and go straight to certain shelves that have Arabic Bibles on them. They buy them, they get back in the car and they go, back to that country I mentioned earlier. Somebody is telling them where to find these books. They are people who have a hunger to know the true and living God.

8. The Jesus film. The Jesus film is translated into a new language every ten days. We hear thrilling stories of people who have watched this film. Some friends of mine took it high up into the Nubian mountains somewhere in Sudan and with a little cranky generator showed it at night in the darkness. The Sudanese were gripped by this film. When Jesus died on the cross, some of these Sudanese were weeping. Then they saw the resurrection and they fired their guns into the air, rejoicing, *rat-tat-tat-tat*! Because they were so gripped by the message of the film. Pray for those who are taking this film all over the world.

9. Religious and spiritual hunger. God has made people that way. Even under Muslim fundamentalism, it is because they are hungry to know something that is secure and satisfying. Behind the Western disillusion with materialism there's a spiritual hunger. The whole New Age movement is basically seeking for answers to this question: What does it mean to be human? Because we are made in the image of God.

10. The huge increase in mission societies, especially in places like Nigeria, India and Korea. The numbers are huge. It's brilliant.

Let's come back to you. Jabez stood out from the crowd and one day he prayed. Who is going to pray a Jabez prayer?

One of the great dangers of Keswick is that we are hearers only and not doers. Isn't it so? It's possible to come from the four ends of the country and even the world, to sit for a week disobeying what the Lord has told us to do. We enjoy the sound of it. Don't just hear! 'If you do,' said Jesus, 'you are deceiving yourselves—not anybody else.' You don't deceive God, of course. We cannot. What you are doing is going through an exercise of self-deception. What a tragedy to pay good money to come all the way here, simply to sit for a week deceiving yourself and then go home, because the Lord might have spoken to you about something and you didn't do the first thing about it. Business as usual, normally next Monday . . . Don't do it!

The challenge tonight is to action, to respond in some way or another. Every year we give an opportunity from this platform for people rise quietly to their feet, while the others sit with their heads bowed, and say, 'Yes Lord, here am I. It's the first time I'm saying it to you without reserve, without regret. Use me, take me, send me.' Will some of you do that here tonight? Every year people rise to say that to the Lord.

There may be many others of you here who want to say something in response to what we've been hearing this evening. Maybe you want to commit yourself to praying more faithfully and regularly for somebody whom the Lord has been putting on your heart, or for some area of need. 'Lord, give me a new consistency, a new faithfulness. I want to pray for doors to open in that 10/40 window and in the 18/25 window up here in Cumbria, North Lancashire. I'm going commit myself to praying. I want to pray for churches to be planted.'

Pray for your children and grandchildren, that they will take their place in this great army that the Lord is raising up.

Some of you may be called to far more sacrificial giving than has been your practice. Most missions that I know of are in financial crisis. I know very few that are saying to us, 'Yes, we've got more than enough thank you, please send it to somebody else.' There is desperate need.

Jabez cried out, 'Lord, would you bless me.' And God granted his request. Are you ready to respond, to say, 'Lord take me, use me, at home or abroad'? Or will you keep your seat and say, 'Lord, you have spoken to me about my prayer life, or about my pocket or the neighbours in my street. Lord I've seen tonight that we are getting closer. I don't want the end to come and me not be one hundred percent involved in obeying you.'

The Lord Jesus is coming back. It's been said in every single message from this platform. To gather together a group of thumb-twiddlers? When the Lord comes back, I'd like to be preaching the gospel somewhere. To be quite honest, I'd rather be there than here.

My time is gone. Let me end with this. Recently the head of the world-wide Coca-Cola company said this: 'We believe that every day, every person in the entire world is going to be thirsty. We in the Coca-Cola Company have the means to quench that thirst. By the year 2000, we want everybody in the world to have tasted Coca-Cola.'

Coca Cola? It breaks my heart. The thirst isn't for Coca-Cola. Brothers and sisters, we have the means to quench the thirst for living water. What a mission statement with which to go out from this meeting! 'I'm going to be committed, God giving me grace and health and keeping His hand upon me; I'm going to be committed to being part of that army for these last days, that sees the job done.'

Communion Service

by Rev. Ian Coffey

1 Corinthians 11:26

> 'For whenever you eat this bread and drink this cup, you proclaim the Lord's death until he comes.'

Paul's friends at Corinth had got it sadly wrong. He had to remind them that this table, rather than being a place where people just indulged (which was what was happening), is in itself a preaching of the gospel. In bread and wine we testify that Jesus Christ the Son of God came in the flesh, was crucified, was dead, was buried, and was raised to life again; and that through his sacrifice on the cross, sinful men and women can come into relationship with a holy God.

I want to direct you to one little word in the middle of verse 26: the word 'until'. Throughout this week at Keswick we've been thinking together about the glorious truth that Jesus shall come again. And here tonight we gather in this tent, and perhaps in the most significant memorable way we can this week, we testify to the truth of that verse which is displayed above my head—'All one in Christ Jesus'[1].

We are used to celebrating Communion, the Lord's Table, the Lord's Supper, the Eucharist—the very fact that we use these different expressions testifies to the different way in which we are used to doing what Jesus told us to do. It is interesting that Paul doesn't lay down any set pattern, prescribing the size of the table, the colour of the table-cloth,

---

1. These words (from Gal. 3:28) are the motto of the Keswick Convention, and for many years have been displayed in the tent and elsewhere as a visual focus of the Convention weeks.

whether the bread should be one loaf or in lots of little cubes—the kind of issues that we might perhaps have strong feelings about. The central heart of what he is saying in this chapter is, 'We proclaim to one another—to the principalities and powers, to a watching world—we proclaim the truth that Jesus died and rose again, and one day shall return.'

That's why that word 'until' is there. And I want you to notice that it is,

A Waiting Word

It's the kind of thing we would say to a friend or a partner, or a child: 'Stay there until I get back.' John records in his Gospel that Jesus said it to His disciples: 'Do not let your hearts be troubled. Trust in God; trust also in me. In my Father's house are many rooms; if it were not so, I would have told you. I am going there to prepare a place for you. And if I go and prepare a place for you, I will come back and take you to be with me that you also may be where I am' (John 14:1–3). 'Until' is a waiting word. Jesus says to His disciples as He says to you and me, 'This meal is until that great celebration in heaven.'

University students get up to some very crazy things. One rag week a bunch of students came up with a great stunt. Outside a large skyscraper office block in the middle of a city centre, they approached a passer-by and held out a surveyor's tape measure. 'Could you help us? We are trying to measure the circumference of this building. Would you hold the end of this tape while we go round it and come back?' Of course, the passer-by agreed. Then they went round to the opposite side of the building and found another innocent bystander. 'We've got some friends who are holding the other end of the tape, and we need to give them some information. Would you mind holding this end until we get back?' I don't know how long the two stood there holding the tape. They may still be there! But they were waiting for nothing.

The people of God are waiting for someone. Jesus is coming again, and in this meal we affirm that fact. Augustine said,

> He who loves the coming of the Lord is not he who affirms it is afar off, nor is it he who says it is near; but rather he who, whether it be far off or near, waits for it with a sincere faith and a steadfast hope and a fervent love.

Not speculation but anticipation—that's been the note this week, we wait. It's a waiting word.

A Working Word

But I want you to notice that 'until' is also a working word. Have you noticed, in the parables of Jesus, how many times that note comes through? Where Jesus speaks about an end coming to the story, and people being held accountable.

Perhaps the best known is Matthew 25, the parable of the talents. It was through reading that parable—without any preacher, without any evangelist, without any Christian service, but just reading that passage of Scripture in a Gideon Bible—that I came to faith in Christ. The man gives to his servants, to one five talents, to another three, to another one. He goes away. He comes back. And that's the sense of this word 'until'; it's a working word. The master says 'Get on, and do what you will with what I've given you until I return.'

And you and I have been encouraged many times this week not simply to listen to the word, but to do something with it. Can I ask you a question tonight? As you get ready to go home tomorrow, what are you going to do with what God has told you? If I can put it this way, without in any sense wanting to be rude or offensive: you've been at Keswick for a week. So what?

So—what? We should never sit to listen to the preaching of God's word, we should never stand to deliver God's word, unless we can answer that question. So—what is God saying to you about your giving? About your praying? About the way that we live within our families? About our community? What's He saying to you and me about that church situation that perhaps we found so difficult and challenging in the last few weeks? 'Until' is a working word.

In the Christian Hospital in Nazareth, there is a chapel

and in the chapel there is a communion table. And there, poignantly, in a place where Jesus grew up and spent those predominantly thirty silent years, the Lord's table—the communion table—is a carpenter's bench. And there on the communion table, the carpenter's bench, are all the tools, the hammer, the plane, every instrument he would have used. But here's the important thing. When you look at those instruments, the handles are all pointing towards the congregation. They are not pointing towards the minister but towards the people. You see, 'until' is a working word; we are called to 'work out your salvation with fear and trembling, for it is God who works in you to will and to act according to his good purpose' (Phil. 2:12)—it's a working word. And it is also,

A Willing Word

It's a word which comes out of our hearts with a great sense of longing. Have you ever wondered about the last few words in the Bible, in the Revelation of John? How he could contain himself, as he wrote some of these things that are so amazing, so hard for the mind to comprehend? But he comes in verse 20 of the last chapter of the book of Revelation, he says this autobiographically: 'He who testifies to these things'—the Lord Jesus—'says, "Yes, I am coming soon." ' And John adds, 'Amen. Come, Lord Jesus.'

I wonder if in the tent this evening there are some who cry out, 'Come, Lord Jesus.' Am I speaking to some this evening for whom every communion service is difficult, as you remember a loved one, a life-partner who no longer sits alongside you? And for you, any communion service is a difficult place to be. But sister, brother, in Christ; can I remind you tonight, this word 'until' is a willing word, that looks forward to that day when Jesus shall come again. Heaven is a place of reunion. It's a place where there are no more tears. It's a place where there is no more separation. And we look forward in faith, to that great reunion of God's people.

I want to encourage any tonight who come perhaps with mixed feelings, and with a sense within of longing that the

Lord might come soon; God has a purpose for you today. You have not been left behind by accident. God has a plan, and you are still to fulfil that plan.

A visiting preacher once stayed in a house of a widow. He'd arrived on Saturday to preach on the Sunday, and the lady of the house, being that sort of person, had given up her bedroom for the guest. When he got up in the morning he threw back the curtains and looked out on a beautiful scene: hills way in the distance, beautiful green pastures. But he was intrigued to notice that in the corner of the window pane child-like writing was scratched in the glass. He could just make out the words: 'This is the day'. At breakfast asked his hostess, was it done by a grandchild who had been playing around with something sharp?

'No,' she said. 'I did it myself, and I did it with the diamond on my engagement ring.'

And she explained how, having lost her husband some years previously, there were many times when she would throw open the curtains and not see a beautiful pastoral scene but pouring rain. She would be plunged into despair and depression, and she would have no wish to go out and face the world. Having lost her life-partner, she felt that meaning had gone.

Then one morning, in a moment of bleak despair, she opened her Bible for her daily reading and saw the words, 'This is the day that the Lord has made, we shall rejoice and be glad in it' (Psa. 118:24). And the Holy Spirit reminded her that God had a plan. And now, as every day began, no matter what the weather, she threw back the curtains and (as she explained to the preacher) 'I want to look into the day through the promise of God. This is the day, and whether the Lord calls me or whether He comes for me, I want to live each day for Him.'

It's a willing word.

A Wonderful Word

For the people of God, it's a wonderful word.

Paul doesn't say, ' . . . proclaim the Lord's death *if* he comes'. He doesn't say, ' . . . *in case* he comes.' He says, ' . . .

You proclaim the Lord's death *until* he comes.' Yesterday morning we read together the words of 1 Thessalonians 4:16, with its great description of the resurrection.[2] Bishop J. C. Ryle was Bishop of Liverpool from 1880–1900, and was regarded by C. H. Spurgeon as 'the best man in the Church of England' (I can assure you, that's a compliment, from a Baptist!). Ryle wrote, 'When we die, where we are buried and what kind of funeral we will have, matters little. The great question to be asked is this, how shall we rise again?'

That is why throughout this week, as we have studied the Scriptures, as we have been encouraged by one another and by hearing of God at work in different places, there has been that note of 'until'. Jesus is coming back—'until'. It's a waiting word; so don't lose patience. It's a working word; so don't lose sight. It's a willing word; so don't lose hope. And it's a wonderful word; so don't lose faith.

A couple of weeks ago I was playing golf with a close Christian friend. As we walked down one of the fairways he took me completely by surprise; he asked me, 'Ian, do you think you will go to heaven to meet Jesus, or do you think He'll come from heaven to meet you?' But as I reflected on my friend's question, I thought, that's a thoroughly Christian question to ask: it's an important question to ask. Is the Lord going to call us to Him, or is He going to come from heaven to meet us? We don't know. We don't want to speculate, but we do want to be ready. Don't we?

When my sons were much smaller than they are now, my wife Ruth had some difficulty convincing them, when Daddy had gone away, how long it would be before he came home. They found it very difficult to comprehend how long I was going to be away. Ruth hit upon a good idea. She got a large potato and stuck into it the same number of match sticks as there were days I was to be away. Every morning at breakfast someone would be chosen to take a match stick out of the potato. In that way they gained some sense of when Daddy was coming back. Early one morning, one of them came downstairs and took out all the match sticks in one go . . . it

---

2. See the Bible Reading by Rev. Alec Motyer, p.55 of the present volume.

reminds me of some Christians! But the fact is that my sons understood, in a childlike way, that one match stick less meant one day nearer.

And I want to say to you, the people of God, tonight —without in any sense wanting to be irreverent or trivial —as we meet around the Lord's table, in this glorious demonstration of our unity in the body of Christ, that it's one less Lord's supper and one step nearer glory.

Let us commemorate; let us celebrate; let us proclaim; until, until, until He comes. Amen!

'Heaven In Us, Before We Are In Heaven'

by Mr Jonathan Lamb

Revelation 7:9–12

> There is darkness without and when I die there will be darkness within. There is no splendour, no vastness anywhere, only triviality for a moment and then nothing.

So wrote Bertrand Russell, shortly before he died. He captured how many people feel about life and also about death; for in this Western world we find it difficult to avoid the conclusion that the material world must be the only true, real one. There might sometimes be a suspicion of an afterlife in some form, but it's an irrelevance. For most people the prevailing philosophy is 'Eat, drink and be merry'—or more commonly, 'Eat, drink and watch telly.'

These days the most important thing is to avoid thinking about those ultimate issues, by maximising on our present experience. Tomorrow's world is little more than a TV programme as far as most people are concerned. For many, all religions are mocked by the hard, white smile of the skull. Of course in England and in other parts of Europe there is what people observe to be a new spirituality: the New Age movement, the interest in occult activities, a great deal of interest in reincarnation. They are all indicators of a restlessness in people, as they reject mere bland materialism, and try to discover what the future holds. Is there any kind of life beyond death?

It has to be said that Christians haven't always projected an attractive image of the afterlife. Ernest Gordon, the author of *Miracle on the River Kwai*, said that before he became a Christian he looked upon us as the kind of people who extracted the bubbles from the champagne of life: 'I preferred a robust hell to the grey sunless abode of the faithful.'

Similarly Laurie Lee: 'Heaven is too chaste, too disinfected, too much on its best behaviour. It receives little more than a dutiful nod from the faithful. Hell, on the other hand, is always a good crowd-raiser, having ninety percent of the action—high colours, high temperatures, intricate devilries, and always the most interesting company available.'

The problem is that we Christians think about heaven in the same way that we think about death. Die? That's the last thing I'll do. Heaven? That's the last thing I'll think about.

A minister was visiting an elderly couple. The husband was quite seriously ill upstairs in bed. Before the minister went up, his wife asked, 'Please, do talk to him about something cheerful and hopeful. Not about heaven and that kind of thing.' . . . We feel too much at home here, don't we? We are too earthbound, we are too secularised; and we fail to realise that the afterlife is not some vague shadowy existence, but that as C. S. Lewis says in *The Great Divorce*, in heaven everything is more real, more solid than it is here. It's this world which is perishing, which is creeping towards decay. But in His great mercy God has given us new birth into a living hope through the resurrection of Jesus Christ from the dead, and into an inheritance that can never perish, spoil, or fade, kept in heaven for you.

If we are living in the light of His coming, then we will be like the Christian who when asked whether he thought he would go to heaven when he died said, 'Why, I live there.' And it was said of Richard Sibbes, the great Puritan preacher, 'Of this good man let this be written, heaven was in him before he was in heaven.'

Now the book of Revelation lifts the curtain. It gives us a glimpse of what heaven will be like—literally, it is an unveiling. And this apocalypse of John from which we have read tonight, is written between one pronouncement in 1:7, 'Look, he is coming with the clouds, and every eye will see him, even those who pierced him', and at the end of the book the confirmation by the exalted Jesus: 'Yes, I am coming soon.' And the response of God's believing people, 'Amen. Come, Lord Jesus' (cf Rev. 21:20). Sandwiched between that opening and that conclusion declaring the return of the Lord, we have a number of songs of heaven which are wonderfully colourful pictures about what heaven will be like.

It is very important, as we think about the second coming, to follow the rules of biblical interpretation; a lot of people see tanks rumbling through Ezekiel and helicopters and gun ships in the book of Revelation. But I think Revelation is also a book to be read with our imagination. The songs of heaven are here in 7:9–12; the multitudes appear, the atmosphere is charged with excitement, with enthusiasm, the worship is demonstrative and noisy. You see, God's people, this great multitude, have come through a great deal of suffering. They have had a tough time. And John's writing was a special encouragement in the first century to Christians who are under pressure.

So let's look at the three characteristics of heaven which we see in these verses, and as we do so, let's also ask whether it is true of us as it was of Richard Sibbes, that heaven is in us before we are in heaven.

The Vision Was Of God's Family (7:9)

'There before me was a great multitude that no-one could count, from every nation, tribe, people and language.' The vision included representatives of every part of the globe. See how he piles up those expressions—'nation', 'tribe', 'people', 'language'. He does this in several other places in the songs of heaven. He does it to show that the redeemed, God's family, aren't from a restricted group. They are from all over the world. It's a universal family, and God aims to be worshipped by converts from every corner of the globe. And this international community is innumerable: 'a great multitude that no-one could count'.

Do you remember when God said to Abraham, 'Abraham, just come out of your tent a moment. Look up at the sky, and try to count all of those stars if you can. So shall your offspring be! I will surely bless you and make your descendants as numerous as the stars in the sky and as the sand on the sea shore.' That is John's vision. All of Abraham's true offspring, all of the servants of God from down through the centuries, from every part of the world, as far as his eyes could see; a countless number streaming in every direction, but each one standing before the throne and in front of the Lamb. If you are a Christian you are part of a world-wide family, the fastest-growing family on this planet. And if heaven is going to be populated by people from every tribe and language, people and nation, then God's mission is by definition world-wide. And if heaven is in us before we are in heaven, we will be passionately committed to that same world-wide mission; we will be deeply concerned to see John's vision of God's family become a reality.

But we must be honest. It has to be said that for most of our churches—certainly in the British Isles—and perhaps for most of us Christians, we find this increasingly difficult, for a number of reasons.

For one thing, there's the mood of our age with its so-called tolerant spirit, so that anyone who stands up for absolute truth is branded as a divisive fanatic: 'You can't be so dogmatic as to assert that the Christian faith is for the whole world.' These days, it's been said, any stigma is good enough to beat a dogma with. And in this atmosphere of relativism it's very difficult for Christians to hold on to this conviction of world-wide vision. 'Oh, it's nice for you, it's nice for Europeans, it's nice for Caucasians—but don't try to absolutise it, don't try to universalise it.'

Another trend that affects us Christians in our society is the paradox that alongside this incredible development of the global communications network, there's a shrinking of our horizons. I was talking to some Christians not long ago who are working for the European Community in Brussels. They were bemoaning the fact that at the very time you would expect greater unity among Christians in Europe and a widening of horizons on the part of God's people, the trend appeared to be the reverse; towards a drift among Christians to a narrow concern for their particular country, their particular city, their particular church.

The same is, I'm afraid, true of the student community whom I seek to serve. I was a student about twenty years ago in the days of student protest and revolt; there were all kinds of sit-ins, and people were very interested in world politics. Recently there was a student protest in Oxford, where I live. I was very encouraged—at last a sit-in! It's not that I'm particularly radical, it was just that I was pleased to think of some interest being expressed beyond the purely personal. What was the sit-in about? Sudan? Bosnia? It was about the university crèche facilities.

It's not uncommon for us Christians to find our main interests and concerns focusing on personal, family or local church life. Those are all proper concerns; but if heaven is in us before we are in heaven, it can't possibly stop there. The tribalism, nationalism and individualism of our culture should not be allowed to extinguish John's vision of God's world-wide family.

The China Inland Mission, which later became the Overseas Missionary Fellowship, was born out of the agony of heart of Hudson Taylor. In June 1865 in Brighton he was worshipping in a church on a Sunday morning with a large crowd. Suddenly he picked up his hat and stormed out of the church. He wrote later in his diary: 'Unable to bear the sight of a congregation of a thousand or more Christian people rejoicing in their own security, while millions were perishing for lack of knowledge, I wandered out onto the sands alone in great spiritual agony.' There he prayed for twenty-four willing labourers to join him in world-wide mission. You see, we can't truly worship God and at the same time appear to have a total indifference to whether anyone else is worshipping Him.

I'm very thankful that in the church I attended for the past few years there have been number of older people who regularly and enthusiastically reminded us of God's world-wide family and God's world-wide mission. One of our older brothers used to pray, 'Lord, we pray for all the people in the uninhabited parts of the world.' But the Lord knew what he meant, and so did we. Here was a man who was concerned for every tribe and tongue and nation and people; heaven was in his heart.

One of the kingdom texts in the New Testament which this particular Keswick Week should not neglect is Matthew 24:14—'And this gospel of the kingdom will be preached in the whole world as a testimony to all nations, and then the end will come.' It's happening. We've been hearing about it. Over the last hundred years or so, we've seen a greater advance of the church's mission than in any previous century. In parts of Africa, in parts of Latin America, the church is growing at rates in excess of ten, twenty, thirty percent a year.

I read a while ago of a church synod in Indonesia, where it was seriously suggested that baptisms should stop for a year or two just to give the church time to catch up with what God is doing. John's vision is becoming a reality, and the vision of God's international purposes must be in our hearts and on our lips, touching our pockets, shaping our prayers, transforming our churches—from all nations. If heaven is in your heart before you are in heaven, that will be your burning prayer, that will be your joy: God's world-wide family.

The Reason Was God's Gospel (7:9–10)

It's a wonderful privilege for me to be working in an international fellowship. In IFES you encounter all kinds of differences: West Indian music, Latin-American embraces, a different view of time with some of our African and Latin brothers and sisters; Russians who stand for prayer and whose pastors greet you with a kiss on the lips—there's all kinds of diversity. And our world-wide Christian family is enriched by all of these differences.

But in a world of fracture and tribalism, how is it possible to live together? Look at verse 10, 'And they cried out in a loud voice: "Salvation belongs to our God . . .".' God's gospel expressed through the saving work of Christ transcends all the cultural, linguistic, racial and national boundaries. And we find that God's family is united through Christ's work.

Look now at three things in verses 9 and 10 about God's family.

What they wear They are wearing white robes. At its simplest this symbolises their right relationship with God. Commentators point out that the Greek noun here signifies long robes—much more appropriate to glorious garments, than to work-a-day clothing. They were standing before God justified, perfect in the righteousness which only Christ supplies. Verse 14: 'These are they who have come out of the great tribulation; they have washed their robes and made them white in the blood of the Lamb.' They are standing there through Jesus' work ready, dressed for the occasion.

What they hold They were holding palm branches in their hands (verse 9). This probably symbolises victory and rejoicing. Palm branches were often associated with the Feast of the Tabernacles, that great joyful party, that holiday at the end of the harvest season when everyone gave thanks for the successful gathering in of the harvest. They had singing processions bearing palm branches, and together they gave thanks not only for the harvest but also for God's deliverance of them out of Egypt and into the promised land.

That feast pointed to the completed harvest in the end time, when God promised through the prophet Isaiah to gather His own from all nations, to swallow up death for all time and to wipe away tears from their eyes (cf Isaiah 25). And John sees the celebration in heaven with people from all tribes and nations, redeemed by the one Lord Jesus Christ, dressed for the occasion, at that great final ingathering of God's harvest. It's a celebration of Jesus' triumph.

What they say 'They cried out in a loud voice: "Salvation belongs to our God, who sits on the throne, and to the Lamb." '—the 'Salvation Shout', as it's been called. John has both God and the Lamb in view.

The reason for all of God's people being united in celebration is God's gospel. Salvation comes from the sovereign act of God in Christ.

John quite frequently uses the expression 'the Lamb in heaven' in his songs in Revelation. There's a similar song in chapter 5, where John is told: 'Do not weep! See, the Lion of the tribe of Judah, the Root of David, has triumphed . . .

Then I saw a Lamb, looking as if it had been slain, standing in the centre of the throne' (5:5–6).

The Lion of the tribe of Judah who comes in triumph is also the Lamb who was killed. It's often been said that the only man-made thing in heaven will be the marks of slaughter upon Him. This conqueror is the one who submitted to God's purposes on the cross. And so John sees, in ever-growing concentric circles, people breaking into praise until all creation joins in that song.

I love F. F. Bruce's comment on this passage: 'The future belongs, not to the mailed fist, but to the pierced hand.' And for hard-pressed Christians in the first century, as for hard-pressed Christians now (and there are many of them), this is the message of hope and encouragement. The future is absolutely sure in the hands of their, and our, crucified and exalted Lord.

Now let me draw just a couple of applications before I come to my final point.

There is no confusion of tongues

In this heavenly choir drawn from different nations, tribes, peoples and languages, there is no confusion of tongues. Babel is a thing of the past. As Philip Hughes puts it, 'This is a shout of unanimity which is heard as a single voice. Single-mindedly the vast multitude ascribe their salvation to God and to the Lamb.'

They are diverse, certainly. It's possible that the original reading of Revelation 21:3 should have 'peoples' in the plural. God's purpose isn't to obliterate distinctions or diversity, but to gather together all of His people in one diverse and unified assembly. God's gospel transcends all of those barriers—cultural, racial, economic, sexual. The banner over my head tonight will be even more appropriate on that day! 'All One in Christ Jesus'[1].

Well, that's heaven. I ask you: is heaven in us before we are in heaven? For Jesus, this is essential for the effectiveness

---

1. These words (from Gal. 3:28) are the motto of the Keswick Convention, and for many years have been displayed in the tent and elsewhere as a visual focus of the Convention weeks.

of Christian mission. 'May they be brought to complete unity, to let the world know that you sent me' (John 17:23) That's the main reason, you see, why Jesus prays that we will be one: so that the world may believe in Him and His mission.

Have you ever tried to nod your head and say 'No' at the same time? It takes quite an effort of the will. A little while ago I was in Bulgaria, the only European country that has reversed certain cultural symbols: and as I preached I saw the congregation shaking their heads, and the more passionately I preached the more vigorously they shook their heads. They were agreeing with me! In our culture, if we did that we would be giving two contradictory signals simultaneously. But it is one of the major problems in Christian mission. We affirm a huge 'Yes' that we are all one in Christ, but at the same time we are shaking our heads—our disagreements, our wrangles, our divisions, our tribalism—all of which convey a very different message.

You may have heard the story of the minister who was asked whether he had an active congregation. 'Oh yes! Half of them are working with me, and half of them are working against me.' Unfortunately it can often be all too true. Richard Baxter in 1656 said,

> The public takes notice of all this division, and not only derides, but becomes hardened against all religion. When we try to persuade them they see so many factions that they do not know which to join; they think it is better not to join any of them. Thus thousands grow in contempt of all religion by our divisions.

I've just returned from Nairobi where I heard the leader of the Burundi IFES movement, the Christian Student Movement, say that the Christian student leaders there in Burundi categorically refused to take sides in the conflict. And now, because those Christians did so, the government has invited Hutu and Tutsi Christian students to visit schools together, to model reconciliation. In fact, on one campus, although the mood is still one of prevailing fear and hatred, Christians are standing together. A group of believers on one campus received the message from the university authorities, 'If this university is functioning, it's because of this Christian group.'

That's wonderful. If God's people can demonstrate that, then we are doing something in this fractured world. But there's a cost. In neighbouring Rwanda, most of the IFES student movement's board, staff and student leaders were all killed during last year's genocide.

I recently prayed with a group of Christians from Croatia and Serbia. Immediately before they prayed, they stood together with linked arms to sing the song, 'Bind us together':

> There is only one God,
> there is only one king,
> there is only one body,
> that is why we sing,
> 'Bind us together Lord.'

So I ask again. Is heaven in your hearts? Is your church celebrating with that one voice that you hear in Revelation 7? Are our churches doing so together? Is our mission committed to partnership with evangelicals, unity with others, co-operation at every point? Because that is God's gospel, and that is heaven.

My second point of application has to do with what Gerald Priestland called 'the scandal of particularity'. Because in heaven, you will see as you look at these verses,

They are united through Christ's work

There at the centre of the countless multitude is the Lamb that was slain.

Today I think, the reason why so many of us are not caught up in telling other people about the Lord, in the task of world-wide mission, is our failure to believe that Jesus Christ is the only way to God. For John's vision demonstrates that there is no other name. And the task of mission has as its greatest motivation, this fact: salvation belongs to our God. What they wear, what they hold, and what they shout, all say: 'Jesus is the only way.'

The Focus is God's Glory (7:11–12)

'They . . . worshipped God, saying; "Amen! Praise and glory and wisdom and thanks and honour and power and strength be to our God for ever and ever. Amen!" '

In the Greek, each of those seven qualities is preceded by the article 'the'. In each case it is not 'a' but 'the' praise, the glory . . . above all others, which should go to our God for ever and ever. The focus of heaven, when the harvest is finally gathered in, will be the glory of God. And that's why, if heaven is in us before we are in heaven, we have cause to anticipate that celebration. Remember what Psalm 96 says: 'Declare his glory'—where?—'among the nations'. If you want the theological term, it's 'doxological evangelism'. Declare His greatness, the greatness of God, above all other gods, 'all other godlets', as I believe Alec Motyer calls them.

Our task is to call our friends, our neighbours, all people, to worship Him. Mission exists because worship doesn't. Jesus came to be an evangelist for worshippers. The reason for our lack of concern, limited giving to missions and half-hearted prayers is our little-felt emotion of burning desire for God's glory.

Last night on the midnight news there was a report of the debate in the American Senate over whether or not to lift the arms embargo in Bosnia. A woman senator said, 'We are outraged at the atrocities. There is one thing we cannot do and that is nothing.' I imagine many of us feel that outrage about the atrocities going on tonight in our own continent.

But when I heard that news item I had to ask myself: what outrage do I feel that people are worshipping other gods and not Jesus? For four years Margaret and I lived in a city that has the second largest Hindu community in the world. Do you know which city that is? Leicester. And just across the Channel, Belgium has four times as many Muslims as Protestant Christians. We see in all of our towns different religious practices by people in our neighbourhoods, in our places of work, even in our local schools.

Henry Martyn was a great Cambridge academic of the nineteenth century. But he decided to leave all of that and go to India; he died when he was younger than I am now. As a missionary he watched people prostrating themselves before pagan images. He even heard someone describe a vision of Jesus bowing down to Mohammed. And Henry Martyn said, 'I was cut to the soul by this blasphemy. I could not endure existence if Jesus was not glorified. It would be hell to me if He were thus dishonoured.' He had a passion for God's glory.

I have to ask myself—I hope we all do—what am I giving my life for? Paul says, 'Let's make it our aim to please him.' A passion for God's glory; that's the focus in heaven, and if heaven is in our hearts, that will be our motivation too.

And that's the reason, you see, why worship, without a missionary burden for men and women of every tribe and tongue, is humbug. Heaven is God's family saved by God's gospel, celebrating God's glory. Is heaven in us?

David Barrett coined the expression, 'World Christian'. He defines it thus: 'A world Christian is someone who is so gripped by the glory of God and the glory of His global purpose, that he chooses to align himself with God's mission, to fill the earth with the knowledge of His glory as the waters cover the sea. The burning prayer of the world Christian is, "Let the peoples praise Thee oh God, let all the peoples praise Thee." '

And all the people said, Amen!

'New Heart, New Desire'

by Mr David Burke

Titus 3:1–8

At the time of the writing of the epistle, Titus, a co-worker of Paul, was pastoring a church in Crete. It was a difficult job. In support of his colleague, Paul wrote: 'For there are many rebellious people, mere talkers and deceivers, especially those of the circumcision group. They must be silenced' (1:10–11).

It's very hard as a young Christian worker to silence people who are coming into your church. And it is very hard to adjust to an aggressive, different culture: verse 12, 'Even one of their own prophets has said, "Cretans are always liars, evil brutes, lazy gluttons." This testimony is true. Therefore, rebuke them sharply, so that they will be sound in the faith and will pay no attention to Jewish myths . . .'. Titus faced the tough job of getting a bunch of people who were at root rebellious, to come into line with God's word. Not just with the doctrine (what God's word says), but also with the practice (what God's people ought to do): 'Remind the people' (3:1)—of all kinds of things. 'Because these,' said Titus probably to Paul, 'are the things that my congregation are forgetting, and I need to keep on reminding them.'

Paul writes to encourage and strengthen Titus in the challenge of reaching this congregation and their friends with the good news of Jesus. We need encouraging. Sometimes God's people have to learn to face down their fears and do things that don't come naturally, so that Jesus Christ might be glorified. Let's trust God and His Spirit to bring His word immediately to our hearts, and to teach each one of us as we need to be taught; so that we may take it home to our churches, to change our lives and to change the situations in which each one of us finds ourselves.

A few years ago I went on a caving expedition with a group of friends in the Yorkshire Dales. Well, I'd *planned* to go with them, but they got the date wrong. So I was sitting outside a cave in my wetsuit feeling very foolish, thinking, 'Well, I know what I'm doing. I might as well just go on in.' So I went underground alone into a cave system that was fairly straightforward—something you should never do, but I did it. I spent a happy hour or two crawling round underground passages and by the time I was ready to leave, my lamp was starting to get a bit dim.

I started to retrace my steps. And then, with a sinking feeling I realised that somehow in this little cave system I'd got myself completely lost. Every passage now turned out to be a blind alley. I went round them again and again and with a dimming light and an increasing panic. There was no way out. I was in a completely closed system, locked in the blackness. I was becoming more and more frightened. Eventually I sat down and thought, 'What on earth am I going to do? How am I going to get out of here?'

After a couple of moments of some of the darkest despair I have ever felt in my life, I finally explored a narrow rock fissure. At the end there was a boulder and on its top a green leaf was lying. Leaves don't stay green long underground; I knew immediately that it must have fallen in somehow and that I must be near the entrance. So I slithered up to the boulder and looked up. Overhead I saw daylight, and the big tree from which the leaf had come from. Then I was out. I was free and no longer locked in this dark closed system. I was in daylight again, smelling the sweet fresh air.

Verse 4: 'But when the kindness and love of God our Saviour appeared, he saved us . . .'. How do you know that there is a heaven, that there is a God? How do you *know*? Because the kindness and love of God our Saviour was literally made visible, in time, in space, on planet earth. Jesus Christ lived and He died and He rose again from the dead.

And just as that leaf was my clue to how to break out of my closed system and into fresh air and freedom, so the life of

Jesus, God's grace, God's mercy made visible to us, is the clue the human race needs to show that this life is not all there is. We are not locked in a closed system with nothing afterwards, to become meat for worms when we die, accountable to nobody. Jesus came and lived and died and rose so that we could be sure.

That's why I can believe and have intellectual integrity. There are reasons why I believe. Jesus really lived, Jesus really died, and Jesus truly rose from the dead. It's a matter of historical fact. Just look at Him, and you will see all the evidence that you need to get out of this closed system and into all the glories that God has for you. In the words of C. S. Lewis's Screwtape,

> Human beings are amphibians—half spirit and half animal . . . As spirits they belong to the eternal world, but as animals they inhabit time.[1]

And our late twentieth-century world says human being are only animals, but the life, death and resurrection of our Lord Jesus Christ screams at us that human beings are amphibians. We are made for two worlds, to live in two habitats —that of planet earth and that of heaven. Jesus came to show us the certainty that heaven is a reality. He is the leaf on the rock at the end of the tunnel, the clue to the fact that there is life outside our animal life—life in the Spirit, life in heaven.

'The kindness and the love of God our Saviour appeared' —it was made visible in the life of Jesus—'and He saved us.' It's interesting that word 'salvation' appears several times in these verses, in 2:11, 3:4, 3:6. I want to ask three questions about the salvation we've been given in Jesus Christ; the answers are given directly in verses 3 to 8.

Why Did God Save Us?

Verse 5: 'He saved us, not because of righteous things we had done, but because of his mercy.' This is the utterly

---

1. C. S. Lewis, *The Screwtape Letters* (1942), ch. 8.

unique dimension of the teaching of the New Testament that you will not find in any other great world religions of the world.

Mankind's religious instinct is performance-related. Many people think salvation is like the gifts for which you become eligible when you have collected enough stamps at the petrol station. But there are no stamp cards in the New Testament. And though to some that is quite obvious, to others it is a life-preserving truth. One of the commonest neuroses in the church is the feeling of not yet being good enough for God to use or to bless. We compare ourselves with the top performers in our churches and our Christian communities, and say: 'I'm nothing like that—I couldn't do that—I'm less than a worm.' And we run away with the curious idea that God has lost interest in us. Some of us go around with such feelings every day of our Christian life. They become a dark cloud that threatens us.

But think about those top performers, whom you consider to have collected lots of stamps at the petrol station. Ask yourself, 'Why did God save them?' Verse 5: He saved them, not because of the stamps they'd collected, but because of His mercy. And if that's why He saved the people whom we think of as high-performers in the Christian community, that's the reason He saved us too. He saved you—the person whose psyche goes into riot mode whenever you feel threatened about your assurance of salvation. He saved you not because of the good that you've done, but because of His mercy.

Maybe you'd like to memorise that verse or write it down somewhere you can see it regularly, because it's true of the greatest saint that's ever lived and it's also true of the person who thinks that he or she is the least saint that ever lived. That's why God saved you; just because He's like that. Our God is simply wonderful. He accepts failures and sinners. Notice the contrast between verses 3 and 4. Kindness and love are made visible in Jesus Christ the Lord who saves you, not because you are a high performer, but because He wants to show His mercy to you. He just wants to be kind to you. That's all; that's why He saved you.

And it focuses down on the cross, our Convention focus for today. 'This is love,' says John, 'not that we loved God,'—not that we are high performers in the love department—'but that he loved us and sent his Son as an atoning sacrifice for our sins' (1 John 4:10). He saved you, just because He's like that, just because He is merciful.

How Did God Save Us?

Verse 5: 'Through the washing of rebirth and renewal by the Holy Spirit, whom he poured out on us generously through Jesus Christ our Saviour . . .'

There has to be a crisis. There has to be a moment when you realise who you are, a sinner trapped in a cave, locked in a closed system without hope; and you need to break out of that cave into the daylight that you know instinctively lies beyond. You know you are an amphibian, you want to break out of that closed system, but you don't know how. Then you come across Jesus, the Jesus who came and lived and died. And you see in Him the clue to breaking out into the life of heaven, and you believe it.

And when you believe, repenting of your sin, turning from the cave and towards the life of heaven, something supernatural happens inside you; something powerful, something that happens once and never again—something that completely changes the balance of power in your life, so that henceforth sin no longer has mastery over you, but the Spirit of God begins to take over. The Bible calls it rebirth or 'regeneration', because you start your whole life over again.

Some Christians can identify the time and the date when that happened to them. I can't—it happened to me some time during 1974. But whether over a period or in a cathartic moment in time, it happens and we are reborn. You can't fudge your way into the kingdom. You must be born again.

He saves us by 'the washing of rebirth'. 'Washing' refers to Ezekiel 36:24, in which Ezekiel looks forward, by the power of the Holy Spirit, to what God will do through Jesus Christ in the New Testament: 'For I will take you out of the nations; I will gather you from all the countries and bring you back into your own land. I will sprinkle clean water on you, and you will be clean; I will cleanse you from all your impurities and from all your idols.'

That washing doesn't come cheap. There was a price tag attached. It was a price that our Lord Jesus paid in His own life, dying on the cross for us at Calvary, the atoning sacrifice for our sins of which John speaks: the sacrifice that will bring the ancient enemies God and man back together again. The price was the life of the perfect Son of God, paid on the nail on the cross, outside Jerusalem 2,000 years ago. And now we can be washed, reborn, our sins forgiven, sprinkled with clean water, weaned off the idols to which we are addicted and brought into the kingdom. Ezekiel 36:26 says what God will do next. 'I will give you a new heart and put a new spirit in you; I will remove from you your heart of stone and give you a heart of flesh. And I will put my Spirit in you and move you to follow my decrees and be careful to keep my laws.'

God is going to do something else to achieve our salvation. Ezekiel predicts it, and Paul picks up that second point in Titus 3. He saved us through the washing of rebirth and through renewal by the Holy Spirit; and the second phase of God's salvation plan in our lives is to put the Holy Spirit of God within each one of us, so that for the rest of our lives we continue to change until one day we resemble in character the Lord Jesus Christ, the perfect man, the Son of God.

When I was a teenager at school we were passionately interested in cars. My friend Derek was car-crazy but couldn't afford one. He came to school one day beaming: 'I've got a car.' We didn't believe him, so after school fifteen of us went round to his house where he showed us an incredibly rusted 25-year old Morris Minor convertible. We teased him mercilessly, but the reason we didn't see him after school for a while wasn't because of that but because he was working on his car. About three months later he arrived at school in an amazing, shiny, perfect vehicle. It even had fluffy dice and go-fast decals. We'd ribbed him about it, but now we turned green. He had a car, and we hadn't. We'd teased him, but he'd simply smiled beatifically. 'It's mine, I bought it, it cost me fifteen quid, I'm going to do it up.'

When people turn to Jesus they are often in lousy shape, just like that car. Others might walk past us and think we don't count, that we're not young enough, rich enough, attractive enough. But Jesus looks at you with a smile on his face, because He bought you, He paid for you, and now He's going to do you up.

The first thing Derek did with his car was to replace the old defunct engine with a new one. The first thing that Jesus does when He's washed us is to put a new engine inside us: the Holy Spirit of God, the third Person of the Godhead, God Himself, come to live in our lives and in our hearts. He gives the power to live the Christian life, to do what we weren't capable of before. And so the balance of power shifts: from being in bondage to sin, to being able to live the way that God intended us to live.

Once Derek got the car going, he discovered with horror that he couldn't make it stop. So he fitted it with brakes. And there are some things that need to stop when we become Christians; not because Christians are negative people, but because there are things that will not enhance or fan into flame the work of the Spirit in our lives. So we cease to do those things and we start to do the things that will enhance the Spirit's work and fan into flame His life within us.

In verse 1 Paul touches on some of these qualities. Let's make no mistake about this. We cannot move a millimetre in the Christian life unless we are filled daily and continually with the power of the Holy Spirit to enable us to live for, and serve, our master the Lord Jesus Christ. 'He saved us through the washing of rebirth', but it does not stop there—He saves us through the renewal of the Holy Spirit whom He poured out on us generously through Jesus Christ our Saviour. The Spirit of God is poured out upon those who ask for Him and are open to His ministry. The Spirit of God comes to the child of God who cries out to God, 'Use me, fill me, forgive me, help me, change me. Help me to live for the Lord Jesus Christ.' That's how God saves us.

The gift of the Holy Spirit came because Jesus died upon the cross. Do you remember that conversation in John 14–16, where Jesus is talking to the disciples? 'I've got to go,' He said. The disciples were full of sorrow, and the Lord said, 'I've got to go, because if I don't, I can't send you the Spirit.' The cross had to come first, before the liberating Spirit could be sent to occupy the hearts of those who are washed in Christ's cleansing blood.

From What Did He Save Us?

About ten years ago in America the mountain rescue team in the Yosemite National Park in California took a man to court. They'd gone to rescue him, but he hadn't wanted rescuing. He'd set out to climb, solo, an enormous half-mile-high cliff called Half Dome, which is almost vertical. After about a week he'd got about half-way, but he didn't seem to be making much progress; some days he seemed to be getting nowhere at all. People were watching him through their binoculars and were getting very worried. So after about ten days the Yosemite Mountain Rescue Team turned out, helicoptered to the top of Half Dome, and winched one of their men down on a steel cable. He said, 'I've come to rescue you. You've been up here for days, we're very worried about you.'

The climber answered, 'Well, I'm on three weeks holiday. I've got all the time in the world. It's my holiday.' He refused to be rescued, and there was a blazing row. I never found out who won the court case.

But when you tell people today that Jesus died to save them, the response is often, 'Well—what did He die to save me from? Because I am very happy, and I don't really feel that I need saving.'

'At one time,' says Paul (verse 3), 'we too were foolish, disobedient, deceived and enslaved by all kinds of passions and pleasures.' It happens to be true that the people among whom we live are blind to the issues to which Jesus Christ wants to make us alive. We don't want to be saved.

What did He come to save us from?

Well, firstly, *from the wrath of God*. Verse 7: 'So that, having been justified by his grace'—set right with God in such a way that God is satisfied with us through the cross, and no longer subject to His wrath on the day of judgement, we have been saved from hell and set on the road to heaven.

Secondly, *from a way of life that is locked inside a cave and says 'This life is all there is.'* He wants to save us from that self-indulgent world view and bring us into a completely new one where we understand that we are amphibians: so that 'we might become heirs having the hope of eternal life'. We are going to inherit a kingdom that will last for ever. We belong in this physical world, but we also belong in the heavenly world. We are amphibians made for both. God wants to save us so that we can start to live differently.

That's the third thing God wants to do. He wants to save us *from a self-indulgent blind way of life*, into a new one oriented around the Lord Jesus and committed completely to Him, to His agenda and His way of living.

Verse 8, He wants to save us *so that we become people who are devoted to doing what is good*. We evangelical Christians are frightened of this, because we know we are not saved by good works; but we are still frightened of doing good works in case people get the wrong idea. But we've been saved for a reason: to commit ourselves to doing what is good. A Christian friend reminded me recently of times when we were pagan rock climbers in our youth, hitch-hiking round Keswick during Convention Week. We reminded each other of the number of times we'd stood together on the road trying to thumb a lift, and seeing car after car driving past with 'You Need Jesus' stickers in their rear windows. We used to look at each other—long hair, greasy tee-shirts—and we'd say, 'That's all very well . . . I might well need Jesus, I'm perfectly open to the idea. But I also need a lift.'

I'm not saying you should therefore pick up every hitch-hiker that you see. But sometimes we are wary of the good works God calls us to do. Sometimes we think that God saved us so that we could sit in meetings like this, getting fed until we burst. But God saved us so that we can do good works, and go out and get at close quarters with the people around us, being in the world, but not of it—being mixed in with the world as salt and light, but not compromised and tainted by it, so that we can change the people around us because we are so obviously different.

He saved us *so that we could live changed lives*. See the clear difference between 3:1–2 and 3:3. As we mix with the world our faith will be seen in our lives. Nobody will listen to your doctrine these days; nobody's interested. They need first to be brought to the point where they are prepared to be interested. And what raises people's level of interest in the Christian message is not good graphics, it's Christians who do good works, who are committed to people, and are in the world but not of it.

Our mistake in the late twentieth century is that we are of the world. We are just like everyone else. But we are not *in* it, and we convince ourselves we are holy because we are separate.

Let's beware this great reversal. Let's commit ourselves to turn it back on its head, and to live once again the design of the Lord Jesus Christ and walk to His tune. This is why we've been saved, saved to do good deeds, saved to live changed lives (2:12). That verse provides our marching orders in the interim between the ascension and the coming again of Jesus. Get involved in and do good works, and, despite the pressure of the world around us, live changed lives, changed from the quality described in 3:3 into the quality described in 3:1–2—'Be ready to do what is good.'

'Slander no one'—that alone will make you different from most of the people in your office, your staff-room, most of the people in your class room. 'Be peaceable and considerate'—if you're under thirty, that will make you immediately different from most of the rest of your generation! 'And to show true humility towards all men'—that will make you different from everyone.

And we are saved *to live for two loyalties*: as citizens of this world, subject to the rulers and authorities (verse 1); and as citizens of the world that will come when Jesus comes again (verse 7). We are saved to hold those two together in our lives, and not to become so spiritual we never mix with anybody nor so mixed in that we become indistinguishable from everybody. We are saved to live in such a way that Jesus is glorified, so that others are attracted and will listen, and so that we never let the passions and pleasures of this world pull us back into the kind of life we once used to live.

I grew up in Sunderland, on the other side of the Pennines. Every weekend during my school years, as soon as I was old enough, I would escape over here to the Lake

District and spend the whole weekend climbing. I've only been here twice to Christian events, however, and the first was earlier this year, the Keswick Speakers' Conference to pray and prepare together for the Convention. The snow had fallen on the tops of the mountains and there was a sprinkling on the hills as far as you could see, right down Borrowdale. Early in the morning I went down to the lake and looked at the scenery I'd been in love with ever since I was a child. And I said out loud a question I've often asked: 'Lord, why can't I live here?'

For the first time in my life the answer came with real power. *The reason the Lord has never let me live here is that if He did I wouldn't want to die.* I would want to hold on to this life—just another year longer!—and be reluctant to live for a kingdom one can't see.

I love this place! But I have to beware of the passions that would pull me away from living in two worlds. I have to remember that I am called to live in the world, but not to be of it.

And that's what you are called to do as well. Let's pray.

'Nothing Beyond Scripture'

by Canon Keith Weston

1 Corinthians 4:6

I read these verses recently in the Revised Standard Version, which my wife and I were reading together some weeks ago at the end of the day. In the RSV, verse 6 reads like this: 'I have applied all this to myself and Apollos for your benefit brethren, that you may learn by us to live according to Scripture.' It was that phrase 'to learn by us to live according to Scripture' that caught my eye. And as the weeks went by I began to think that maybe that was what we ought to be talking about in the opening meeting of the 1995 Keswick Convention. And having thought and prayed and studied, I do honestly believe (as I trust all the speakers at our Convention can say when they get up to speak), that this is what the Lord wants me to tell you from His word.

Here is surely the aim of each one of us who has come for the Convention: to learn to live according to Scripture. And that surely must be the burden upon the heart of every Convention speaker, whether in these great meetings here in the tent, or in the little groups with your children in the tents during the day: it is our desire, as Paul said to the Corinthian Christians, that you may learn by us to live according to Scripture. For the speaker that is a big responsibility, and we have urged you to be praying for us as we have been preparing for this Convention. And to that end these speakers have been studying and praying themselves; all the while, as Paul also says here, 'applying the truth to ourselves first of all.' For a preacher can only preach what he has learned for himself and applied in his own life. We come as very humble clay pots, but by the grace of God we have tried to apply the lessons that God has taught us, so that from these all unworthy clay pots something of the rich wine, the wonderful truth of God's word may be poured out for our thirsty souls.

So let me try tonight simply to develop what the apostle Paul said in these verses. First of all, I want to affirm without any hesitation that what we read here is,

The Ground Rule Of All Our Teaching

It needs to be said in these days, because tragically many people have lost sight of the word of God as the ground rule for all their teaching. Our aim by the grace of God is to learn to live according to Scripture. So we are unashamedly a Bible Convention, we believe with all our heart that this book is the word of God, and that when you handle it God speaks to you through it; and that though men and women seem today in our society to have largely abandoned Scripture, as irrelevant to their lives, we affirm here with all our heart that what is written here is utterly relevant to our lives today. Indeed, it is absolutely essential for our society and for the world. So let's pray that by the grace of God we will learn, during these Convention weeks, what it means to live according to Scripture.

For some years I had the privilege of being rector of a church in Oxford. One Sunday morning a college chaplain who'd drifted into the service, no doubt to find out what went on at that church, shook me by the hands afterwards and said, 'Do you know, I never believed that anyone took the Bible seriously these days, as you appear to do.' A college chaplain! God have mercy on us. Well, we take the Bible seriously here. It is the lamp for our feet and the light to our path, through these most confused and confusing days (cf Psa. 119:105). It is the truth that is 'sweeter than honey . . . from the comb' (Psa. 19:10). It is the Spirit's sword (Eph. 6:17), which is sharp and effective and clearly divides the opinions of men from the truth of God.

It is able to make us wise unto salvation, Paul wrote to

Timothy. And therefore it is profitable. When we often feel so helpless to understand what on earth is going on in the world around us, here is the profitable book for *teaching*. It is profitable says Paul, for *reproof*, when we stray into the ways of the world and allow our minds to be infected by the ideas of the world. It is profitable for *correction*; and how often we need that, when we fall into that temptation to believe the opinions of the world instead of the truth of God. And what's more, it *trains us for righteousness* says the apostle, so that we may be mature and equipped for the Lord's service, in these difficult days. I believe that in the mercy of God, there are going to be many who will be sent home from this Convention to their own churches—or maybe called by God in His mercy to go to the furthest ends of the world—equipped for service, to learn to live by Scripture (cf 2 Tim. 3:15–16)

And if that is true, then beware how you handle your Bible during this week of Convention. It is alive, and 'sharper than any two-edged sword' (Heb. 4:12), and God will use it if you will Him to. He's waiting to do that for you through the Convention meetings here. This is our conviction, this is the ground-rule for all our teaching—to learn to live according to Scripture. I say again, pray for our speakers, that every one of them may be able to come before us and say with that same total conviction, 'Thus saith the Lord.'

Let us pray also for one another during this Convention: that we may sit with reverence under the word of God, to believe that in this place God will speak through His expounded word, and that we will know that He has spoken. Let us come then expectant, to be taught, to be reproved maybe, to be corrected, to be instructed and trained in righteousness, so that we indeed may serve God the better in these extremely problematic days.

The Discipline For All Our Hearing

The modern translations bring out a most helpful aspect of what the apostle is saying in this passage. The phrase 'Do not go beyond what is written' (NIV) is placed in inverted commas. In other words, it's a saying which the Corinthian

Christians would have recognised. Perhaps it had become familiar because in the time Paul had been with them, perhaps in his first letter which we don't possess, he had made it emphatically clear to them that in the confusing situation in which that Corinthian church was situated, with pagan religion and false teachers abounding all round them, Scripture was the bench mark. 'Nothing beyond Scripture' was to be their inviolable rule, in all matters of faith and practice.

Look now at the context. In 1:10 Paul had begun to unburden himself with the great concern he had, because the church in Corinth had been split into parties—'I belong to Paul' said one lot; 'I belong to Apollos', 'I belong to Cephas', or even (perhaps with a ring of pride), 'I belong to Christ'. Some from the household of Chloe had reported that to the apostle. He was concerned that these Christians were splitting themselves up into sects.

The spiritual issues involved are then explained to them in detail in the first four chapters. In chapter 4 you find the climax of this introduction to the epistle: 'This is how one should regard us, as servants of Christ and stewards of the mysteries of God' (RSV, 4:1). That's the spiritual basis, the Scriptural basis, on which their ministry was based. That's how they will stand or fall before the judgement seat of the Lord Jesus Christ (4:4). 'Your attitudes to us', Paul is saying to those Corinthian Christians, 'in the party labels you attach to each other, is most disturbing and most alarming for me. For if you regard this man or that man as better than this man or that man—something more than a servant of Christ perhaps, more than a minister of the gospel—then you are going beyond what Scripture says.' That's the context.

As if the apostles were supposed to gather around themselves these rival factions amongst disciples! What would it do to the unity of the church? It would destroy it. What would it do to the hearts of the apostles, what does it do to a Peter or a Paul? Hearing that you have a following is bound to sow the temptation to pride. 'No, no, no,' says Paul, 'don't you remember the oft-repeated thing we said to you? "Nothing beyond Scripture." So regard us as we are, nothing more and nothing less: servants of Christ and stewards of the mysteries of God.' And Paul adds, 'I have applied these things to myself and Apollos for your benefit, so that you may learn from us the meaning of the saying, "Do not go beyond what is written".'

'All that is very interesting,' you may say, 'but what has it got to say to us? I am sure that none of us is so spiritually immature as to try to exalt one Convention speaker above another.' For this is how you are to regard us as Convention ministers—nothing more nor less than servants of the Lord Jesus Christ and ministers of the mysteries of God. But if our context here is different from the context in the Corinthian church of Paul's day, with its personality cults and party spirit, I believe that there is an application of the principle which we ought to bear in mind for us this week: nothing beyond Scripture.

Brothers and sisters, I want to speak humbly but very directly to us all. We shall during these coming days, God willing, be addressing one of the most thrilling of all themes of Scripture, and one which is in fact most frequently spoken of in the New Testament out of all the doctrines of Scripture. I refer of course to the glorious coming again of the Lord Jesus Christ, the promise which He Himself repeatedly gave us, that He will return at the end of the age and that every eye will see Him. It is a 'blessed hope' that is set before us, stated and re-stated, emphasised and re-emphasised, over and over again in Scripture, as though the Lord would say to us, 'Take it on board! This is the most glorious truth to which you as Christians look forward.' He is coming again.

Did not Jesus Himself teach us to pray in the Lord's prayer, and many of us use it frequently in our worship, 'Thy kingdom come, Thy will be done, on earth as it is in heaven'? We pray for this fulfilment of the promise whenever we pray the Lord's prayer, because we believe that He meant what He said. We don't just let it roll off our tongues because we learned it from childhood. Surely, we must pray it with conviction. 'Lord, look at Bosnia. Thy kingdom come! How long, O Lord, must it go on? Come again Lord Jesus, so that justice may reign in our world.' Surely you find yourself praying the Lord's prayer with meaning every time you read your newspaper, every time you turn on the television news. 'O God, how long has it got to go on? Have mercy, Thy kingdom come, Thy will be done, on earth as it is in heaven.' And that is indeed what will happen, when the Lord Jesus Christ comes again.

Thus the very last words of the Bible are the promise of the Saviour: 'Yes, I am coming soon', followed by the very last prayer of the New Testament—the promise and the prayer go together—'Amen,' says the church. 'Come Lord Jesus'.

Scripture always represents this thrilling truth first for *our great encouragement* in a world of such confusion and such depressing news, but secondly for *our eager response* in terms of readiness and service for that great day. And for this twin purpose, our encouragement and our edification to readiness and to service, enough is revealed in Scripture to excite the heart of the spiritual man or woman of God, and to nerve that man or woman's will to live for Christ according to Scripture and to witness for Christ in the remaining days before He comes again.

Enough has been revealed . . . but not everything. Ah, there's the crunch! Even the day and the hour when He shall come again is not known, even to the Son of God Himself (Matt. 24:36). The precise details are not revealed, fascinating though it may be to speculate, of how it will happen and what will happen. But enough is said to excite the will of Godly men and women to re-dedication of their lives to serve God, in the days remaining to us before that great day when He comes again.

How often down the centuries has the mind of human flesh delighted to pretend to know what Scripture has not revealed! And I want to say this—because I do not want our study of this glorious truth in Scripture to be spoiled in the slightest way by us—'Nothing beyond Scripture'. In this respect we have to learn, over and over again, to live according to Scripture and not to trespass beyond Scripture. That has been a great detriment to the work of the Lord down the years.

How we love speculation! It is the mark of our times. The news that John Major had resigned as Leader of the

Conservative Party gave rise to two or three weeks of sheer speculation. I said to my son who works at the BBC, 'You'll have to rename the Nine O'clock News programme "Speculation at Nine." ' He replied, 'But it's the summer months; there's so little news.' Sadly, some of the media make up news in order to speculate on it.

Let's not do that when we handle the word of God. As we sit under the word of God this week, and as we take it home to the various places where we are staying, beware lest we are tempted to go beyond Scripture. We've got to learn to live according to Scripture. Let's rejoice in it, because enough is there for us to be excited about the day of the Lord's coming. But don't go beyond Scripture, don't speculate, don't trespass where God hasn't taught us how to go. This is the discipline which we must practice not only here in our Convention, but when we get home to our churches and all our conversation with our fellow Christians.

Let us affirm what God has said, reject what God has not said, rejoice in what God has made clear and not be tempted to speculate on what God has not made clear.

The Jerusalem Bible translates our verse 6 very nicely —'So you can learn', it says, 'how the saying "Nothing beyond what is written" is true of us.' This must be the discipline we submit to in all our hearing and in all our speaking during these weeks of Convention.

The Prospect For All Our Living

But there's a third thing I want to say. Paul also speaks of the prospect for us for all our living; putting these things into practice and living these days for the Lord Jesus Christ.

Paul puts his whole appeal to the Corinthian Christians into the context of the Lord's coming. There it is in verse 5: 'Do not pronounce judgement'—that is to say, on this or that person and their views—'before the time'. And what is the time? 'Before the Lord comes'. And then all that is hidden will be revealed and the purposes of every heart will be disclosed. So live in the light of His coming, and let everything be under that glorious truth, because that's when the judgement will begin.

So, verse 6: 'All this I have applied to myself.' Isn't that lovely? It's the humility of the apostle, which says, 'I have done this myself. In the quietness of my own heart I have got on my knees and applied this truth, the 'nothing beyond Scripture' principle, to myself'—in his context here—'in terms of what my ministry is as a servant of Christ and as a steward of the mysteries of God.'

I think if he was on this platform speaking on this subject tonight he would say, 'I've applied this all to myself in terms of how I handle the glorious truth of the coming again of the Lord Jesus Christ. I've applied it therefore to my own life and to my own thinking and to my own living, and it's a matter of very little import to me how people may judge what I say. The truth of God's word is what I stand on.'

The word he uses is an interesting one, because it's the only time it ever occurs in the New Testament: 'I have applied this to myself'. The commentaries suggest that it has a strong affinity with the idea of transformation; there is a verbal parallel in the Greek. The truth revealed in Scripture he's applied to himself, by which he means that the result is Spirit-wrought transformation in his own thinking and living. So in the Corinthian context it means that he knows himself to be simply a servant of Jesus Christ and a steward of the mysteries of God: nothing more, nothing less. And it has transformed his whole view of himself as he ministers to those people. 'I've applied this to myself,' he says, 'and it's a very small thing therefore what other people may think of me.'

How much more we should learn that same lesson for ourselves, and apply all this to ourselves this week: to apply all the glorious truth of the hope that is set before us and apply it to our lives; so that the wonder of the realisation of the promise of our Saviour which He has made and which He will never recant should be applied to our lives. That, even if He came back this very night, we might be transformed through the Spirit's use of the word of God and application to our need; that we should be ready for that coming, and working eagerly toward it.

I close with an illustration. Many years ago I had the joy and privilege of being sent by the Convention to the Indian continent for the Keswick Conventions there. During my visit I flew to Kathmandu and on to Pokhara in Nepal to visit missionaries from our church. And I remember thinking 'I am looking forward to this immensely, because all the missionaries in Nepal tell us about the Annapurna range and how glorious Fish-Tail Mountain is, and they send us postcards of the unbelievable view you get from Pokhara.'

I arrived at Pokhara in the afternoon and looked for the view. It simply wasn't there. Just a few low mountains with trees on them, looking rather like a poor imitation of the Lake District. I thought, is this the Nepal I was taught to anticipate, the wonder of what I was told I would see? I went to bed disappointed, because it had not come up to expectation at all.

I was woken early next morning by the bells of cattle moving along the street beneath my window. I looked out to see what was happening. And there was the Annapurna range! And I had to stoop down in the window to see the top, because a wall of snowy crags rose up, and up, and up. What I had seen the previous night was simply the little foothills. And as the sun rose, the whole view changed colour—purple, gold and silver. It was the most exhilarating sight I've ever seen; I used almost a whole film photographing the range from that little window. It was a glorious sight!

And by coffee time, it had disappeared again. The mists and clouds had covered it, and you couldn't see it at all. But I'd seen it, I'd seen it.

'Nothing beyond Scripture', says Paul. But oh, what glorious truth is here in Scripture concerning our topic for this Convention week! Don't be content with the foothills, perhaps repeating the words parrot-fashion as people sometimes recite the Lord's Prayer or the Creed parrot-fashion. Don't be content with the foothills. Launch out into the glorious sight that God has revealed to us in Scripture, that His day will not be long coming. It's coming! And that glorious truth will absolutely enlighten your mind and your heart, and thrill you with the prospect of the blessed hope set before you as a Christian.

And don't let the mists of unbelief, or the fog of denial, or dismissal of the subject, or the sheer pollution of untruth or half-truth, speculation and distortion, remove from your sight the view that Scripture gives you. What glory shines from Scripture! 'Nothing beyond Scripture'—but I'm content with what Scripture does say, and in that I will rejoice.

What's more, I want to do what the apostle says. 'All this I will apply to myself', so that the truth of the Lord's second coming may make its impact upon my life with transforming results. May God grant for all of us during this week, that we may hear the promise again: 'Surely I am coming soon.' And that we may join in the heart-felt prayer of the church: 'Amen, come Lord Jesus'.

KESWICK 1995
TAPES, VIDEOS AND BOOKS

Audio tapes of the Keswick platform ministry, including much not included in the present book, are available from:

ICC (International Christian Communications)
Silverdale Road
Eastbourne
East Sussex BN20 7AB

from whom catalogues and prices can be obtained. Details of videos of selected events can be obtained from:

Mr Dave Armstrong
STV Videos
Box 299
Bromley, Kent BR2 9XB.

Some previous annual Keswick volumes are still in print, as is the anthology *Keswick Gold*, ed. David Porter (OM Publishing, 1990), which contains a selection of 22 addresses from the 1978–1989 volumes. Details are available from local Christian or secular bookshops, or in case of difficulty from the present publishers, whose address is on the reverse of the title page of this book.

KESWICK 1996

The annual Keswick Convention takes place each July at the heart of England's beautiful Lake District. The two separate weeks of the Convention offer an unparalleled opportunity for listening to gifted Bible exposition, experiencing Christian fellowship with believers from all over the world, and enjoying something of the unspoilt grandeur of God's creation.

Each of the two weeks has a series of five morning Bible Readings, followed by other addresses throughout the rest of the day. The programme in the second week is a little less intensive, and it is often referred to as 'Holiday Week'. There are also regular meetings throughout the fortnight for young people, and a Children's Holiday Club.

The dates for the 1996 Keswick Convention are 13–20 July (Convention Week) and 21–27 July (Holiday Week). The Bible Reading speakers are Rev. Michael Wilcock and Rev. Stuart Briscoe respectively. Other speakers during the fortnight include Rev. Steve Brady, Mr Hugh Palmer, Mr Charles Price, Rev. Alec Ross, Rev. David Coffey, Rev. Colin Sinclair and Rev. David Row.

For further information, write to:

The Administrator
Keswick Convention Centre
Skiddaw Street
Cumbria CA12 4BY
Telephone: 017687 72589